Off the Edge

Photos   Department of European Ethnology, page 6
Susanne Ewert, pages 13, 24, 37, 46, 92, 97, 98, 102, 114, 120, 131, 132, 142
Pernille Sys Hansen, pages 20, 28, 88
Richard Wilk, pages 14, 58, 64, 70, 160
Orvar Löfgren, pages 54, 69, 126, 150
Anne Pyburn, page 80
Anne Marie Palm, page 154
Lars-Eric Jönsson, page 76
Kirsti Mathiesen Hjemdahl, page 108

Offprint of Ethnologia Europaea. Journal of European Ethnology 35:1–2 (2005)

Museum Tusculanum Press
University of Copenhagen
Njalsgade 94
DK-2300 Copenhagen S
www.mtp.dk

Off the Edge

Experiments in
Cultural Analysis

Edited by
Orvar Löfgren
and Richard Wilk

MUSEUM TUSCULANUM PRESS · UNIVERSITY OF COPENHAGEN
2006

CONTENTS

IN SEARCH OF MISSING PROCESSES

Orvar Löfgren and Richard Wilk

This collection of essays* is out to revitalize discussions about cultural processes of stability and change. Researchers have always been busy developing new analytical concepts, but usually in a piecemeal fashion, as they are needed. This collection reverses the direction, explicitly inventing new processes and reviving some forgotten ones as a means of suggesting what kinds of analysis are needed in a rapidly changing world. Have you ever heard of the cream effect or the power of cultural backdraft? Have you watched the slow process of fossilization or the tactics of cultural stealth? Are you familiar with the need for cultural bracketing? Perhaps you are just waiting for the right word to describe what you have seen.

Conventionally we think of research as discovering something about the way the world works, and then finding an existing label to describe it. But in practice because we think metaphorically, we are always in an oscillation between labels and processes. Often we may be unconscious of the way our metaphors and labels affect our thinking. Here we will make this movement more explicit, by considering the labels directly, and by playing with the reversals, when the labels and metaphors precede and directly affect our observations. We hope this reveals the ways that areas of analysis become stunted because we lack the right vocabulary. We are trying to catch up on the cultural lag when old terminologies don't match new research questions.

We gathered twenty scholars from different fields (European ethnology, anthropology, sociology and archaeology) for a workshop in December 2004 and asked them to invent (or re-invent) an interesting cultural process, a fresh perspective for analyzing some kind of cultural dynamic. After the workshop we expanded the group and here is the result, 25 essays experimenting with very different approaches and reflecting on overlooked or understudied perspectives. Our aim is not to force 25 new concepts onto the world, but rather to illustrate how different perspectives may enrich cultural analysis and allow a bit of playfulness and experimentation into the process. We are peeking into blind spots, peering around corners, looking under the furniture, and trying to understand how some kinds of social life become visible, while so many others remain unseen. The participants were sent out to invent a process, but luckily (and predictably) their quests took on very different forms. Our project became an experiment in finding different styles of cultural analysis.

In our introduction we will discuss some problems of inventing processes, starting with a historical look at how the tool kit of cultural vocabulary has been transformed over the last century. What kinds of fads and fashions can be observed, what interests become typical academic subjects at different times? We also want to explore the potentials and problems of the metaphors which help some kinds of explanations "make sense" to particular audiences. In what ways do metaphors channel or conserve certain approaches? We want to emphasize that the line between process and condition is blurred in our collection and we think it should stay so. We are as much interested in those processes that maintain

stability, and freeze a status quo, as with dramatic transformations. From the world of changing metaphors we move to a discussion of over- and under-exploited fields in cultural analysis and finally we very briefly introduce the essays.

Mapping Landscapes of Metaphors

Leafing through old textbooks in anthropology, sociology or European ethnology is sometimes like visiting a graveyard of dead and buried concepts. You encounter words and ideas that are now completely forgotten. Who remembers *dynamic equilibrium, replacive integration, system homeostasis, logic-aesthetic dynamics,* or *acculturative stress?* They were listed in Fred Voget's 1963 review of disciplinary trends on the cutting edge of the anthropology of cultural change.

Concepts come and go, and even reading contemporary textbooks you feel that many of the processes used and defined will soon fade into oblivion, although they seem powerful at the moment. There is a constant wear and tear on terminology that make some concepts tire very rapidly, while other have staying power and/or a high potential for constant revision and eventual recycling. A historical comparison of anthropological textbooks from the 1920s up to the present tells a lot about constant and changing conceptual frameworks. Different theoretical schools had their own favourite sets of processes and keywords. As long as societies were thought of as clearly delineated systems with characteristic patterns and structures, processual thinking was focused on the ways those individual cultural objects interacted with each other, colliding, rebounding or blending. Since cultures were likened to species, machines or nations, the key metaphors were often borrowed from biology, technology or military strategy. Within an evolutionary framework of trees and staircases, cultures ascended, climbed, deteriorated or degenerated. Cultures in contact travelled, spread, clashed, penetrated, merged, or gave submission through acculturation.

Functionalism portrayed cultures as systems or organisms, and used metaphors like growth, equilibrium, and disorder to diagnose function and dysfunction. More recently we have seen cultural analysis going through several theoretical "turns". The textual trend of the 1980s consciously used concepts from literary theory and discourse analysis to portray culture as "texts" inscribed on bodies and commodities, to be decoded and read by the observer with the right language skills. There was the nomadic trend in the 1990s that emphasized travel and migration metaphors as well as terms which emphasized flux and motion, like displacement and deterritorialization.

Each trend in cultural metaphor production provokes its own opposition, and we can see how the language of mobility, cosmopolitanism and placelessness was countered by "a spatial turn", bringing space and place back into the debate with the help of concepts from cultural geography. These included cultural mapping, mental cartography, earth-writing and all kinds of -scapes (see Falkheimer & Jansson 2006). In a similar manner the poststructuralist reaction against the misplaced concreteness of cultural groups, and the fabrication of the ethnographic present often used graphic tensile and textile metaphors. This was a new cultural world of not only fragments and bricolage but also rifts, threads, weaves, sinews, knots, looms and tangles.

We have no argument with the creative use of metaphor as a means of thinking about the social world. In fact many prominent linguists believe any kind of thought is impossible without metaphor (Lakoff & Johnson 1980, 1999). But this knowledge should make us think critically about the metaphors we choose to use, and reflect on their potentials and problems. Metaphors can open up creative new avenues, and help us find pattern and rhythm we had not seen before, but they also have the potential to "frame" particular questions and issues and thereby channel our vision, making some problems invisible, and suppressing questions, in much the way Kuhn saw established research paradigms operating in science. We have trouble seeing things for which we have no mental image or template.

The Metaphorical Transit System

"Metaphorai" is a sign painted on tramcars in Athens, a motto which should help us remember the importance of knowing when to jump aboard a metaphor and when to get off, as Gregory Bateson (1973) once stressed. We also need to remember that all borrowed terms carry stowaway and unwelcome passengers. Metaphors are seductive, and some have a magic that blinds us. Sometimes we just get carried away.

What does the choice, focus, or invention of processes tell us about the theoretical and methodological landscape at given times, in particular academic settings? Do choices of metaphor reflect strategic alliances between groups and factions? We can learn a great deal from tracking the trajectories and transformations of concepts as they travel between disciplines, areas of study, and generations.

Many different fields have contributed to the large and disorganized historical tool chest of social analysis. Digging through our collection, we find examples drawn from biology (*ecotypes, memes*), gastronomy (*smorgasbord, simmering*), metallurgy (*forged, melting pot*), linguistics (*creolization, grammar*), psychology (*projection, attachment*), physics (*osmosis, entropy*), medicine (*symptoms, diagnosis*), warfare (*guerrilla tactics, manoeuvres*), and even the construction industry (*building, framing*) – just to name a few.

We need to explore the kind of hidden undertones and unwanted baggage that comes along when concepts are transplanted from one arena or discipline to another. Do we borrow some of the legitimacy or stature of a powerful discipline like economics along with their terminology? The flow of metaphor may define a hierarchy of power, or provide a vehicle for more balanced transactions between groups of scholars.

We can illustrate this process by looking at the cultural field of consumption and consumerism, where the metaphorical construction of consumption has had a major impact on the way scholars approach the topic (Wilk 2004). Because the key metaphors for consumption have been "burning" and "eating", scholars tend to look for prototypical acts which take raw materials, use them in a destructive way, and leave degraded wastes behind. The whole process is driven by a deeply embodied urge akin to hunger and thirst.

Because of the "eating" metaphor, consumption ends up carrying many of the same moral polarizations of gluttony and starvation, empty and full, health and illness, lean and fat which are so characteristic of discourses about eating food. The metaphor of eating frames the issues of consumption in ways which foreground the acts which are most like burning or eating – burning fossil fuels while driving, for example, while pushing other equally important forms of consumption, such as reading a book or walking the dog, into marginal, atypical categories. Likening consumption to eating also obscures the dividing line between needs and wants, in a way which can be manipulated in various ways by those with different moral and political agendas.

Another metaphorical tradition that has been prominent in discussions of mass consumption is the use of Newtonian physics and hydraulics, for example in discussions of (over-)abundance: overheating, overloading, overflowing, and pressuring. Such metaphors may trap us into a thinking of culture as a kind of liquid in a container which exists in a set quantity, making it a limited good. Excess is then produced through the mechanisms of pushing, swelling, spilling over, and this hydraulic thinking may mislead us into taking for granted that an overflow or elaboration in one cultural field must result in drainage, scarcity or thinning out somewhere else. Pressure must lead to release or destructive explosion.

The Power of Key Words

Historians and social scientists have turned attention back on themselves, thinking about the history, functions and activities of academia, including the social life of academics. In contrast, they have paid much less attention to the role of language and key words in intellectual movements and programs. They fail to take into account the results of other academic research, in linguistics, anthropology and cognitive sciences, which show that there is a very close relationship between language and thought.

We believe that language and terminology are generally a conservative influence on creative thinking in social science. It is not hard to find support for this contention. Williams in his famous "Keywords" argued that social science language encodes power relationships, and generally acts in the interests of those who have power and intend to keep it. In doing so he makes a convincing argument that change in the status quo requires the invention of new language, new lexicons, and new terms.

The power of conceptualization is often easier to spot away from home, in other sciences. In medicine, for example, official processes for defining terms and classifications are often out of synch with the latest research. There is generally a considerable lag in the terms for diagnosis and labelling of diseases, or defining what kinds of toxins are dangerous and how levels will be measured. These classifications can exert tremendous power in the real world by slotting particular forms of behaviour into labelled pathologies with recommended treatments. Yet the elements of power are hidden in a maze of committees which operate with little oversight and without public debate. Thus you end up with, for example, an international classification of diseases which makes fine distinctions among various afflictions of affluence, while lumping the diseases of poverty together into many fewer categories. The cultural values of one particular group of people become globally recognized diseases, and the maladies of others are "folk" ailments (Bowker & Star 1999).

In our own world of cultural analysis, we can see many instances where the choice of metaphors for cultural processes has influenced the choice of subjects, the kinds of examples chosen, the moral implications of findings, and even the kinds of fieldwork pursued and forms of presentation. There are always tensions between the language we use and the kinds of things we see and seek to understand. We are not arguing here for a simple model of progressive scientific discovery, where social sciences simply "advance" and leave old sets of ideas and terms lagging behind. Instead we would argue that we live in a world which is always changing, and that new phenomena are always appearing. It is perfectly understandable that at first we try to fit these new things into existing categories, and we try to stretch the meaning of our existing vocabulary to accommodate them. One lesson from this is that we must allow ourselves to experiment with labels and concepts. When you re-label, all of a sudden you see aspects that were previously hidden. The metaphor is cut loose.

Overexploited and Underdeveloped Fields

An important critique that came out of the workshop concerned what many felt to be the current overemphasis upon processes of speedy renewal, fluidity and hybridity. This is related to what Elizabeth Shove has called "a preoccupation with the explicit, the visible and the dramatic" (2003: 1). During the last decades the use of metaphors from theatre has underlined this preoccupation with "front stage" scripted and intentional cultural processes, using metaphors like performance, plots, scenography, and choreography.

At the same time the postmodern critique in the 1980s and 1990s was a reaction against the old fashioned cultural theory of the superorganic and sociological thinking of cultures as having agency, acting purposively or strategically. Postmodernists attacked the heroic actor as the product of a modernist master script, and emphasized the accidental and liminal, the products of pastiche, and bricolage, using metaphors of flow, flux and flexibility. These more recent concepts focus attention on the parts of the world in constant change, emphasizing processes of cultural fragmentation and individualization. Such processes are undoubtedly an important part of contemporary society, but these concepts can overshadow equally important cultural forces of cohesion, stability and routinization.

Many of the contributions to this volume emphasize the need to explore cultural processes that turn the dramatic, exotic or explicit into inconspicuous elements of the mundane habitus. These processes often carry negative connotation of banalization and trivialization, but they should be seen as a strong undercurrent in everyday life, gaining their power from their invisibility and their being taken for granted. This space in between choice and habit is a rich terrain that has not been named and is consequently poorly explored. There are classic discussions of routine and habituation in works by Gregory Bateson (1973), Pierre Bourdieu (1977) and Michel de Certeau (1984), and more recent studies which emphasize the ambiguities of routines. Jean-Claude Kaufmann (1997: 195ff.), Elizabeth Shove (2003) and Ben Highmore (2004) develop a more nuanced understanding by examining the micro-physics of making and breaking routines and the ways in which they structure everyday life in time and space. Routines are often seen as tools for economizing because they may help actors conserve time and energy by developing their auto-pilot. They can be described as territories of restfulness or security where "you just know what to do," but they can also be seen as cultural straitjackets that constrain actors, block creativity and stifle change. As habits, they may be seen as obstacles which have to be "broken" and at their worst they blend into the pathologies of addiction and habituation. The lives of routines are much more complex than any simple polarity can capture. Sometimes in the inconspicuous practices of daily life, these small repetitive actions can work to subtly change larger social structures, cultural values, and gendered notions of self and society.

The realm of routinization is closely linked to another underdeveloped one, namely that of *cultural maintenance*. So much that appears to be seamless "inertia" or "stasis" is actually active, requiring huge and often concealed effort. Cultural maintenance includes the activities needed to keep the appearance of order, which we can explore through metaphors of housework and gardening, tending, straightening-up and pruning. Like all maintenance work it tends to be done best when it is noticed least, and those who do it tend to be unrecognized, or even stigmatized and treated as boring plodders (academia provides many examples).

Cultural maintenance can also be a more dramatic battle for order and the aesthetics of symmetry, harmony and logic. This reminds us of the need for more studies of cultural messiness and disorder,

including topics like anachronism, uncoordination, dissonance and clutter. It is easy to forget that far from being "natural" consequences of orderly human activity, messiness of all kinds is usually a human creation, sometimes with clear purpose. Reverting to the theatre metaphors, many of the essays thus advocate a greater interest in the backstage, the prosaic construction of props and preparations rather than the stage itself.

From Aisthesis to Zero-making

The following 25 essays give some examples of underdeveloped themes in contemporary cultural analysis. We have organized them into five sections:

Sensing

After a long preoccupation with discourse analysis and textual metaphors, social scientists have developed new interest in the kinds of cultural phenomena that are hard to catch and describe in words – fleeting or mixed emotions, sensory and bodily experiences – things felt but not easily verbalized. This section explores the potentials of some sensual approaches. How does *the cream effect* work as a sensory high that comes from adding that little bit of extra? And why is it that *warming* is seen as such an effective way of domesticating the new and alien, making it more cosy, hospitable and authentic? Of all the senses, tactility is most often overlooked. *Aisthesis* is about the ways in which the sense of touch works together with all other senses, whereas *smoothing* is about tidying up cultural messes, cutting corners and flattening experiences.

Ageing

As we pointed out earlier, there has been ample interest in renewal, innovation and development, but less on the flip side of the coin: disintegration, disappearance and going out of fashion. The papers in this section explore related underexploited themes. *Wasting* deals with the ways in which objects, activities and people are sorted out, redefined as waste or just wasted, while *bracketing* is about putting culture on hold, in waiting and latency. How can different forms for *cultural wear and tear* explain that all of a sudden a theoretical concept, a ritual or a family car becomes unfashionable, faded or tacky? *Fossilization* is a special variety of cultural ageing. What happens when objects or activities are petrified into social fossils – and can they be brought back to life? *Composting* is the mystical process of mixing cultural stuff and letting it decompose into something which nourishes new developments.

Moving

In the modern world perceptions of movement carry a heavy symbolic load; some are bad, some are good. Good movements often equal change: breaking up, moving on. Usually this is a heavily gendered sphere of male adventure, associated with the fear of being stuck or left behind. Thus a slowing of pace is often associated with stagnation or lack of initiative. The essays in this section deal with temporal movements that are often invisible and are seen as unproductive or disturbing. What if we borrowed the soundscape of the *Doppler effect* to look at our distorted perceptions of past and present, or focused on the kinds of *slow motion* that are often mistaken for inactivity? The dynamics of *sync/unsync* can help us understand the workings of anachronisms. Cultural *stealth* is about knowing when to be invisible and when to make a surprising appearance, whereas *still life* may be a machine that distils events and scenes into a liquid potency.

Transforming

Cultural transformations may evoke images of dramatic metamorphosis, but the drama is often preceded by seemingly trivial routines. Think for example about the hidden work of the left hand that is so important for the magician, who captures our attention by waving his right hand up in the air in order to make us forget what's actually happening. *Zero-making* is the art of wiping the slate clean, producing a fresh start or a cultural discontinuity. Why is *artificialization* so pervasive and popular and what happens when you silence certain experiences and they return as a powerful and surprising *backlash*? The sudden explosion of *backdraft* may teach us to focus on the slow and often invisible build-up be-

hind it. *Customizing* promises the freedom of extreme makeover and individual styling but often turns into new forms of homogenization. *Menuing* helps people make choices through a kind of pre-packaging which is not confined to the restaurant table or the computer screen.

Mystifying

Cultural theory often seems preoccupied with making sense, trying to understand the workings of the world through order and rationality. This section deals with the irrational and mysterious, but also with social practices of imagination and make-believe, fears, dreams and daydreams. *Self-mystification* is about looking with bafflement at the stranger in the mirror, whereas attempts at *camouflage* bring out hidden rules of normality. *Silence* can be both restful and fearful but also ominous, while *sanchismo* is about self-destructive and inexplicable behaviour. Finally, *sleeping* is a nightly mystery – a retreat into a private world full of shared cultural elements.

Coda

Reverting to the world of metaphors, these essays represent a smorgasbord of very different approaches. Botanizing among them you will also be reminded of what's not on the menu. For the curious we have footnoted the original shopping-list we made up before the workshop, just as a reminder of all the alternatives spurned by the authors and the rich potentials of further inventions.[1] There are of course no missing processes out there, just waiting to be discovered. They will surface as creations of a dialogue where ideas of labelling are confronted with analytical perspectives and ethnographic materials. Not a manual of new processes, this collection is meant to stimulate ethnographic experiments and analytical playfulness in the service of serious research. And remember: all research metaphors are tramcars. Know when to step on and step off, waiting for a new one to appear around the corner.

Notes

* A special thanks to Magdalena Tellenbach Uttman, Ph.D., for her editorial assistance.

1 **A check-list for potential cultural processes**

Speed and direction

Fast/slow, (cultural inertia and lag), static/mobile (cultural freezing), flexible/inflexible, one-directional/multi-directional, moving upwards, downwards, backwards, onwards, sideways (evolution, devolution, progress, decline), rerouting

Centripetal and centrifugal forces (integration, disintegration, fragmentation)

Friction, flow, momentum, spin, acceleration, braking

Ageing and rejuvenation (cultural amnesia, recycling)

Vanishing, disappearing, reappearing, haunting

Material characteristics

Hard/soft (cultural software), sticky, fuzzy, polished, uneven, dense (cultural condensation)

Temperature, heating up, chilling, freezing, burning, vaporizing

Evaporation, crystallization

Liquidity, viscosity, dilution, concentration

Raw/cooked

Scale, size and weight

Miniature, Small, Medium, Large and Extra Large cultural phenomena

Expansion, growth, shrinking (cultural downsizing)

Heaviness and weightlessness

Floating and sinking

Combinations

The spectrum from amalgamation (elements transformed in a way that cannot be reversed) and physical mixes (elements may separate again after a time).

Blending, osmosis, dissolving, synergy, solvency/insolvency

Exposure and sensual presence

Over- or underexposure, hiding, highlighting, vocalizing, visibility/non-visibility, shadowing, haziness, clear/unclear, tactile, reachable, slippery, ephemeral

Reduction, redundancy, intensive/extensive

References

Bateson, Gregory 1973: *Steps Towards an Ecology of Mind.* London: Paladin Books.

Bourdieu, Pierre 1977: *Outline of a Theory of Practice.* Cambridge: Cambridge University Press.

Bowker, Geoffrey C. & Susan Star 1999: *Sorting Things Out.* Cambridge: MIT Press.

de Certeau, Michel 1984: *The Practice of Everyday Life.* Berkeley: University of California Press.

Falkheimer, Jesper & André Jansson 2006: *Geographies of Communication. The Spatial Turn in Media Studies.* Gothenburg: Nordicom.

Highmore, Ben 2004: Homework: Routine, Social Aesthetics and the Ambiguity of Everyday Life. *Cultural Studies,* 18 (2–3), 306–327.

Kaufmann, Jean-Claude 1997: *Le Cœur à l'ouvrage. Théorie de l'action ménagère.* Paris: Nathan.

Lakoff, George & Mark Johnson 1980: *Metaphors We Live By.* Chicago: University of Chicago Press.

Lakoff, George & Mark Johnson 1999: *Philosophy in the Flesh.* New York: Harpercollins.

Shove, Elizabeth 2003: *Comfort, Cleanliness and Convenience: The Social Organization of Normality.* Oxford: Berg.

Voget, Fred 1963: Cultural Change. *Biennal Review of Anthropology,* 1963, 228–275.

Wilk, Richard 2004: Morals and Metaphors: The Meaning of Consumption. In: Karin Ekström & Helene Brembeck (eds.), *Elusive Consumption.* Oxford: Berg Publishers, pp. 11–26.

SENSING

THE CREAM EFFECT

Regina Bendix

"Would you like that with whipped cream?" the waitress asks the customer. Perhaps he is already feeling mildly guilty for having ordered a hot chocolate. Then, perhaps, a "what the heck" feeling overcomes him and he says "yes, I do!" Or maybe he has entered the café fully intending to go for the full hit, satisfying the craving for a dose of gustatory and nutritionally utterly unnecessary, fat-enriched pleasure. In a time where supermarket shelves offer vast arrays of products in many grades of fat-deprivation and where countless subdisciplines of medicine have banded together with good old-fashioned social control to keep us looking for low fat and lean, it takes courage to order whipped cream.

The cream effect names, not entirely arbitrarily, a patterned process involving sensory experience and subsequent longing for more. The term stands here for the collectivity of manipulable sensory pleasures which, as a rising anthropology of the senses will argue, require differentiation – both in terms of the human senses (be they five or more) and different cultural settings and historical eras (Corbin 1991; Howes 2003). Hence, another researcher might speak of the Chanel N° 5 effect, or the harp, sunset or velvet effect. I chose taste and gustation to stand for the whole and leave it to another to empirically and ideologically challenge the choice of term. There is no argument entailed here, however, that gustation is hierarchically above the other senses in the cream effect (and I acknowledge that for some the choice of this substance for a label might be all but pleasing or even allergenic; I apologize and hope they will

humor me...). Two salient features of the cream effect that are to be explored further below are 1) its almost anti-Cartesian logic (I sense, therefore I am pleased) and 2) its availability both for an individual's self-gratification and for manipulative use in human interaction.

Many cultural practices feature creaming as a literal and metaphoric component: it is the additional touch, the extra that creates or enhances pleasure and thus is particularly suited to pamper, mollify or, as we will see, influence another. Those who have been lucky enough to experience the cream effect and the excess of nice, bodily experience it offers, will fantasize about it during times of the opposite experience of deprivation: a body and mind exposed to harshness, pain, and scarcity may long for that sensory high that spreads warmth through the body. Embodied pleasure provides such a sense of affirmation of the union of body and mind in human existence, that by contrast its absence – a state of sensory deprivation and lack – fosters desperation and doubt.

Popular literature provides all kinds of appropriate references for the cream effect's powers. While subtler than a land of victual plenty such as *Cockaigne* or the German *Schlaraffenland*, the joys of creaming appear as sources of solace and pleasure in diverse settings. To offer just two: In the prose of the nineteenth century Swiss serial novelist Jeremias Gotthelf, depictions of harvest feasts conjure up images of mouth-watering richness rewarding day laborers for weeks of backbreaking work (e.g. 1846).

And what does Goldy, mystery author Diane Mott Davidson's present-day catering sleuth do when she has suffered scratches, bruises or worse in her pursuit of murderers? She reaches into her pantry and bakes mouth-watering and especially rich sweets or, better yet, lets her policeman husband pamper her with Tex-Mex creations slathered in sour cream, followed by further pleasures in the marital bed (e.g. Davidson 2000). Creaming is an optional addition, a value added, an improvement on the level of "embodied mind".

The cream effect produces first and foremost a sensory experience, lodged between physiological and cognitive, individual and cultural awareness. Taste and touch, smell, sight and hearing are nothing if not eager for "cream" – for while the senses naturally provide us with many crucial signals for our bodily survival, they are also the primary conduit for experiences of pleasure. Creaming works internally or externally, and it comes in literal and figurative forms. Potions and lotions that heal and pamper skin make us touch and rub, please and relieve the biggest organ of our own or someone else's body with gentle hand motions. There is a bridge between the sensory stimulus, the luxurious feeling it releases, and the memories and longings it opens. Hence the effect of creaming is supremely individualistic and perhaps egoistic revelry.

As the smooth richness spreads slowly and pleasurably through the body, the mind seems to slow down, helping the body capture all the goodness that can be had from a dollop of cream. Yet given this effect, and given human communicative rules and ruses, the cream effect is also available for manipulation: I am not the only one who can order hot chocolate with whipped cream. Someone else can decide to offer it to me, literally and metaphorically, lovingly enjoying the sight of my pleasure or cunningly preparing me for some kind of action or opinion that I might, uncreamed, fail to warm up to. Unlike the proverbial "buttering up" – clearly a derivative or rather a too intensely stirred cream effect... – creaming undertaken by another is subtle: a hint of warmth in a gaze usually neutral, a honeyed hue in the voice, a chair pulled imperceptibly but comfortably closer. All these techniques potentially raise, somatically or just seemingly, the body temperature, thawing a chill and forestalling the resistance that a proposition might otherwise provoke.

Creaming offers a slightly guilty, but oh so pleasurable luxuriation. Its bodily experience is different though perhaps related to what is in German called "getting soaped" or "soaping someone" (einseifen) that is, feeling well and pleasured under the influence of someone who seeks to make literal or metaphorical profit from us or, to use an English expression, "pulling the wool over one's eyes". Proverbial expressions for creaming in different languages could be an empirically interesting and trying avenue to clarify just which sensory-cognitive-rational mix-up is being plotted and executed.

It is easiest, naturally, to document the cream effect within the realm of foodways. A carrot soup transforms from a wholesome food into a delectable one with the addition of cream or a dollop of sour cream (or, for the really fat conscious, a spoonful of plain yoghurt...). There are gustatory pleasures where richness of flavor can spread from palate to stomach to body, signaling comfort and satisfaction, a bodily warmth. Creaming thus pushes the palatable into the realm of the pleasurable. The greatest challenge posed by modern forms of asceticism such as dieting is to find substitutes for the cream effect's particular sensory-bodily stimulus. Generally this is done by shifting the aesthetic emphasis; the sense's collaboration in creating pleasure has long been recognized in aesthetic philosophy (Burke 1958; Baumgarten 1983). A modern spa, perhaps even located in a former monastery, will serve its meager meals on exceptional porcelain, often on plates whose absurd size vis-à-vis the tiny portion reinforces the "I am doing something good for myself" feel. Scented air, thick, soft towels and robes will pamper the skin, musical selections add to this sense of well-being and together (although cumbersomely), the pleasures served to eyes, ears, nose and skin make up for the lacking cream. Whether cognition can be willed to translate such sensory substitutes into positive experiences depends entirely on how strongly an individual subscribes to the ideological precepts surrounding the cream effect in a given cultural context.

Naturally the pleasures of creaming are culturally shaped and passed on: the pleasure of biting down on a fatty looking grub is likely to be inaccessible to someone who was not enculturated in the Brazilian rain forest, as Lévi-Strauss observed. The smell and taste of delectable, desirable cheeses are abominable and utterly unsuited to evoke the cream effect for many non-Europeans. A lulling tune and voice in one place may be disharmonious and disturbing in another, though the creaming of sound is probably more recognizable cross-culturally than that of gustation.

The cream effect may reside between body and mind, between individual and culture – but culture works hard at prying it out of this liminal state by offering guidelines and restrictions on the appropriateness of "creaming". These are most evident in efforts to portion, restrict and ideologically discipline what our sensorium would gladly endure in great amounts. Religious critiques and disciplines of pleasure on the one hand, and the eager absorption of medical knowledge into everyday practice on the other, have left us with a number of confusions regarding the simple pleasures of creaming, inserting a cerebral monitor between sensorium, bodily experience and feeling.

Real cream clogs some people's arteries, and it favors our fat deposits rather than our muscles, and hence the global diet of the health conscious excludes the rich substances whose fatty smoothness are also happy-making. We learn new discourse and eating practices that attempt to teach us to cerebrally substitute the experience of creamy pleasure with the virtuous knowledge of oat bran and celery. The number of creamy lotions for application externally to ever more muscular and yoga-steeled bodies has, however, grown exponentially. Yet external creaming is no longer a simple pleasure between one, two or more – its value has risen, studios and parlors that cream and massage us for a fee have sprouted even beyond metropolitan areas. The luxury of creamy touch has accrued more status and like the gustatory deprivation of cream, it is cerebrally enhanced through the scientific and multiculturally-branded knowledge that we are "doing something good" by paying for (perhaps not so nice smelling) creams and creaming services (Lau 2000).

The cream effects of taste and touch requires management and considerable capital investment which raise their price. But there remains, it would seem, a human capacity to locate "cream" in places where cultural ordering and market forces have not yet reached. There are perfumes and room deodorizing substances that guide our scent-repertoire in culturally approved and economically priced directions. But the child returning from school and catching a whiff of a cake that has just left the oven will experience a brief and unexpected high, having their happy home reentry further "creamed" by a pleasing sensory experience (I am aware, of course, that "the smell of baked goods" is probably available in a spray can). A parent discovering the smell of a newborn, a couple in love recognizing the scent of the other's sweat – these are pleasures so idiosyncratic in their nature, and in the way we appreciate them, that the positive experience is hopefully shielded from cultural control and capitalist profit.

Sight has long undergone severe schooling, regarding what we are supposed to process as aesthetically pleasing, but beneath the surface there must still be a capacity to experience the visually beautiful or surprising with the capacity Goethe called "the enlarging of the soul". This experience gives us an unexpectedly pleasurable, and sometimes nearly painful, jolt to body and mind.

Sound, finally, is perhaps our greatest alternate realm for the culturally mediated cream effect. Sound designers have long figured out how to make car doors and blow dryers emit sounds they think we like (and then make us pay for their efforts). But we still know how to find and gorge on music that satisfies a particular bodily and emotional craving, employing new technological gadgets to bring the cream ever closer to our nervous system. There is of course a ready cultural critique of headphone-carrying joggers and youths ruining their hearing by blasting music much too loudly. But this is aimed at the lack of care for the sense of hearing, not at the basic auditory pleasure of music.

The "cream effect" is the extra, the "unnecessary" to speak in the vocabulary particularly to cultures patterned by Protestantism. Cultural history and ethnography have yet to explore the complex connection between guilt and pleasure and the victory of one over the other in specific instances and settings. Late capitalism with the assistance of scientific research has achieved a certain return of sensory pleasure, but it is, as is typical of Ulrich Beck's risk society (1992), pleasure laden with reflection and cost.

Dogs and cats are brought to old age homes because it has been scientifically established that the pleasure of touching their breathing and purring fur-clad bodies improves the wellbeing of lonely, elderly people – but only once a week, since of course it costs something. Newborn babies receive foot massages, because it enhances their sensory awareness and improves parent-child bonding, so say the studies, but parents have to enroll in a course on how to do it properly. Should you accidentally discover a sensory pleasure not yet charted and disciplined, you will face the difficult choice of relishing it (guiltily?) all by yourself, or carrying it to the market, after it has been properly studied, so that others might purchase it, in moderation, with guidance and thus avoid the otherwise unavoidable uncertainty and guilt over what might be too much of a good thing.

References

Baumgarten, Alexander G. 1983 [1750–58]: *Texte zur Grundlegung der Ästhetik*. Edited and translated by Hans Rudolf Schweizer. Frankfurt: Felix Meiner Verlag.

Beck, Ulrich 1992: *Risk Society: Towards a New Modernity*. London: Sage.

Burke, Edmund 1958 [1756]: *A Philosophical Enquiry into the Origin of our Ideas of the Sublime and the Beautiful*. Edited by J.T. Boulton. London: Routledge and Kegan Paul.

Corbin, Alain 1991: *Wunde Sinne: Über die Begierde, den Schrecken und die Ordnung der Zeit im 19. Jahrhundert*. Stuttgart: Klett-Cotta (French original 1991), pp. 197–211.

Davidson, Diane Mott 2000: *Prime Cut*. New York: Bantam.

Gotthelf, Jeremias 1846: *Uli der Knecht*. Berlin.

Howes, David 2003: *Sensual Relations: Engaging the Senses in Culture and Social Theory*. Ann Arbor: The University of Michigan Press.

Lau, Kimberley 2000: *New Age Capitalism: Making Money East of Eden*. Philadelphia: University of Pennsylvania Press.

WARMING

Güliz Ger

Making the New Familiar and Moral

As the adage goes, the only thing that does not change is change itself. In the contemporary world of global interconnections, change is even more significant. New objects, spaces, and procedures emerge incessantly. If "a universal human need is familiarity" (Tuan 1993: 113), these ever-changing life worlds pose a challenge. Faced with ongoing change and pervasive novelty, how do individuals cope? I will argue that the process of warming provides one way through which people negotiate change and stability, the new and the old, the unfamiliar and the familiar. In the cold, insecure, and risky (post)modern times, warming is a strategy which individuals use to make their daily lives more romantic, cozy, hospitable, inalienable, and authentic.

While much has been written on aesthetization of life, the feelings that are part and parcel of aesthetization have not been emphasized. However, the feeling of warmth is an aspect of aesthetics: the aesthetic experience involves not only sensory beauty but also feelings. Warming makes material culture humane. This essay claims that warming is crucial in shaping habitats, that is, warm aesthetics underlie the beautification of spaces. I discuss how people warm their spaces in order to make themselves feel at home in a changing world. Modern subjects shape their living spaces to make them romantically and nostalgically warm.

One example of warming appeared in a study of families who moved from the village to the town of Alaşehir in Turkey (Ger & Balım 2005). For migrants to the town, the decoration of the home was not merely a visual beautification or a functional endeavor, but rather it entailed making the home both modern and warm. The homemakers refer to the ideal home as *güzel*, which literally means beautiful and good. A home is considered *güzel* if it is both modern and warm. These homemakers, keen on expressing their new urban identity, were also keen on maintaining their links to the village and what they considered to be the "warmth" of the old rural ways. Warming serves to connect life in Williams' (1973) city of progress, modernization, and worldliness to the country of the past, old human and natural ways, and simple virtue, peace, and innocence.

The transition from the country to the city is negotiated by warming the modern urban home in various ways. One astonishing sight to us, researchers from bigger cities, was the abundance of embroideries, crocheted doilies, and laces in Alaşehir flats – much more than anywhere else we had seen. There were many more such covers in Alaşehir than in the village, to adorn the many modern goods in these city flats. These textiles, decorating the kitchens, bathrooms, and the rooms in both the rural and urban homes, provide a continuation of "tradition" in modern lives. Handmade laces, which are from a woman's dowry, make the home in the town inalienable. The dowry entails textiles and other objects that mothers make and buy for their daughters. While modern kitchen appliances are nowadays also included in the dowry, the most important are the knit or embroidered textiles such as laces and pillow covers.

Dowry links the generations as mother and daughter make many pieces together, or pass them along as heirlooms. It also links friends, relatives, and neighbors: daughters and mothers embroider with others, while they socialize in various homes, and embroideries are contributed as gifts by a large circle of people. The dowry thus records social relations of girlhood. And even though the contemporary dowry also includes electronics and modern furniture, the cherished handmade textiles epitomize "our customs" and embody the memory of social relations and things left behind – girlhood and village life.

Each and everything of value, such as crystal, china, decorative objects, gifts, souvenirs, encyclopedias, television, music sets, and appliances are placed on or covered with laces. Tables, show cabinets, sofas, and armchairs are also decorated with handmade textiles. Cold and "naked" factory-made electronics, from food processors, telephones, computers and televisions to washing machines, are dressed with doilies and embroideries. Delaney (1991) suggests that covers serve to conceal the naked materiality of objects which must be bound and kept in place. However, doilies are also used to reveal and display: for example, the modern glassware and trinkets in modern show-cabinets are displayed standing on lace. Thus, laces and embroideries seem to do more than conceal naked materiality. They warm valued, but cold objects from the market.

Furthermore, coordinated sitting and dining sets, which provide a modern aesthetic readymade by the market, are dressed up with lace or pillows with embroidered cases. Thus, doilies and embroideries that mark and remind about social relations and the past are used to cushion, trim, beautify, and personalize, and essentially to warm the modern. What Hetzel and Schuman (1999) refer to as the "aestheticization of the present using the past," not only aestheticizes but also warms the present.

Perhaps such decoration is as much a self-communication of achieved urbanity/modernity as a display to the public. The self as an agent in decoration gets subsumed into displays, which are about relationships with urban friends and rural relatives, as well as about the public recognition of urbanity. Feeling confident in being a possessor of modern objects and a modern urban life, the modern subject draws from the past and the rural in order to make her new space warm and thus familiar.

Warming fuses the new and the old, the unfamiliar and the familiar. The aesthetics of the novelty of urban life and its things are warmed by the aesthetics of the old, by the nostalgically and socially warm textiles. While the new is aspirational, the old is the identity: the traditional provides a sense of warmth because it is both distant, and at the same time constructed to be "us," "our customs." The traditional is wistfully warm; these informants becoming modern wish to leave the peasantry and the past behind, but they feel nostalgic when they do.

Warming also moralizes the uncertain and risky new. The word *güzel* (beautiful and good) for the ideal home is noteworthy. A home is to be made both beautiful and good. This term resonates with the view that "[c]ulture … is a moral-aesthetic venture, to be judged ultimately by its moral beauty" (Tuan 1993: 240). "… [T]he good and the beautiful, the moral and the aesthetic, are inextricably intertwined – doublets, deeply rooted in common human experience and yearning" (Tuan 1993: 226). "Relationship with the other is at the heart of morality… Material culture … plays a necessary role in the invention, elaboration, and maintenance of structures of moral behavior" (Tuan 1993: 241). Laces and embroideries of the past/country that warm the modern objects of the market, serve to make these new/urban objects and hence their newly urban owners/users moral.

The emphasis on warmth emerges precisely due to the focus on the modern in the process of becoming urban. Beautification of homes seems to entail the key struggle of modern life – to retain both a sense of authentic locality and claim rights to a global modern status (Miller 1998) or the struggle of "seductive globalism and authentic localism" (Wilk 1999: 248). In their struggle to become modern, the informants warm the modern. Then this new modern becomes inalienable to those who create it. And it implies a modernity that entails continuity rather than a clean break with the past.

If we live in an era of rapid flows of people, in a

mobile world, in transition from one way of living to another, faced with choosing or ending up with new lifestyles in new places (Appadurai 1996), and if familiarity is a human need (Tuan 1993), then making our new world, lives, and spaces familiar is an ever-more important (and challenging) task. On one hand, the present is laden with aspirations, uncertainties, contradictions, every-day problems, and the mundane. On the other hand, other times and spaces, for example, the past and the distant country provide a romantic, idealized, utopian image (Illouz 1997; Williams 1973). Romanticizing and construction of utopian images come in handy to deal with the new and the present. Williams (1973) argues that creating idealized images is a means of coping with the present and providing a sense of stability. Experience of romance affords a secular access to the experience of the sacred and utopian visions of romance appeal to the past of our lost authenticity, and to the lost pastoral simplicity, innocence, and intimacy (Illouz 1997).

Material culture, such as handmade textiles, objectifies (see Miller 1987) a sense of the familiar other – distant and bygone times and places as well as social relations with people of the bygone and distant times and places. If utopian images help us cope with the present and provide a sense of stability, then warming entails using things that objectify the utopian "once-us-other" to make the present familiar. Warming requires the creation of a remembrance of things past; it draws on the idealized objects that embody the nostalgia for a romanticized time, space, and social relations.

References

Appadurai, Arjun 1996: *Modernity at Large: Cultural Dimensions of Globalization*. Minneapolis: Minnesota University Press.

Delaney, Carol 1991: *The Seed and the Soil: Gender and Cosmology in Turkish Village Society*. Berkeley: University of California Press.

Ger, Güliz & Yeşim Balım 2005: Material Culture of Urbanization: Making Turkish Homes Modern and Warm. Working paper.

Hannerz, Ulf 1992: *Cultural Complexity: Studies in the Social Organization of Meaning*. New York: Columbia University Press.

Hannerz, Ulf 1996: *Transnational Connections*. London: Routledge.

Hetzel, Patrick & Robert Schuman 1999: Aestheticization of the Present Using the Past: A Socio-Semiotic Analysis of Some Service Places in Contemporary Markets. *European Advances in Consumer Research* 1999:4, 188–189.

Howes, David (ed.) 1996: *Cross-Cultural Consumption*. London: Routledge.

Illouz, Eva 1997: *Consuming the Romantic Utopia: Love and the Cultural Contradictions of Capitalism*. Berkeley, CA: University of California Press.

Miller, Daniel 1987: *Material Culture and Mass Consumption*. Oxford: Basil Blackwell.

Miller, Daniel 1998: Why Some Things Matter. In: Miller, Daniel (ed.), *Material Cultures: Why Some Things Matter*. London: University College London Press, pp. 3–21.

Tuan, Yi-Fu 1993: *Passing Strange and Wonderful: Aesthetics, Nature, and Culture*. Washington D.C.: Island Press.

Wilk, Richard 1999: 'Real Belizean Food': Building Local Identity in the Transnational Caribbean. *American Anthropologist* 1999:101 (2), 244–255.

Williams, Raymond 1973: *The Country and the City*. Oxford: Oxford University Press.

SMOOTHING

Richard Wilk

There is nothing regular, planned, symmetrical or consistent about culture; it has no geometry. Cultural processes of change are equally messy and unpredictable. Even in retrospect we rarely find trends over time which fit straight lines or simple logarithmic curves, and simple repetitive cycles are equally rare. From a contemporary standpoint, directions and trends are even more chaotic and difficult to discern. Every rule seems to have exceptions, no boundary is completely fixed, and culture seems to constantly burst out of whatever category we use to contain and describe it.

Cultural smoothing describes a variety of ways people simplify, regularize, paper over, and flatten experience, knowledge, history and social life, making culture and cultural processes easier to see, describe, and codify. The idea of smoothing invites us to think about the gap between experience and description, events and memory, nature and the naturalized. Smoothing is a process of interpretation and representation which finds order in chaos, direction in a random walk, and geometry in a messy tangle. Often we perform various kinds of smoothing entirely unconsciously, because finding patterns in nature was for so long an essential survival skill. The ability to see the trail of a running rabbit across loose sand covered with other tracks can become an automatic and unconsciously-applied skill.

But a great deal of smoothing is intentional and even strategic, a tactic of persuasion, a method of manipulating information, and a means of solving social problems. The term "smoothing over" is used in English to describe situations where everyone has been persuaded to agree to ignore a social rift, a quarrel or dispute, to act as if something never happened. In this case social smoothing requires two steps – forging agreement on a common definition of what has happened, and getting everyone to agree to act as if they have forgotten that the disorder was ever there.

Building a roadbed through rough terrain is a good analogy for the two movements of smoothing. Road-building requires two basic operations; cutting and filling. The hills in the way are removed, and the waste is dumped into valleys and low spots. The ideal path has an even balance between cutting and filling so there is no excess or shortfall in material and the road grade is constant. Similarly, the cultural process of smoothing involves removing obtrusive, unexpected, unusual or anomalous events, and filling in gaps in memory, records, groups, with symmetrical arrangements and surfaces.

While smoothing is an ethnographic reality-something which can be observed in every social setting, it is also one of the primary activities of social scientists. Even the most basic levels of ethnographic work involve a great deal of smoothing. We choose to ask questions which flow logically one into another, smoothing the path of speech and story-telling instead of constantly changing courses and topics. We filter out the "noise" from our field recordings, choose particularly uncluttered or clear views for our photographs, and keep our attention carefully focused when recording direct observations, pushing events into a smooth linear sequence. Often we

enlist the people we work with as our collaborators in creating a smooth ethnographic record which has direction, flow and order. At other times we may not even know about the cracks and crevasses in the stories they tell us, their recollections and explanations, for they are carefully hidden and concealed.

The technology of reporting and recounting historical narratives and ethnographic detail has its own role in creating smooth flows in text. The process of crafting a book or article requires constant choices about what to include and what to leave out, which actors to bring on stage and which to leave hidden in our field notes. Like a gardener creating topiary from an unruly bush, we chop and trim until a coherent narrative emerges. We smooth months of unruly notes, piles of scribbled reminders and hasty drafts, boxes of reprints and lumpy quotes, and end up with a coherent sequence of paragraphs, pages and chapters which moves smoothly from introduction to conclusion.

In the process of writing and teaching, academics sort theoretical perspectives neatly into opposing camps, collaborators, and distinct schools of thought; whole groups of scholars have specialized in the work of *theoretical smoothing*. They survey an unruly gaggle of working scholars, and nominate a few whose thoughts are "central," representative and influential. They choose the particular parts of the whole messy production of an academic career which will stand as the intellectual motif for a theorist's life's work. They tell and retell the founding myths of a discipline and trace the descent of ideas through time as a continuous and coherent sequence – very little of which was actually visible to the people who lived through those times and played major parts in the story. Smooth stories exist in retrospect and prospect, but rarely in the present.

Smoothing is such a pervasive process that examples can be found almost anywhere. To smooth out this unruly abundance, I have chosen some arbitrary categories which encompass most of the kinds of smoothing that ethnographers and ethnologists generally encounter.

Realignment is a kind of cultural chiropractic, which seeks to connect events into a seamless chain leading from a founding event to the present. Think of Winston Smith, the hapless hero of Orwell's *1984* (1949), rewriting history daily in order to better explain the changing alliances and wars of the fictional superstate of Oceania.

One of the most famous ethnographic cases was recorded by ethnographer Paul Bohannon, when he worked with the Tiv people of northern Nigeria. The Tiv are patrilineal, and their lineage organization is extremely important in politics and jurisprudence. Alliances and coalitions are often based on how patrilineages are related to one another, and those relationships are reckoned based on birth order and descent many generations back into the past. The right to settle and use land is also grounded in ancestral relations. During one fieldwork session Bohannon recorded these genealogies, because they explained existing alliances and the distribution of offices. Returning a few years later, he wanted to verify his earlier genealogies, but found that many had changed. When alliances broke up, the genealogies were adjusted accordingly, and new allies were discovered to be relatives by previously unknown ancestors. A newcomer to the area, if accepted, could become a long-lost relative. Another might fall from power or be expelled from a settlement, and people might remember that there was a dispute over whether the person ever belonged to the lineage at all.

The smoothing of history to accommodate political change is common in modern states as well. As recounted in *The Commissar Vanishes* (King 1997), Soviet photo retouchers were busy after every purge or rehabilitation to remove or restore faces in historical photographs. The present Bush administration in the USA has refined this art of political smoothing into a policy of state; never admit errors, rename disasters as victories, call every bad judgment an instance of "strong leadership," and ignore or silence alternative interpretations. Two major methods many governments use in their smoothing enterprises are "throwing money," and the appropriately named "cover up." The former consists of giving the appearance of fixing cracks or filling gaps by appropriating and spending money. Then a government can assert that it has taken care of a problem. The cover up just hides irregularities under a blanket of secrecy. While the internet has made some kinds of secrecy and cover-up more difficult, computer technology has also brought the tools of retouching onto every desktop. No form of published photographic evidence can be assumed to be in its original unsmoothed state.

While these smoothing strategies deal with eliminating or concealing special or anomalous events which break the "alignment" of a regime's narrative and performance, other kinds of smoothing are so thoroughly institutionalized that they are part of the normal routine of governance. This variety of realignment, which could be called *Textbooking*, selects one from all possible accounts of events and officializes it, authorizing a public version which will be told to outsiders and taught to the next generation. This very public form of communal remembering requires an equal measure of forgetting, once again demonstrating that smoothing requires cutting and filling in equal measure.

As I have already implied, smoothing takes place at many social levels, from the family that develops a single communal narrative of holidays, meals, and key events, up to the global functions of organizations like UNESCO which authorize a single narrative of the direction the world is moving. As individuals we maintain our own ongoing smoothing efforts. Cognitive scientists have recently demonstrated that people have a tremendous power to unconsciously smooth their own visual field. Told to concentrate to catch the appearance of one character in a video, most subjects manage to screen out unexpected objects. A man in a gorilla suit enters the scene, but most subjects do not consciously register it, or recall it after the film.

Individual memory is itself a wonderful instrument for smoothing, allowing us to forget particular events and elaborate others. Narrative therapists argue that personality develops through a life-long process of telling and retelling events and stories in an internal monologue, by telling stories about ourselves and our past, thereby creating a biographical narrative. A process like this presents many opportunities for selective cutting, pasting, and trimming to build a smoothed and coherent identity, from what would otherwise be a chaotic jumble of memories.

Retrodiction could be seen as a variety of historical smoothing which creates a directional narrative to make the present seem like an inevitable consequence of natural forces or past events. Many myths retrodict the present, explaining that some particular aspect of the world is a direct result of supernatural events; "earth woman was given fire by the creator, which is why women cook today." Mythological retrodiction like this has a theological counterpart in teleological stories which interpret events as the consequence of past sins or good deeds. Fundamentalist Christians in the USA have honed retrodiction into a political art form. Pat Robertson, for example, said that New Orleans was destroyed by hurricane Katrina because of its sinful history and bacchanalian Mardi Gras celebrations. A fundamentalist church recently held a demonstration at a military funeral in a town in Indiana. The man had died fighting in Iraq; the demonstrators carried signs saying that his death was punishment for the country's toleration of gay people. They "reasoned" that open homosexuality in the USA was bringing God's wrath on the country.

The logic of retrodiction is also familiar territory in many of the sciences and social sciences. Evolutionary psychology, a rapidly growing interdisciplinary field of research, explains all kinds of modern human behavior by reference to human evolutionary events in the far distant past. So for example, people today like to gamble in casinos because three million years ago when australopithecines were learning to hunt big game, young males could improve their "reproductive success" by taking risks to outhunt their peers (Gray 2004). Other evolutionary psychologists have hatched scenarios which purport to explain monogamy, male dominance, the invention of money, various kinds of political systems, and even standards of female beauty and fashion trends by retrodicting back to primordial evolutionary events or pressures. I have a retrodiction of my own about the origins of evolutionary psychology. I trace its intellectual ancestry back to the "Scientific Racism" of the nineteenth century and the social evolutionism of Herbert Spencer, and connect it forward along a smooth historical trajectory through the eugenics movement and Robert Ardry's (now discredited)

"Territorial Imperative" arguments of the 1960s, when he explained the war in Vietnam as a consequence of Australopithecine cannibalism (1966).

Retrodiction can function in the other direction, where instead of explaining the present by using past events, we refigure and reorder current events in order to fit them to prophecies and predictions. We could call this *Nostradaming*. Again the religious right in the USA provides many examples, as they use the Book of Revelations as a template for interpreting all events in the Palestinian Intifada as a foretold prologue to the "rapture" followed by apocalypse. They have even become powerful enough to try to force current events along into the pattern foretold by prophecy, supporting the invasion of Iraq because it will hasten the second coming.

My paternal grandmother was an expert at genealogical nostradaming, especially when aimed at my mother. When I was a rebellious misbehaving teenager, my grandmother constantly reminded my mother about all the times she had warned my mother that this would happen. Grandma had prophesied that because mother was too indulgent, or too strict, or fed me the wrong food, or let me run around without proper clothing, I would end up badly. And look what happened! There is a certain aesthetic pleasure to tying up causes and effects, predictions and actual events, into a neat and ordered package, at least when the predictions are your own.

I have played with many other smoothing metaphors. Some of them seem to lead in creative directions, for example *Stretching* and *Compression* can be used to describe the manipulation of time sequences to make them longer or shorter. The spatial metaphors of *Coiling* or *Winding* apply to methods of turning a linear sequence of events into a series of cycles or repeated patterns. We can also think about the way people *Fold up* narratives and stories into smaller packages, or *Wrap* one process, concealing it inside another. All of these have the effect of smoothing and *Untangling* the complex and unruly knots of events, personalities and institutions into neat elementary geometrical forms of lines, circles, boxes, and trees.

Specialized areas of study can require their own

metaphorical toolbox for particular kinds of smoothing which are topically specific. I have used *Blending* and *Stewing*, for example, to describe ways that different cuisines are combined to create new local hybrids and mixtures which are then smoothly formalized in cookbooks (Wilk 2001). I have also thought about *Veneering* as a useful metaphor for smoothing in tourism studies. It describes the thin coating of regularity and simplicity which is presented to the outside world. In Belize, for example, complex multiethnic politics are concealed from touristic vision by a veneer of multicultural "harmony among all the ethnic groups." The theme of unity in diversity is regularly performed in public when each culture is represented through the safe formats of an ethnic musical style, a form of dance, a typical dress, or a unique food.

If smoothing belongs to a larger category of processes, that superordinate group might be called "cultural cosmetology." This could be the basis for a much larger taxonomy of cultural processes which regularize and conceal disorder and chaos. My only worry is that the gentle and superficial connotations of all the metaphors I have used in this essay could themselves conceal the violent and destructive nature of smoothing. It may be necessary to develop a more active set of metaphors to describe the armaments and methods of smoothers, like shaving, hacking, smashing, bulldozing, blasting, disappearing, atomizing, and even murdering.

References

Ardry, Robert 1966: *The Territorial Imperative*. New York: Random House.

Gray, Peter 2004: Evolutionary and Cross-cultural Perspectives on Gambling. *Journal of Gambling Studies* 20, 347–371.

King, David 1997: *The Commissar Vanishes: The Falsification of Photographs and Art in Stalin's Russia*. New York: Henry Holt.

Orwell, George 1949: *Nineteen Eighty-Four, a Novel*. London: Secker & Warburg.

Wilk, Richard 2001: Food and Nationalism: The Origins of "Belizean Food." In: Bellasco, Warren & Philip Scranton (eds.), *Food Nations: Selling Taste in Consumer Societies*. New York: Routledge, pp. 67–89.

AISTHESIS & AN-AESTHESIA

Jojada Verrips

In this essay I seek to highlight the importance of the 'knowledge' of the world we get through *all* our senses, not only the eye and the ear, and to argue that tactility is always more or less implied in the other sensorial modes. Touch is more fundamental in mastering and understanding our social and natural environment than is frequently assumed by rational ocular-centric scholars (cf. Hetherington 2003).

In a recent article on screens, I tried to formulate this rather over-confident viewpoint with regard to the touch as follows:

> Finally I think that it would enrich the work of anthropologists, if they paid more attention to the fact that the relations of human beings with their fellow human beings, other animals as well as things, such as screens, always imply tactility. Though we westerners have learned to think that there are only five different senses with sight at the top and the touch at the bottom, because the former is associated with the mind and the latter with the body, we should do everything to get rid of this five-fold, Judeo-Christian and Cartesian type of hierarchical classification. It blinds us to the fact that we relate to the world through the touch of the cornea of our eyes, of the tympanum in our ears, of the receptors in the mucous membrane in our nose, of the papillae on our tongue, of the sensors in our skin and/or our whole body. Instead of the anthropology of the senses, we need an anthropology of the touch and how people have learnt to fragment this basic human experience (Verrips 2002: 39).[1]

Before I present the concept that expresses this provocative idea in a succinct way I deem it necessary to first say something about my (religious and therefore particular sensorial) background that can be held responsible for my radically putting upside down the sensorial hierarchy as it became common in the western world.

I was raised in a rather orthodox Calvinist environment, like many people in the Netherlands, where a sharp distinction was made between body and mind, where the flesh, on the one hand, was associated with a lack of reason, distracting and therefore negative emotions, and in its wake with abject practices called sinful, and where the spirit, on the other hand, was associated with the promising presence of reason and rationality, the imprisonment of all kinds of irrational feelings, especially sexual and aggressive ones, and the inclination to behave as if these feelings did not exist. God was an ever-present eye watching over people, seeing each and everything one thought and did, and keeping account of all the times one became a victim of dark bodily desires, irrational longings and thoughts as well as forbidden fantasies cropping up from the crevices of a corrupted and therefore impure mind. Though I managed to say goodbye to this rather depressing type of Protestantism, I guess that it was due to this outspoken dualistic, ocular-centric and reason-oriented religious background that I later developed a keen interest in alternative ways of perceiving the relation between body and mind and especially in the importance and meaning of irrationality, emotionality and other sensorial sensations than the visual, in our relations with the landscape and humanscape we and others are part of.[2] On several occasions I have tried to come to grips with these intriguing issues, with the importance of the body, unreason, emotions and the other sensorial experiences next to the ones we get through our eyes and in its wake through our rational mind capable of thinking and accumulating so-called 'true knowledge'. Yet I always felt handicapped by the idea that I lacked the concepts to properly express or describe what I was after, in particular with regard to the senses.[3]

And then, some time ago, I came across – I have to admit rather late in my career – the concept *aisthesis* as it was defined in the preface of the book *Bodycheck: Relocating the Body in Contemporary Performing Art*:

> *Aisthesis* comprises more than just visual perception; it stands for general perception with all the senses, as well as the impression that the perceived leaves on the body. In the original meaning of the concept, tactile and visual perception constitute a whole, and it was not until later (e.g. in the Kantian tradition) that this meaning was reduced to merely an eye that observes, without a body (Bleeker et al. 2002: v).

I really had a kind of *eureka*-experience when I read this passage.[4] *Aisthesis* is the concept I was looking for, so I thought at the time I discovered it and stored it away in one of my notebooks.

So when I was invited to contribute a concept to put on the stage of the social sciences, I immediately thought about *aisthesis*. I would like to launch *aisthesis* in order to express my idea that the touch forms the cornerstone of our perception of the world and that all the other sensorial modes are in the last instance based on or even reducible to tactility. In a euphoric mood I let the editors know that I would come up with this fantastic concept. However, what I thought to be a rather easy thing to accomplish became an intellectually unsettling kind of endeavour. For I discovered that armies of scholars with divergent disciplinary backgrounds have already,

for ages, written about and worked with this complex philosophical concept and that it would take me more than a lifetime to find out what exactly it meant in the work *De Anima* by Aristotle where it was launched, and in the works of its numerous later interpreters. I nevertheless want to present here some thoughts with regard to *aisthesis* that I think might at least help to critically reflect upon what we learn to take for granted with regard to the dominance of the eye over the other senses in gathering particular knowledge of, and insights to, the world we live in.

In *De Anima* Aristotle deals with the question of how the 'psyche,' conceptualized by him as a non-material entity with specific powers or a kind of life energy with certain potentialities, uses the material body of human beings and other animals to realize these potentialities or powers through and in their bodies. The 'psyche' is the source of: 1) our potentiality to feed ourselves, 2) our potentiality to perceive the world through our (five) senses (*aisthetikon*), 3) the powers to make representations of (*phantastikon*), 4) the power to think over (*nous*) and 5) the power to develop desires in (*orektikon*) this world, on the basis of our sensations.

Of all our senses the touch is considered to be fundamental by Aristotle, because it forms the condition of our survival through reproduction (sex) and defence (violence). Though he did not see the other senses as variations of the touch in the way I suggested above, he saw our perception of the world through our five senses in the last instance as a kind of an undividable whole. And that is what he meant by *aisthesis*, our corporeal capability on the basis of a power given in our 'psyche' to perceive objects in the world via five different sensorial modes, thus in a kind of analytical way, and at the same time as a specific constellation of sensations, as a whole, for instance, an apple with a texture, a taste, a smell, a sound and a visible shape and colour. An apple makes an im-pression or has on im-pact (on us) as a whole as well as in different sensorial ways at the very same moment. *Aisthesis* then refers to our total sensorial experience of the world and to our sensitive knowledge of it.[5]

In the course of history this type of knowledge

has gradually been pushed to the background in the western world. Emphasis came more and more to rest on sensations through the eye, representations based on eyes alone and finally abstract thinking and reasoning based in their turn on these representations. Especially after Descartes presented his *cogito ergo sum*, expressing his sharp division between body and mind, the *aisthesis* of Aristotle, the *aisthetic* way of knowing the world, the knowing through our body, rapidly lost ground in intellectual circles. Baumgarten's introduction to the aesthetica in the middle of the eighteenth century as the science of sensitive knowing in the classical sense was a hallmark, but it did not mean the return to a more balanced relation between *aisthetic* and rational 'knowing' of the world.[6] However, with the rise of phenomenology, especially as it was developed by Merleau-Ponty in his work on perception (2005 [1945]), *aisthetic* experiences and knowing re-appeared on centre stage again (cf. Marks 2000; Mackendrick 2004; Sobchack 2004). Merleau-Ponty's *Causeries* (2003 [1948]) explicitly dealt with *aesthetic* experience in connection with the rise of modern art.[7] Artists were after representations of reality that were more in accord with the fact that we do not perceive it through our eyes alone, but with all our senses, our whole body.[8]

It is my sincere conviction that ethnologists, anthropologists and sociologists can enrich their disciplines if they start reusing the Aristotelian notion of *aisthesis* in its original meaning. This would require that more balanced attention be paid to *all* our corporeal sensorial sensations in daily life, not merely the (audio-)visual. These sensations form an indissoluble whole in which the touch seems to be more fundamental than is often assumed. It would imply a break with our ocular-centrism and our heavy emphasis on the role of the mind, reason and rationality, and would bring back an interest in our somatic experience of reality. We would then focus on such difficulty to grasp phenomena as deeply felt emotions and desires (especially those related with *eros* and *thanatos*) as well as the irrational and the fantastic, the absurd and the surreal. In other words, re-using the concept *aisthesis* may generate an interest in a (basically tactile) way of knowing the world

other than the rational one that seems to need no body and fully relies on the capacities of our mind.

An apt illustration of what I have in mind when talking about the relevance of taking into consideration *aisthesis* or the whole spectrum of sensorial sensations in experiencing the world can be found in the work of Milena Veenis (1999), a Dutch anthropologist who did fieldwork in the former DDR. She extensively deals with the perception and experience of material objects before and after the *Wende*. She was struck by the fact that her informants were almost always very explicit about the sensorial impressions of Western products, when they received them as gifts from relatives and friends before 1989, and bought them for themselves thereafter. When comparing them with the products they were used to during the socialist period, they sketched the differences in colour, glitter and glance, their smell and taste as well as in their tactile properties. On the basis of the fact that Western products were said to have made such a strong and multifaceted sensorial impression, Veenis criticizes the approach of material culture studies, especially of consumer goods, as it developed in the last decade of the twentieth century. Next to the meaning of material objects, what they represent, on the one hand, and the role they play in the life of people, on the other, one also needs to take into consideration, so she convincingly argues, the fact that people 'very often "know" material objects through all their senses' or, as I would say, *aisthesis* in relation to these objects or commodities. This broad appeal to the senses also features in the ways they are advertised. In his book *Sensual Relations* David Howes deals with the increasingly conscious use of all sensory stimulation in consumer capitalism:

> consumer capitalism, in fact, would make its business to engage as many senses as possible in its seduction of the consumer. The "right look" must, depending on the kind of product being sold, be reinforced by the right feel, the right scent, the right sound, and the right taste (2003: 211).

Using the concept *aisthesis* might also play a useful sensitizing role in the study of processes of in- or exclusion and discrimination of people, for it demands that serious attention be paid to the role of our sensorial experience in classifying and evaluating these 'others'. So far the literature is rather scarce in which the *aisthetic* appreciation of fellow human beings in socially incorporating and excorporating them is dealt with.[9] If anthropologists pay attention to the sensorial impressions others make, they often concentrate on one in particular, e.g. the role of smell, and not on the whole range, as I think would be necessary for gaining a more encompassing insight in all kinds of discriminatory practices or the micro-politics of human interaction. In this connection the concept of the 'somatic norm image' coined by Harry Hoetink might be helpful.[10] A fascinating project would be to make an inventory of the number and nature of *aisthetic* repertoires as they occur in particular societies, especially multicultural ones. Knowledge about the *aisthesis* of, for instance, classes, ethnic and religious groups could be very relevant for a better understanding of their (friendly, neutral or hostile) relationships and bring us closer to an insight in processes of (dis)integration.

Taking *aisthesis* as a starting point may also generate a fresh approach of the question as to how and under what conditions the total *aisthetic* experience of human beings is formed,[11] transformed, deformed, restricted, mutilated or partly put to sleep, narcotized or 'an-aisthetized.' This brings me to a related concept that I would also like to put in the foreground, namely social or cultural anaesthesia.

While I was pondering the sensitizing value of the Aristotelian concept *aisthesis* for social scientists, I also became fascinated by its counterpart: *an-aisthesis* or anaesthesia. I realized how valuable it could be for finding out more about the particular ways the *aisthesis* of societies, communities or groups is shaped, implying that certain sensorial sensations are pushed to the background where they seem to lie dormant, waiting for awakening and others are, on the contrary, put at centre stage (see Zelinsky 2001).[12] Besides the cultural narcosis of certain sensorial sensations in favour of others (for

instance, the visual ones as these are deemed to be the cornerstone of getting knowledge of and insight into the world), I also thought of this narcosis or anaesthesia in a more general sense. It can refer to the process of making people more or less sensible, and its flipside, making them insensible to certain aspects of the landscapes and humanscapes they live in, for instance, by power elites using a specific ideology, discourse or language.

Here one can think of what Klemperer tried to make clear in his work *LTI* or *Lingua Tertii Imperii*, published for the first time in 1947, on the poisoning effects of German fascist language. In this book he states, for instance,

> ...der Nazismus glitt in Fleisch und Blut der Menge durch die Einzelworte, die Redewendungen, die Satzformen, die er ihr in millionenfachen Wiederholungen aufzwang und die mechanisch und unbewusst übernommen wurden. (...) Worte können sein wie winzige Arsendosen; sie werden unbemerkt verschluckt, sie scheinen keine Wirkung zu tun, und nach einiger Zeit ist die Giftwirkung doch da (Klemperer 1999 [1947]: 26–27).

Though Klemperer's work has been criticized as being biased (cf. Maas 1984), I still find it valuable, because it pays attention to how particular language use can play a role in tuning the *aisthesis* or more generally the habitus of human beings.[13] But, of course, next to being anaesthetized by powerful ideologies and discourses, people can also (temporarily) anaesthetize themselves through alternative means.

In this connection the use of drugs and/or various driving behaviours can also be instrumental. As a consequence of utilizing these means people might get differently tuned, so that they end up with radically altered states of consciousness (e.g. Lex 1979). Since anaesthesia does not necessarily imply a loss of all sensorial experiences, as the term suggests, but only of a few, such as the ability to feel pain, and often calls forward a whole range of other sensations, images, and thoughts, there is even reason to look for a more adequate term. In this connection Colás' article on how nitrous oxide developed in the mid-nineteenth century from a means of having fun at so called 'laughing gas parties,' into a fully accepted narcotic in medical circles, is particularly relevant. In this article he sketches why the term anaesthesia, literally meaning no *aisthesis* at all, was coined and accepted for the application of this narcotic in spite of the fact that Humphry Davy, who experimented with it at the end of the eighteenth century, not only pointed to its analgesic potential, but also and very explicitly to its *aisthesis* transforming capacity.[14] The term implied a diversion of the attention from 'aesthetic knowing through, rather than in spite of, the body' (Colás 1998: 350; see also Lingis 1994: ch.1 and Greenfield 2001: 624) that was being rejected because it was considered unscientific and was therefore relegated to the realm of the arts. Colás uses this case history to emphasize what I also deem important: a re-evaluation of the importance of 'our physicality, our bodies, our senses, our experiences' (ibid.: 352).

Much can be gained by re-appreciating *aisthesis* as a crucial instrument to develop a specific sort of knowledge of the world that is not easy to capture in words, but nevertheless forms an undeniable guide for conduct, as much as the knowledge developed on the basis of our capacity to think and reason. Though Colás signals that anaesthesia can be seen as a misnomer, he does not suggest a more appropriate term such as, for instance, *al-aisthesis* (or *al-aesthesia*) which seems to better cover what happens when people are narcotized in order to not suffer from certain pains.[15] This term could be used in a figurative sense by social scientists for all the phenomena which temporarily transform the normal mode or variety of *aisthetic* experience of a category, group or other conglomerate of people.

I would like to emphasize that others have written about social or cultural anaesthesia as suitable concepts for social and cultural processes. In the late 1970s, almost hundred years after Féré and Binet launched this concept (see note 12), Donald Meyer wrote about social anaesthesia in a work on religion in the USA (see Massa 1997). The historian Barbara Ann Day (1992: 688) used it in passing in an essay on the representation of aging and death in French culture. In anthropology Allen Feldman came up with the concept cultural anaesthesia in a thought-provoking article in the *American Ethnologist* (1994).[16]

While others[17] invented social or cultural anaesthesia, I find it most important that it has enormous sensitizing value, along with its counterpart *aisthesis* (and eventually *al-aisthesis*). It can be useful for a wide range of social scientists in tracing, describing and analyzing certain important facets of the societies and cultures they study. For me the use of these concepts means one step further on the road to a full rehabilitation of the body, in particular of the role of *all* the senses – seen as specific variations of the touch – in creating *in unison*, though sometimes with a different vigour, a mode of perceiving and knowing the world. Westerners have learned to devalue this mode of perception (as in the religious circles in which I was raised), in comparison to rational or scientific types of knowing and perceiving. Against the backdrop of the immense increase of *(n)e(w)motions*[18] and the resulting bizarre fantasies and disturbing behaviours with regard to others which we see in our glocalized world, it is most important that we pay more attention to *aisthesis* and social and/or social an-aesthesia. However, if one is prepared to take seriously what I outlined in this essay, then one should realize that our challenge will be to look for and/or to develop a kind of language that will enable us to express more accurately this *(al-)aesthesis*, and the social or cultural an-aesthesia of others and ourselves. This might imply the launching of a new literary turn in anthropology, for I think that it will be impossible to adequately describe in scientist terms what we will find.

Notes

1 See for a strikingly similar viewpoint Mackendrick, who notices a 'tactile trace in all our senses': 'We move our eyes over surfaces, hear the sounds rippling across our tympani, taste what comes into contact with our taste buds, smell tiny particles that bump the linings of our noses' (2004: 61–62). See also Classen (1993: 54–55) and Harvey (2003) who gave the introductory chapter of her book on the touch in early modern culture the title: 'The "Sense of All Senses."'

2   It formed an important part of what I called the anthropology of the wild (in the) west which I began to develop in the early nineties, which focused on the 'dark' sides of Western civilisation (see Verrips 2001).

3   One of the books that come closest to what I was looking for is Johannes Fabian's dazzling work (2000) on the drunken encounter of Africa explorers with indigenous populations. This study explicitly tackles the role of the senses and ecstasis (seen by Fabian as a loss of control implying a detachment from the rules of scientific inquiry) in the production of knowledge of the Other. However, it does not contain an 'embodied anthropology' in which all the senses are equally dealt with and does not present the touch as fundamental, whereas the concept ecstasis relates to a rather altered and certainly not normal sensorial state of consciousness.

4   I remembered that I had read earlier about the concept in, for instance, the work of Classen (1998: 2), but her reference to it did not arrest me, maybe because it was so casual and the notion did not pop up again in the rest of her book.

5   I used the translation of *De Anima* by Schomakers (2000). This work contains a clear introduction and several guidelines for a proper understanding of this difficult philosophical text.

6   The aesthetica developed into a science of the beautiful and the philosophy of art; in other words more and more away from the Aristotelian conception. One of the reasons for this development might be that Baumgarten was raised as a pietist and reckoned the senses to belong to the body or the flesh standing at a lower level than the mind (Shusterman 2000: 301; see also Barck et al. 2002 [1990]: 461–62).

7   See also his essay on film and the new psychology in which he tersely states: '…ich nehme… eine ungeteilte Weise mit meinem ganzen Sein wahr, ich erfasse eine einzigartige Struktur des Dings, eine einzigartige Weise des Existierens, die alle meine Sinnen auf einmal anspricht' (Merleau-Ponty (1999 [1945]: 230). On the relation between art and the senses see Classen (1998).

8   Howes (one of the founders of the anthropology of the senses) propounds a negative attitude towards Merleau-Ponty's work because 'his doctrine of the synergy and intertranslatability of the senses in his *Phenomenology of Perception* covers up the potential disunity of the senses in cultural practice' (2003: 239n6). I disagree with this overly cultural relative viewpoint, for it throws out the baby with the bath water.

9   But see the work of Hall, for example his programmatic article on proxemics (1968) in which all the sensorial dimensions relevant in human interaction are brought together in an enlightening scheme. This is why I consider him a pioneer in the exploration of the phenomenon *aisthesis*, though he does not use the term.

10 Hoetink defines somatic norm image as the entirety of somatic traits that the members of a specific group have learned to share as norm and ideal (Hoetink 1962: 202) and he uses it in connection with somatic distance, that is the degree to which differences between one's own somatic norm image and another somatic type are subjectively experienced (ibid.: 251). Important somatic traits are, of course, colour and decoration of the skin, hairdo, 'soundscape' and 'smellscape.' However, if one wants to include other traits, such as proxemic behaviour and dress, then the concept somatic *Gestalt* might be more to the point, as I have argued elsewhere (Verrips 2001).

11 A culturally patterned *aisthesis* is what has been called a *sensotype* by Wober (in Howes 1991: 33).

12 Crary refers to the work of Féré and Binet who in the nineteenth century described 'the simple fact of attention' as 'a concentration of the whole mind on a single point, resulting in the intensification of the perception of this point and producing all around it *a zone of anesthesia*; attention increases the force of certain sensations while it weakens others' (1999: 39).

13 For fascinating reflections on 'the tactility of language,' which is manifest when repetition occurs, see Mackendrick (2004: 50ff.).

14 During his experiments Davy had all kinds of pleasurable sensations and saw 'trains of vivid visible images' that 'were connected with words in such a manner, as to produce perceptions perfectly novel. I existed in a world of newly connected and newly modified ideas. I theorised; I imagined that I made new discoveries' (Davy in Colás 1998: 339).

15 It would certainly be rewarding to have a look at all the forms of 'aesthesia' distinguished in the medical sciences, such as hypoaesthesia, hyperaesthesia, macroaesthesia, par-aesthesia, poly-aesthesia, pseudo-aesthesia, and sin-aesthesia. Al-aesthesia does not yet seem to have been coined. See Howes (2003: 211) for the use of hyperaesthesia.

16 His sketch of cultural anaesthesia and what to understand by it resembles what I have tried to present, but there are differences. Feldman, for instance, does not work with the concept aisthesis in the way I propose. For him cultural anaesthesia is his interpretation of 'Adorno's insight that in a post-Holocaust and late capitalist modernity the quantitative increase of objectification increases the social capacity to inflict pain upon the Other… to render the Other's pain inadmissible to public discourse and culture' (1994: 406). Though he remarks that a political anthropology of the senses can be elaborated upon this insight, his article does not contain such an elaboration, but at most a sketch of the direction it might take. And though he extensively deals with beating up bodies, especially the body

of Rodney King, he does not say anything on the fundamental role of the touch and tactility in our lives in a positive as well as negative sense. In almost everything he wrote thereafter Feldman refers to his seminal article that was reprinted in Seremetakis (1994). See for example his essay on the South African Truth Commission in which he speaks of anaesthesia by alcohol or physiological anaesthesia as a component of a wider socio-cultural anaesthesia which informed the racial treatment of prisoners of the police (Feldman 2002).

17 In this connection I would like to point to the lively and thought-provoking discussion that the work of the German philosopher Wolfgang Welsh on an/aesthetics has triggered. He stated, for instance, '[K]ein *aisthesis* ohne *anaisthesis*.' (cf. Carroll 2001).

18 I coined the term *newmotions* for a number of striking (post-modern) emotions that people air, for instance, after somebody has fallen victim to so-called senseless violence in public spaces.

References

Barck, K. et al. (eds.) 2002 [1990]: *Aisthesis: Wahrnehmung heute oder Perspektiven einer anderen Ästhetik.* 7. Auflage. Reclam-Bibliothek Band 1352. Leipzig: Reclam Verlag.

Bleeker, M. et al. (eds.) 2002: Bodycheck: Relocating the Body in Contemporary Performing Art. *Critical Studies* Vol. 17. Amsterdam, New York: Rodopi.

Carroll, J. 2001: The An/aesthetics of Wolfgang Welsh. Http://www.gradnet.de/papers/pomo2.archives/pomo01.paper/Carroll01.htm.

Classen, C. 1993: *Worlds of Sense: Exploring the Senses in History and Across Cultures.* London, New York: Routledge.

Classen, C. 1998: *The Color of Angels: Cosmology, Gender and the Aesthetic Imagination.* London: Routledge.

Colás, S. 1998: Aesthetics vs Anaesthetic: How Laughing Gas Got Serious. *Science as Culture* 7(3), 335–54.

Crary, J. 1999: *Suspensions of Perception: Attention, Spectacle, and Modern Culture.* An OCTOBER book. Cambridge, Mass.: The MIT Press.

Day, B.A. 1992: Representing Aging and Death in French Culture. *French Historical Studies* 17(3), 688–725.

Fabian, J. 2000: *Out of Our Minds: Reason and Madness in the Exploration of Central Africa.* Berkeley: University of California Press.

Feldman, A. 1994: On Cultural Anesthesia: From Desert Storm to Rodney King. *American Ethnologist* 21(2), 404–18.

Feldman, A. 2002: Strange Fruit: The South African Truth Commission and the Demonic Economies of Violence. *Social Analysis* 46(3), 234–65.

Greenfield, S. 2001: Altered States of Consciousness. *Social Research* 68(3), 609–27.

Hall, E.T. 1968: Proxemics. *Current Anthropology* 9(2–3), 83–109.

Harvey, E.D. (ed.) 2003: *Sensible Flesh: On Touch in Early Modern Culture.* Philadelphia: University of Pennsylvania Press.

Hetherington, K. 2003: Spatial Textures: Place, Touch, and Praesentia. *Environment and Planning* A 35, 1933–1944.

Hoetink, H. 1962: *De gespleten samenleving in het Caribisch gebied: Bijdrage tot de sociologie der rasrelaties in gesegmenteerde maatschappijen.* Assen: Van Gorcum & Comp. N.V.

Howes, D. (ed.) 1991: *The Varieties of Sensory Experience. A Sourcebook in the Anthropology of the Senses.* Toronto: University of Toronto Press.

Howes, D. 2003: *Sensual Relations: Engaging the Senses in Culture & Social Theory.* Ann Arbor: The University of Michigan Press.

Klemperer, V. 1999 [1947]: *LTI. Notizbuch eines Philologen.* Reclam-Bibliothek Band 125. 18. Auflage. Leipzig: Reclam Verlag.

Lex, B. 1979: The Neurobiology of Ritual Trance. In: E.G. d'Aquili, C.D. Laughlin Jr. & J. McManus (eds.), *The Spectrum of Ritual: A Biogenetic Structural Analysis.* New York: Columbia University Press, pp. 117–52.

Lingis, A. 1994: *Foreign Bodies.* New York, London: Routledge.

Maas, U. 1984: *"Als der Geist der Gemeinschaft eine Sprache fand." Sprache im Nationalsozialismus: Versuch einer historischen Argumentationsanalyse.* Opladen: Westdeutscher Verlag.

Mackendrick, K. 2004: *Word Made Skin: Figuring Language at the Surface of Flesh.* New York: Fordham University Press.

Marks, L.U. 2000: *The Skin of the Film: Intercultural Cinema, Embodiment, and the Senses.* Durham, London: Duke University Press.

Massa, M.S. 1997: A Catholic for President? John F. Kennedy and the 'Secular' Theology of the Houston Speech, 1960. *Journal of Church and State* 39(2), 307–28.

Merleau-Ponty, M. 1999 [1945]: Das Kino und die Neue Psychologie. In: R. Konersmann (ed.), *Kritik des Sehens.* Reclam-Bibliothek Band 1610. 2. Auflage. Leipzig: Reclam Verlag.

Merleau-Ponty, M. 2003 [1948]: *De wereld waarnemen.* Inleiding, vertaling (van *Causeries*) & aantekeningen Jenny Slatman. Amsterdam: Boom.

Merleau-Ponty, M. 2005 [1945]: *Phenomenology of Perception.* Translated by Colin Smith. Routledge-Classics. London, New York: Routledge.

Schomakers, B. 2000: *Aristoteles. De Ziel. Vertaling, inleiding, aantekeningen.* Leende: Damon.

Seremetakis, C. N. (ed.) 1994: *The Senses Still: Perception and Memory as Material Culture in Modernity.* Boulder: Westview Press.

Shusterman, R. 2000: Somaesthetics: A Disciplinary Proposal. *The Journal of Aesthetics and Art Criticism* 57(3), 299–314.

Sobchack, V. 2004: *Carnal Thoughts: Embodiment and Moving Image Culture*. Berkeley: University of California Press.

Veenis, M. 1999: De zinnelijke verleiding van dingen. *Kennis & Methode. Tijdschrift voor empirische sociologie* XXIII(1), 11–37.

Verrips, J. 1988: Holisme en Hubris. *Etnofoor* 1(1), 35–57.

Verrips, J. 2001: Kleine anatomie van in- en uitsluiting. In: F. Lindo & M. van Niekerk (eds.), *Dedication & Detachment: Essays in Honour of Hans Vermeulen*. Amsterdam: Het Spinhuis, pp. 285–300.

Verrips, J. 2001: The *Golden Bough* and *Apocalypse Now*: Another Fantasy. *Postcolonial Studies* 4(3), 311–35.

Verrips, J. 2002: 'Haptic Screens' and Our 'Corporeal Eye.' *Etnofoor* 15(1–2), 21–47.

Zelinsky, W. 2001: The Geographer as Voyeur. *Geographical Review* 91(1–2), 1–9.

AGEING

WASTING*

Lynn Åkesson
Photographs by Susanne Ewert

Waste is a word with complex connotations. As in T.S.Eliot's famous poem "The Waste Land" from a war-torn Europe of 1922, it may include the double meaning that signifies both "deserted" and "rubbish". Then there is wasting away, as in disappearing or losing strength, wasting as squandering or destroying, wasted as in consumed. We may talk about a wasted life, a waster, a wasteful activity or a waste product. But what happens when you use cultural phenomena like waste disposal and the production of refuse as an entrance into a world of overlooked or underdeveloped types of cultural processes? My starting point is an ongoing project concerning refuse, *The Universe of Waste: On Culture and Decomposition*.[1]

Refuse or waste has to do with cultural order – and disorder. Everyday sorting and classification is a natural expression of such ordering. We are constantly "sorting things out", redefining some objects, activities, people as waste or just wasted. It seems fruitful to look at the ways, in which such redefinitions occur, to take a closer look at the transformation, the moment of wasting.

Sorting Things Out

Such loaded moments can be observed at public refuse collecting centres. In a small local refuse station, voluntarily staffed a few hours a week by representatives of an athletic association, twelve containers stand neatly lined up. Here you can leave your ordinary sorted refuse – plastic, metal, wood, glass, old refrigerators, and so on – along with unsorted waste, medicines and hazardous chemical waste like leftover paint. It costs 50 kronor for a car and 100 kronor for a trailer, to get rid of your refuse. In this small locality, most people know each other, and it happens that someone who is leaving junk will encourage the attendant for the day to ask whether anyone else might want a good used silencer or something else that is too good just to throw out. People also often ask which container things are supposed to be left in. But if they don't, the rule is not to meddle in the doings of other refuse-leavers. Until the person who is leaving refuse initiates the conversation him-or-herself, or until it is time to pay, the attendant stays discreetly in the background, near the shed that gives shelter from the wind and weather. The rules of the public sanitation department for the person who is supervising the little refuse station are very clear as regards the relation to the person who is leaving refuse. "Remember," read the instructions, "never to get into a dispute with the refuse-leavers. Refer complaints to the utility's sanitation section." The attendant is also reminded never to "make comments about the leaver's refuse, such as medicines." In spite of this discretion, some people prefer to leave some rubbish in the more anonymous refuse station in the city. There, private secrets blend and disappear more easily into the crowd.

Refuse sorting becomes an invocation in which the consumer's bad conscience is assuaged. Without really knowing the actual facts with regard to recycling and what is best for the environment, many people still sort their waste because it feels good and is morally right. In some way it works as a disciplining task.

Worthless – Valuable. A Round Trip

Another perspective on waste and scrap considers their capacity to be transformed; to become something else, such as art, exhibited at well-reputed gal-

leries and museums, or available to Internet shoppers, where an abundance of artists now advertise their products. One example is www.nycgarbage. com where you can buy cubes of Plexiglas, guaranteed airtight and odourless and filled with genuine refuse from the streets of New York. A concertina-like coffee mug from Starbucks, discarded chewing gum and old banana skins are transformed into art. While junk art is nothing new, the public has to be tempted by greater challenges if the artists are to be heard above the noise of the metal crushers and attract people's attention. An example of this is when the artist Michael Landy invited twelve people to destroy everything he owned. A total of 7,006 things were destroyed in front of prospective onlookers in rented premises in Oxford Street in central London (Yaeger 2003).[2] To what extent scrap art actually finds its way to the homes of art buyers is a question that remains to be answered. The public's fascination with junk art seems to be mixed with anger and disgust, and the eternal question on what art really is. Art made of rubbish challenge the concepts of aesthetics and beauty, and nourishes the fascination with the secrets of waste and its possible transformations.

Another set of completely different quick-changes transform refuse into musical instruments, tools, houses and other serviceable artefacts. Some people literally live on refuse tips or rummage among street refuse, like "los cartoneros" of Buenos Aires, Mexico's "los pepenadores" or the homeless in today's Sweden on the hunt for copper cables that can be sold to scrap-dealers. Only a few decades ago, the art of remodelling hand-me-down clothes from older to younger family members, turning food leftovers into tasty suppers, or making new tools from old, was considered a way to keep the tradition of thrifty housekeeping alive; these vestiges of recycling are now reincarnated in other, high-tech guises. The western world's growing mountains of refuse have, like necessity itself, become the mothers of invention. Discarded plastic bottles can be turned into material for making fleece jackets, specific bacteria can be used for cleaning up contaminated environments, waste paint can be transformed into composite material and the slag from incinerated refuse and rubber clippings from old tyres can be used as road building material. In Japan, researchers are looking into converting compostable domestic waste into electricity. Building waste can also be recycled into new constructions.

But there are other forms of recycling. In the Experience Economy waste and wastelands can become a tourist destination. There is so-called shock-tourism that is nourished by the allure of misery and misfortune. Shanty towns and slum areas can thus be experienced and scrutinised from the safety of sightseeing bus windows, or outings can be taken to landscapes devastated by chemicals and poisons. Time can also transform an old rubbish dump into a cultural heritage site. One Swedish example of such a development is *Kyrkö mosse*, a bog- and woodland area, used for decades to dump old car wrecks. When the man who ran the dump finally became too old to remain in business and moved out, a heated discussion burst out about whether to remove or to save the remains of the old cars. The later alternative won, and *Kyrkö mosse* is now a valued attraction. Visitors from all of Europe find their way to the bog where the wrecks slowly decompose, covered with rust and moss.

Social systems that are removed to ideological refuse tips can also be resurrected as both unpleasant memories and nostalgic scenery. In former Eastern Germany, with its high unemployment and bitterness at the price of unification, there are plans to create an amusement park with the theme of the DDR. Lithuania already has *Stalin World*, a theme park that has been designed as a Soviet concentration camp and filled with statues from Communist times. Monuments representing a particular time period and its significant personalities are converted to refuse and then may be recycled again. They make use of an emotional charge that can be re-used to gain new value (see Jonas Frykman's contribution in this issue) like the statue of Lenin now standing outside a McDonald's restaurant in Dallas, Texas, furnished with a sign proclaiming "America won" (Burström 2003).

Recycling tells us about the constantly changing relationship between waste and value (Hawkins & Muecke 2003). It says that what is worthwhile can only be understood in the light of what at a given time is defined as worthless. Refuse is never constant. It is transformed and slides along a grading scale of worthless –> valuable –> invaluable. What someone discards, someone else covets. Things can always be re-charged and acquire new meanings (Kopytoff 1986). Refuse thrown away can become someone else's desirable property. Bargain hunting continues at flea-markets, in second-hand shops and on refuse tips. Whole sciences – like archaeology – may build on the foundation of waste and refuse.

Clean and Unclean Waste

Refuse can be categorised according to several different principles. Empirically, refuse tips can be categorised according to content. They can also be classified in terms of refuse that can be converted into energy in the shape of heat or fertiliser, refuse that can be recycled, or that which is dangerous and must be locked away, rendered harmless or stored for the foreseeable future. Another way of regarding the diversity of refuse is to see it as being either clean or unclean.

Clean refuse can be composed of things, places and buildings consisting of discarded objects that can be reused and acquire new meaning and new aesthetics in another context. Castle ruins gave free rein to the imagination and nourishment to visions of noble knights and royal soldiers. Abandoned farms and cottages in process of being enveloped by the landscape raise questions about the people who once lived there, their living conditions, their reasons for rejoicing and their hardships. Think of a small foundry that closed its doors for the last time in the 1950s, where the workers went home but the machines remained. Old agricultural tools sinking into oblivion, large unused silos or entire industrial complexes all bear witness to times gone by. Or an old school with its classrooms restored by the local folklore society: the teacher's elevated desk, wall charts representing the agricultural seasons, biblical quotations and school benches in straight lines. The schoolhouse accommodates a past with its ideas, values, norms and perceptions of authority that have inexorably landed on the ideological refuse tip. Even terrible places like extermination camps or battle grounds are washed clean by time and liberated from their nauseating stench and unbearable visual impressions. Clean refuse generally allows itself to be touched and visited, the old school's outhouse included. Clean refuse has a high nostalgia factor.

Things are quite different when it comes to unclean waste: fermenting, rotting, stinking biological waste, exhaust and chemical pollution, hospitals' hazardous waste, waste from slaughterhouses and radioactive waste. Just like a subterranean mycelium, the communal sewage system connects people with each other. Bodily secretions and slops find their way towards the sewage treatment plant. Sewers are the motorways of separation, carrying what has become untouchable and hidden after leaving the body and the sink, tub or shower. The remains of the delicious meal starting to smell in the refuse bin, a piece of mouldy melon in the fridge, or potatoes that have rotted and now leak their stinking and disgustingly messy liquid into a plastic bag in the pantry. This is waste that must be touched, but quickly and with a certain disgust.

Dead animal carcasses can, like dead people's bodies, be transformed from unclean to clean waste by ritual techniques. Animal crematoriums take care of dead pets at set prices. Domestic pets can also be buried in special animal cemeteries, in collective memorial areas, or in their own separate graves. It is quite obvious that animal owners who pay extra for an individual cremation and burial place for their dead pets regard the animal's body as something more than an impure carcass.

For us humans, the rituals that accompany a death, when the dead body is washed and clothed and undergoes a funeral ceremony, with or without a religious element, mean that a dead body is something other than a rotting cadaver. In this context even time lends a helping hand. Time has picked at the bones of animals and people and the complete skeletons or skull collections in museums clean of their disintegrating flesh. Carcasses have been transformed into relics through ritual practices (Bell 1997; Bloch & Parry 1989; Åkesson 1996).

There is a grey zone between clean and unclean, a fluid area that accommodates the possibility of movement between both categories, that can be both symbolic and material. Symbolic uncleanness or impurity can, for example, attach to certain foods or certain people on cultural, traditional or religious grounds, rather than because of actual inedibility or infection and filth. From this perspective, the fixation on the best-before-date displayed on modern food packages (which means that perfectly edible food is thrown away), is comparable with ancient religious food taboos. In both cases, the idea of inedibility overshadows the food itself. In a general process of secularisation, a religiously conditioned impurity is replaced by a scientific one.

A Secret Life

The grey zone of waste has other dimensions as well. The transformation from unclean to clean often marginalises the very people that handle refuse or dead bodies. These workmen and women concerned with waste management have often been reduced to untouchables on society's fringe. Although this stigma is not attached to today's professional refuse collectors, the location of the refuse tip on the city outskirts also implies that the job of refuse collecting has a certain air of mystery and uncontrollability attached to it. For example, in the popular TV series, *The Sopranos*, the mafia boss Tony Soprano assumes a waste handling company as an outward façade, diffuse enough to allow all kinds of activities to shelter behind it. In Sweden, the connection between scrap

prove their innocence or guilt. In reality, refuse tips are dramatic settings of enormous machinery, cranes and metal crushers. The drama is enhanced by the waste's personal roots, coupled to specific people, dreams and actions. Finding conclusive evidence in gigantic refuse heaps is like looking for a proverbial needle in a haystack. It is an enormous challenge.

Both the hidden and the secretive are forceful literary themes. There is both a tempting mystery and the repulsion of something that we absolutely don't want to know anything about; that which the eye turns away from. Guy Hawkins talks about the "the force of the hidden", what we don't want to see or concern ourselves with. It takes up space, seeks control, and becomes an important tool in the preservation of social order and political authority (Hawkins 2003). A similar perspective is presented in Dominique Laporte's intriguing book *History of Shit* (2000). Laporte shows that the will of the state (i.e. the king) to take control and make value out of the latrine in the 15th century France was embedded in claims to power and forces of repression.

The hidden and the secretive seem to hunt us, and it constantly reminds us of what we want to forget. This perspective is used in the socially critical novel *Underworld* (1997) by Don DeLillo. DeLillo uses enormous amounts of refuse and landfill areas as backgrounds for repressed individual memories, the garbage of the mind and soul. In this way, as pointed out by Patricia Yaeger (2003), waste can be seen as an archive, a private or societal memory that bears witness to culturally relevant categories of order, management, production and consumption. That which is thrown away can also be seen as an archive of actions and preferences, time-bound truths and ideologies. It's significant rubbish, "a mess with a message".

dealing and criminality, where tax enforcers were not always informed about what was going on, goes back to gypsy trading and is hard to eradicate.

The secretive element also has connections to things other than shady dealings. Domestic waste is private and belongs to the personal sphere. That someone else should ferret around in one's own dustbin is an insult to personal integrity. It is hardly surprising that famous people unwittingly subjected to their waste being emptied and exposed to TV audiences react very negatively.[3] Refuse is revealing and ought to be kept secret.

The desire to conceal and hide, combined with discovery, revelation and the keen gaze, provide grist for the story mill in whodunits, detective stories and what might be called documentary reconstructions of violent crimes. Similar things also appear on refuse tips, where skilful experts root about in the refuse of those under suspicion – likewise in their homes or cars – in search of evidence that can either

The Moral Dimensions of Waste

As a result of culture-creating principles of order and segregation, the management of waste is impregnated with ethical value judgements, and with feelings of shame and guilt. What has been separated from the body, the dining table and the household, has also become symbolically unclean, disgusting,

repugnant and untouchable. This transformation has nothing to do with the laws of nature, however. Filth and repulsiveness vary according to time and place so that which is disgusting is also a powerful and often invisible upholder of cultural order. Disgust rapidly moves from the world of ideology to the body as a spontaneous gut feeling. The fact that different values or entire worldviews are the basis of the sense of the disgusting becomes visible only when value systems meet, collide, or change. Jonas Frykman and Orvar Löfgren demonstrated this in *Culture Builders* (1987) with examples taken from the Swedish middle and peasant classes at the end of the 1800s and beginning of the 1900s. People learned how to feel ashamed in accordance with bourgeois judgments about dirt and uncleanness.

Moral overtones and ideologies that lie behind the distinction of what is clean and what is unclean are, like everything else, easier to discern by looking through history's rear-view mirror. Today we are taught, with greater or lesser degrees of success, to be ashamed of the gigantic refuse tips formed by past consumption. But the absolutely essential work of reducing the amount of waste, of protecting land, water, air and also people from the dangers of refuse in all its diversity, doesn't escape appraisal today either. Morality and ethics are constant presences in the kingdom of waste.

Cultural Attrition

Waste follows in human tracks. Waste is about making decisions about saving or discarding, forgetting and remembering, ignoring or resurrecting. Waste is handled, taken care of, transformed and overlooked. The universe of waste therefore offers an enriching panorama of investigation of the ways in which different types of attrition processes interact. How are ideas about cultural ageing coloured by metaphors and models of biodegradation or material fatigue failure? How are the discursive elements of material, cultural and bodily transience interwoven? How can we respond to questions regarding aesthetics, the critique of the civilisation process, the global divisions of labour, and nostalgia, recycling and regeneration? What kinds of culturally based decisions are we making as we stand in a moment of hesitation before we slip an object or an idea into the waste-bin or dump it on the refuse tip? The analysis of such moments may teach us how ideas of repugnance and the untouchable are constructed, but above all how sorting and segregation are basic cultural practices.

Returning to the general question, "why study wasting", we can address classic ethnological themes. Wasting can be used to shed light on processes of classification, ordering, transformation, and stigmatization. In my opinion, the secret dimensions of waste, the force of the hidden, is one of the most powerful themes to explore. Lots of cultural energy is used to keep the hidden and disgusting at distance. What becomes hidden and untouchable does not disappear, it lurks under the surface of the ground and the mind and demands cultural handling techniques. That ritual and religious practises are used to keep the disgusting things or thoughts in place, makes wasting an even more exciting topic.

Notes

* Some of the ideas presented here have been published in *Axess* No. 7, 2003 (Åkesson 2003), and in *RIG* No. 3, 2005. Photographs by Susanne Ewert published (in colour) in *Axess* No. 7, 2003.

1 The project is financed by The Bank of Sweden Tercentenary Foundation and carried out at Lund University's Ethnology Department. The project also includes collaboration with Kulturen in Lund – which means that exhibition and research activities become mutually inspirational and enriching.

2 Michael Landy has been working with the theme of refuse for quite a long time. The exhibition *Scrapheap Services* is an ironic reflection on the theme of humans who need to be thrown out and destroyed (Landy 1996).

3 See also Rathje & Murphy (2001: 17f.) about a journalist's investigation into the refuse of people like Bob Dylan and Henry Kissinger.

References

Åkesson, Lynn 1996: The Message of Dead Bodies. In: Lundin, Susanne & Lynn Åkesson (eds.), *Bodytime: On the Interaction of Body, Identity, and Society*. Lund: Lund Univ. Press.

Åkesson, Lynn 2003: The Religion of Refuse. *Axess* No. 7, 2003.

Bell, Catherine 1997: *Ritual Perspectives and Dimensions*. New York: Oxford University Press.

Bloch, Maurice & Jonathan Parry (eds.) 1989: *Death and the Regeneration of Life*. Cambridge: Cambridge University Press.

Burström, Mats 2003: The Value of Junk. *Axess* No. 7, 2003.

DeLillo, Don 1997: *Underworld*. New York: Scribner, Simon & Schuster Inc.

Eliot, T.S. 1940: *The Waste Land and Other Poems*. London: Faber and Faber.

Frykman, Jonas & Orvar Löfgren 1987: *Culture Builders: A Historical Anthropology of Middle-Class Life*. New Brunswick: Rutgers University Press.

Hawkins, Guy & Stephen Muecke (eds.) 2003: *Culture and Waste: The Creation and Destruction of Value*. Lanham: Rowman & Littlefield Publishers, Inc.

Kopytoff, Igor 1986: The Cultural Biography of Things: Commoditization as Process. In: Appadurai, Arjun (ed.), *The Social Life of Things: Commodities in Cultural Perspective*. Cambridge: Cambridge University Press.

Landy, Michael 1996: *Scrapheap Services*. London: Chisenhale Gallery, Ridinghouse Editions.

Laporte, Dominique 2000: *History of Shit*. Cambridge, Mass.: MIT Press.

Rathje, William & Cullen Murphy 2001: *Rubbish! The Archaeology of Garbage*. Tucson: The University of Arizona Press.

Yaeger, Patricia 2003: Trash as Archive, Trash as Enlightenment. In: Hawkins, Guy & Stephen Muecke (eds.), *Culture and Waste: The Creation and Destruction of Value*. Lanham: Rowman & Littlefield Publishers, Inc.

BRACKETING

Jonas Frykman

The concept of "cultural bracketing" can be a tool for describing how diffuse and changeable is the world in which people move – full of possibilities and open to admit new experiences. Words combined with "cultural" otherwise can easily take on a deceptive clarity. But things are often latent, waiting to be put to use; they live an unnoticed life. If things are not clearly arranged in taxonomies and categories, what about people, thoughts, and mental processes?

Averted Remains

The benefit of thinking in terms of "bracketing" became clear to me in connection with my fieldwork in the region of Istria in Croatia at the end of the 1990s. At that time I had not yet become interested in the many monuments that I saw around me, commemorating the victory of socialism. Instead, I found the emergent regional movement seemed analytically rewarding. It differed in many ways from other contemporary efforts to shape local cultural identity in Europe. Instead of stressing autochthony, purity, and exclusion, the Istrian people celebrated ethnic and linguistic diversity. They emphasized today's landscape more than that of the past, they looked forward rather than searching for roots, and were more interested in change than permanence (Frykman 1999, 2003). This was all the more remarkable in view of the fact that the nation to which they belonged, Croatia, in the aftermath of the war, closed itself in and concentrated on itself.

And yet partisan monuments still stood scattered in the landscape like inaccessible atavisms, averted, brooding on a completely different history – as if they were not there. They were at crossroads and lookout points, in city squares, and wherever people gathered. Sometimes it was just a memorial tablet on a wall or some painted symbols and slogans. Others were impressive in format, sacral like sarcophagi, monuments to dead people from an alien world (Frykman 2001). Many were in decay, the inscriptions on the pedestals overgrown with lichen. For the people in charge of museums and cultural heritage management they were a classificatory dilemma, since they were not protected by legislation or by their artistic qualities. In people's everyday lives, these objects were difficult to handle since they claimed a very definite ideological affiliation.

The fact that they were still standing at all was an indication that people in the region really did have openness and tolerance as a distinctive cultural feature. In other parts of Croatia the war had led to far-reaching iconoclasm. These objects were the remains of a state that no longer existed. Moreover, they represented the ideological and political repression from which the new state of Croatia wished to liberate itself. But here in the post-Yugoslavian Istria they still stood, half-forgotten, and – like any enigma – they invited questions. How can people live with something that so obviously *exists* – such as political monuments – when what they stand for no longer is there?

It is a characteristic of any political monument to withdraw into a very special shadow world. Memorials are only forced out into the open on red-letter days and historic occasions. In the book *Nachlass zu Lebzeiten* the Austrian author Robert Musil has derided the invisibility in which they shroud themselves.

> They are no doubt erected to be seen – indeed to attract attention. But at the same time they are impregnated with something that repels attention, causing the gaze to roll right off, like water droplets off an oilcloth, without even pausing for a moment. You can walk down the same street for months, know every address, every show window, every policeman along the way, and you won't even miss a coin that someone dropped on the sidewalk … Many people have the same experience with larger-than-life-size-statues … (Anderson 1998: 46).

It is, Musil says, as if it were against our very nature to notice them.

In the Middle of the Square

The memorial park in the middle of Liberty Square, *Trg Slobode*, in the city of Pazin is one such cultural parenthesis. There are dozens of busts and statues of celebrated freedom fighters and politically important figures from the region. A central granite monument depicts a half-naked worker with bulging muscles, his arms raised in combat posture. On the pedestal are the words: *SMRT FAŠIZMU – SLOBODA NARODU* "Death to fascism – freedom for the people".

The park is deserted and poorly maintained, as if it were slowly sliding into the seclusion of ruin. People hurry to shops and workplaces; pensioners exercise their dogs and visitors take a short cut to the car park. On some dilapidated benches in the shade, schoolchildren turn their backs on the heroic figures, more interested in each other than in history. The wires on the three traditional iron flagpoles – one for the Party, one for Yugoslavia, and one for the Republic – are rusty from lack of use. No flowers adorn the pedestals, no wreaths with messages from old combatants or city dignitaries. This is yet another of the many places that Katherine Verdery (1999) has written about, where socialism derived its strength from death and gave hope of delivery through eternal progress. Now the place is itself on the road to oblivion.

Here they stand, predecessors of a system and an ideology that many of them had not even heard of – the priest and evangelist of enlightenment Juraj Dobrila, who lived in the nineteenth century, the composer and recorder of folk music Ivan Matetić-Ronjgov alongside the anti-fascist Vladimir Gortan, and "heroes of the people" in the partisan struggles. In the shade of the trees they have been brought together, from many places and times, like the gods in a local pantheon. The resemblance to a site of pilgrimage is striking. The heroes must once have been honoured at annual ceremonies where dignitaries strode in stately pomp, wreaths of flowers were laid, red banners waved, bands played, and a ritual meal was served. *Partizanski grah* – a stew of beans with meat or sausage – was the traditional fare of the partisans.

But today people have tried to find a new use for the busts. As in the half-concealed "non-places" in the city, the ground is strewn with rubbish and the statues are painted with graffiti. Over the breast of the heroine of the people Olga Ban, someone has sprayed an anarchist A, and the same symbol covers Ivan Matetić-Ronjgov, who has also had his eyes, ears, and mouth painted white. Another hero of the people, Guiseppe Budici Pino, has been decorated with a nationalist U on his brow and someone has written the full form Ustaša on the pedestal. Doctor Matko Laginja has a piece of chewing gum stuck up his left nostril, and the hero Vladimir Gortan – who has roads, factories, and schools named after him – has had his ear plugged with chewing gum. Another bust bears the inscription *Komunjare* – "damned communists".

Things in Waiting

The partisan monuments in Istria may serve here to illustrate the concept of cultural bracketing. It can be used to describe areas of culture which are pendant, in waiting mode. As a cultural researcher one focuses on what *exists* – symbols, narratives, rituals, and objects. With the "linguistic turn" in the 1990s it became taken-for-granted to focus on text or discourse. The socialist ideology represented by the monuments could then be seen as something ever-present, as an interpretation to be uncovered. What are the messages carried by the monuments, the contexts to which they belong, the intertextuality that prevails between them and other representations? What are the rituals, oral traditions? How are they distributed in time and place? In what media do they occur? And so on.

Or if the researcher is inspired by studies of symbols and structures, it is then important to think about hierarchization, categorization, and classification. What is their place in the cognitive systems in people's minds? How do covering categories such as state symbolism relate to local compliance? How are categories distinguished with the aid of pollution, and how is the fear of mixing categories expressed in the local, and so on?

But what is a researcher to do with all the phenomena that hardly exist at all, those which do not create meaning? The ones that have been put into brackets, made temporarily invisible by being taken out of use? Is it possible to describe the oscillation between what could also be called "cultural latency" and explicit presence? Can we describe the things that do not speak to people by virtue of their usefulness, but which have not yet been categorized as refuse and thrown on the rubbish dump? The items that have ended up among the waste have thereby been given their set place in the universe of things (Åkesson 2005).

We are thus looking at something other than the eliminated categories, the ones placed in their respective pigeonholes outside normality. Things which have been sorted out are not infrequently labelled with words like *sacred, taboo, limbo, disgusting, dangerous*. These are things that have been pushed aside after being associated with dirt, repulsion, and fear (Douglas 1966). But something that is in brackets is not explicit but vague; it lacks the charge and the magical aura that pervades tabooed spheres. No power flows from it, and no effect is exercised. It is much closer to normality than to the extraordinary. It makes people yawn, not scream.

Everyday life seems to be full of things like this, which we once put aside "in case they become handy sometime", but we have lost interest in them. Farmers collect old trailers and parts of tractors behind the barn, to have them handy. The family fills the attic with the children's toys and grandfather's suits, just in case. Books gather dust on the shelves, but we still refuse to take them to a second-hand bookshop. Things are often in-between, neither used nor ready to be thrown away. And they are far too ordinary to end up in a museum.

Memories and Mortals

If the concept of cultural bracketing is a methodological tool that helps us to understand how things can be put in waiting mode, it may also be applicable to other spheres of culture – such as mental and social processes. Extensive research on memory and culture has clearly demonstrated that memory is not the same as an archive and that it is today, not yesterday, that gives clarity to what once happened (Aronsson 2004). The strong influence from psychology has made many look upon memory as a faculty that you can lose, something that is profoundly influenced by time, culture and society. What we call memory is a toolbox where the objects have numerous and varied uses.

Here in Istria there are oceans of knowledge which people have been unable to get rid of, but have chosen to put on hold. During the 1990s, unsorted stories began to appear about how the partisans had behaved at the end of the Second World War. They had summarily executed people who were suspected of collaborating with the fascists. These were memories that had been banished for a generation, poorly remembered and only furtively uttered. Some of this knowledge would have led to imprisonment if it had been aired in public. Now, in a war-torn country, it was suddenly filled with a different meaning, becoming a sharp weapon in the debate about the hidden horrors of socialism. It could justify the need of the nation state of Croatia to break away from the federal socialist state of Yugoslavia (Frykman 2004).

This is how it almost always is with politically risky memories: they wait for the day when they can come to the surface. It is an obvious example of the way cultural brackets can function as more or less withheld memories. But one should not exaggerate intentionality. In 1991, people had not been sitting and waiting for liberation since 1945. But there is also another phase of latency, one which has received less attention. Throughout Eastern Europe the everyday memories of living under socialism have ended up in a no-man's-land, half-way between oblivion and recollection (Vuokov 2003).

The author Dubravka Ugrešić writes in her essay collection *The Culture of Lies* (1998), about how she felt like one of the survivors of Atlantis – but with the important difference that the things, the material remains, are still there while the narratives have disappeared. The links to the land in which she grew up have ceased to exist. The objects – the houses built in socialist functionalist style, the characteristic holders for the three flags, the offices with the low-placed windows through which visitors spoke to officials, the furniture of blue and orange plastic – all this is still there, as palpable as the monuments. But if people start to recollect the content of everyday life it immediately becomes problematic – the celebration of Father Frost, the initiation as a pioneer, and the congratulations to Comrade Tito on the Day of Youth. These are events which make people bite their tongues (cf. Mathiesen Hjemdahl & Škrbić Alempijević, this volume), not to speak of the many narratives about the home, friends, and upbringing under socialism. They easily become stamped as expressions of Yugo-nostalgia – with an undesirable political charge in a new nation that gained independence through war. This situation describes very well how memories are put in cultural brackets, even without a dictatorial policy directed against them.

Can one also apply a social perspective in order to see how individuals and groups view themselves as being inscribed in cultural brackets – living somewhere between marginalization and full membership? What happens, for example, to a person who is excluded from the labour market or sick-listed – without being stigmatized as criminal, deviant, or socially different? Such people live seemingly normal lives among other people, but they notice that their voice has become weaker and they cannot make the same demands on those around them. This is much more common and far more crucial in society than the classical exclusion, which is a matter of distinct categorization.

A telling example of people who have not been given the status of outsiders – but just put in a state of readiness for it – are those who have been diagnosed with "burnout" (see Löfgren, this volume). They struggle with their social namelessness and homelessness, desperately trying to find out whose fault it is: the job, the boss, stress in general, or inadequate medical knowledge. Labels do not stick to them, and their lables are only approximate. This is a state of cultural latency which serves to exacerbate the condition of those afflicted by the diagnosis (Frykman & Hansen 2005; Lundén 2005).

In Praise of Vagueness

The concept of bracketing could be extended beyond the purely material. Its merit is that it helps the researcher to describe a diffuse world full of opportunities and open for receiving new experiences. It also helps us to question the deceptive clarity often ascribed to concepts combined with culture. Most things in culture are not in fact clearly categorized. Things are not properly ordered, not defined by function except when they are used or put on display in museums. It is only in exceptional cases that people belong to neat exclusive groups defined in terms of age, ethnicity, or gender. Most of the time they are a *you* in an intersubjective relationship; *people* in a crowd. Or perhaps *travellers* on a bus through Europe, who may be alternately friends, mothers, relatives, children, rich or poor, old, unmarried – and it is only when they cross national borders and have to take out their passports that they are defined according to *ethnic* and national affiliation. Their identification changes with the situation (cf. Povrzanović Frykman 2003).

Correspondingly, it is a gross simplification to say that symbols are bearers of messages. They are only rarely interpreted in accordance with the author's intentions, as the anthropologist Anthony Cohen writes (1996). People always add and subtract. Some are accustomed to reading the idiom, others are not. Yet it is not a question of right and wrong, of skill and ignorance in interpreting symbols. The power that proceeds from them depends on *whether they make people think at all*. Do they have the ability to activate the observer? Do they give scope for interpretation? If so, about what? Do they open the way for actions and interpretations which are meaningful in the situation where the observer finds himself? Can they be incorporated into concrete plans – short or long – for individuals or for society?

It was not so much the symbolism in the monuments that spoke to people, but people's use of monuments to create action and meaning. The inhabitants of the city assembled before them annually on the special days; the guests of honour were there, brass bands played *Bandiera Rossa*, friends met, and people had an opportunity to show their loyalty to the party. When the occasion was over, the statues once again slipped back into Robert Musil's characteristic unnoticed state. After the break-up of Yugoslavia in 1991, gatherings like these did not bring any rewards. The world they pointed towards was a shrinking company of old veterans, but scarcely today's world, and definitely not the future.

Correspondingly, rituals around the monuments were not bearers of meaning in themselves. Like all rituals, these were filled with content in relation to the society surrounding the actors. If there is no such context, the phenomenon inevitably ends up in cultural brackets, awaiting a new interpretation.

Things as They Are

The things or phenomena that have ended up in cultural brackets become available for redefinitions through the force of circumstances. They can be taken up and filled with a different message. In this respect the concept resembles the way Edmund Husserl used the word *bracketing* or *Einklammerung* in phenomenological theory. Putting something in brackets means trying to see how it shows itself to experience. This means endeavouring not to think of the intellectual or power-inspired superstructure of interpretations, histories, analyses, and reconstructions in order to be able to see "things as they are" (Moran 2000).

In philosophy this is a method for making progress in the analysis and interpretation of how a directly experienced world could be described. In cultural studies we can use the concept to study how people in their everyday practice manage to live in a given material world – despite changing external circumstances. We can examine how people, as in Istria, handle the dramatically different ideological conditions and divisive experiences of life in a country at war. What is put in brackets is set on neutral ground, banished to a place where one need not consider established definitions. It opens itself, it is "liberated" from intentions forced by the situation. Usually, every such move is mostly mental.

Tools

In a few years the many monuments of the partisans' struggles with the fascists will probably become tourist attractions. In Budapest the memorials of socialism have been resolutely moved to a special theme park – *Szobor Park*. Here, on an industrial estate on the outskirts of the city, they stand, urging each other to progress. It may seem like a bizarre experience, but the tourist brochures provide detailed descriptions of which buses to take to get there. In the theme park *Stalin World* or *Grutas Park* near the city of Druskininkai in Lithuania, the powerful leaders of the Soviet era stare straight into the forest, as tape-recorded revolutionary songs from bygone times resound between the spruce trees and over the popular children's playground. Theme parks like these show that the monuments have now been given a very different story to tell.

When the partisan monuments step out of their anonymity in Istria, they will probably tell of a region that not only hails ethnic and linguistic diversity, but also views itself as steward of an ideological pluralism. But then the symbols will have lost their political meaning and will have been incorporated into the cultural heritage. Perhaps, in a more distant future, they will once again be taken out of their political latency so that they can once again urge people to unite and fight.

The benefit that we as cultural researchers can gain from a concept like cultural bracketing is that we may become more attentive to diversity, change-ability, the situational character of every sphere of culture. Things – like rituals, symbols, memories, stories, and texts – are generally tools which people use in order to perform tasks and resolve problems. Some of them are highly visible and vocal, while others exist as hidden resources which can be taken out when needed. Something that is in brackets is ambiguous, uncertain – a palimpsest for future messages. Brackets are temporary stopping places, something into which things, thoughts, and people are put – and from which they also emerge. This is their enormous significance for culture. It is strange to see how monuments, which were supposed to stand for all eternity proclaiming their messages, were quickly set in motion, so that even those cast in bronze and concrete soon became the most changeable parts of culture.

References

Åkesson, Lynn 2005: Sopornas universum. *RIG*, no. 3, pp. 140–151.

Anderson, Benedict 1998: *The Spectre of Comparisons: Nationalism, Southeast Asia and the World*. London: Verso.

Aronsson, Peter 2004: *Historiebruk – att använda det förflutna*. Lund: Studentlitteratur.

Cohen, Anthony 1996: Personal Nationalism: A Scottish View of Some Rites, Rights and Wrongs. *American Anthropologist* 23 (4).

Douglas, Mary 1966: *Purity and Danger: An Analysis of Concepts of Pollution and Taboo*. London: Routledge & Kegan Paul.

Frykman, Jonas 1999: Modern Identities in Minds and Places. *Ethnologia Europaea* 29 (2).

Frykman, Jonas 2001: Till Vladimir Gortans minne. En fenomenologisk studie av monumentens förvandling. *Kulturella perspektiv* No. 4, 2001, pp. 23–35.

Frykman, Jonas 2003: Between History and Material Culture. In: Frykman, Jonas & Nils Gilje (eds.), *Being There: New Perspectives on Phenomenology and the Analysis of Culture*. Lund: Nordic Academic Press.

Frykman, Jonas 2004: The Power of Memory. Monuments and Landscape in Croatian Istria. In: Kärki, Kimi (ed.), *Power and Control: Perspectives on Integration and Multiculturalism in Europe*. Turku: The Population Research Institute.

Frykman, Jonas & Kjell Hansen 2005: Att leva på kassan. Allmän försäkring och lokal kultur. Stockholm: *Försäkringskassan Analyserar* 2005:4.

Lundén, Mia-Marie 2005: The Price of Burnout or Burnout Prize. *Ethnologia Scandinavica*, vol. 35, pp. 68–85.

Moran, Dermot 2000: *Introduction to Phenomenology*. London, New York: Routledge.

Povrzanović Frykman, Maja 2003: Bodily Experiences and Community-Creating Implications of Transnational Travel. In: Frykman, Jonas & Nils Gilje (eds.), *Being There: New Perspectives on Phenomenology and the Analysis of Culture*. Lund: Nordic Academic Press.

Ugrešić, Dubravka 1998: *The Culture of Lies: Antipolitical Essays*. London: Phoenix.

Verdery, Katherine 1999: *The Political Lives of Dead Bodies*. New York: Columbia University Press.

Vuokov, Nicolai 2003: Death and Desecrated: Monuments of the Socialist Past in post-1989 Bulgaria. *Anthropology of East Europe Review*.

WEAR AND TEAR

Orvar Löfgren

Every summer I visit an old abandoned farm house in a deserted woodland, far away from the bustling holiday life out at the coast. For 30 years I have returned to a landscape of gradual decay and ageing. Each time I track the effects of a past winter season. The planks are rotting, the roof is caving in, nails work themselves out of the grip of wood and stand exposed until they rust and disappear. Plants and sprouts sneak into widening gaps and cracks. Moss and lichen create new color combinations and surface structures. The roof tiles become brittle and fall apart. Changes between warm and cold, wet and dry, speed up the decay process.

Indoors the curtains fade, the wallpaper looses its grip on the walls, old bottles turn opaque and the clothes in the wardrobe are attacked by mildew. Outdoors objects are ensnared by the grass, drawn into the ground by gravity, slowly disappearing. Only the handlebars are still visible on the old bike, waving above the high grass like the arms of a drowning person.

A swarm of activities are going on in the stillness of this abandoned landscape. Objects and materials are transformed into new forms and combinations. Most of these changes are so slow that they would hardly be noticeable if I was living next door. Only because I visit this farmstead once a year, can I observe and record them. New orders and disorders are created all the time. For the visitor, the boundaries between discarded and saved objects become more and more unclear. The disintegrating belongings inside the house look more and more like the trash accumulating behind the old barn.

The special atmosphere of this deserted farm is produced by the intertwining of the life of objects and its former inhabitants. Up in the attic you can find old tax returns, wedding photos and funeral invitations. They give off a melancholy mood of decay – scattered remains of both a family life and a home.

Ruins like this are culturally productive; they open themselves up to all kinds of daydreams. A fascination with decay runs through Western history, often filtered through the romantic mood of the bittersweet, mixed feelings of nostalgia and alienation. It is a mood often charged with moral or ideological values. The ways in which a ruin captures our attention vary with who we are and where we are looking from. Ruins can be invigorating as well as depressing. Children may be fascinated by what they see as the openness produced by decay and disorder. This setting can invite action and set their imaginations in motion. Elderly people may experience nostalgia or even bitterness, projecting their own situation onto the landscape, interpreting it in terms of loss or approaching death.

But a site like this old farm could also be used to explore the micro-processes of cultural wear and tear. One summer I brought a Mayan archeologist to the farm, and she enthusiastically started to list the transformative processes she saw in the building and among all the scattered objects: oxidation, glass crazing, percolation, osmosis, implosion, cryoperturbation, erosion, and hydration. It struck me that her vocabulary from the natural sciences meant

that what some see as death and decay, others view as rebirth, new forms of life and information.

The rich terminology from biology, physics and chemistry made me envious; all of a sudden the cultural vocabulary for ageing seemed so poor. What if we turned some of these biological or physical processes into cultural metaphors? Can there be cultural *corrosion, erosion* or *dehydration*? Can a cultural phenomenon, an object, an idea, a routine or a symbol *fade* or *rot*? What kinds of cultural forces correspond to the work of weather, wind and water up at the old farm?

There may, for example, be cultural worlds or phenomena that could be characterized as *brittle*. They may look well-organized, intact and alive, but only a minor change or a slight touch may cause them to crumble or disappear. The Austrian author Stefan Zweig has described a classic case of brittleness. Writing in 1941 from exile he remembers the overwhelming feeling of stability, security and tradition people felt during his childhood Vienna, just before the collapse of the Hapsburg empire at the outbreak of the First World War in 1914. He calls it "The Golden Age of Security". Members of the well-established bourgeoisie kept reassuring each other that they were living in a thousand-year-old monarchy that would remain forever. The economy was stable, everybody knew the interest rates ahead or in what year you would get the next rise in wages and what your pension would be. The year and family life had a ritualized rhythm. You could insure yourself against any eventuality. "Nothing could change in this well-organized order. Nobody thought about war, revolution or upheavals. Everything radical or violent was an impossibility in this era of rationality." Then came the war and the old culture just fell apart. Nobody had seen the warning signals ahead (Zweig 1943: 2ff.).

Life Cycles

Cultural wear and tear varies in speed and scope. How is it that all of a sudden I see a theoretical concept, a shirt, or the family car with different eyes? One morning it just jumps out as unfashionable or tacky, and you are ready to throw it away or sell it.

Most cultural phenomena have a life cycle that make them fade, lose their attraction or usefulness, but the striking thing is that the rhythm or tempo of these cycles vary so much. Some phenomena age very rapidly, others hardly at all. As Michael Thompson has shown in his book *Rubbish Theory* (1979), physical and cultural wear and tear are rarely synchronized.

From the perspective of fashion and longing for the "brand new", ageing is often seen as unappetizing, shabby or dismal. The unfashionable is always just round the corner, which gives the shining "new" a short life span. The first dent in car, the tear in the fabric or the fading of color will transform something into a *used* object, a worn idea, a second-hand commodity. It is obvious that our senses are taught to trace and evaluate cultural wear and tear. The hand defines the threadbare, our taste buds detect spoilage, our eyes note the paling, our ears the squeaking. Among thrift-shop managers it is well known that what really puts customers off second-hand objects is the smell of age.

Shining newness is thus a very vulnerable condition, as Rem Koolhas points out in his discussion of "junkspace" (2003). He talks about the nightmare of the manager of a new mall. One day he might wake up and find out that his establishment has aged overnight, and all of a sudden there is moss growing on the walls, the pipes are dripping, the parking lot is cracked and empty.

Consuming the new makes last year's model obsolete, or at least old-fashioned. This has long been an important theme for marketing specialists. The American car industry had already in the 1920s started to copy the idea of "this year's fashion" from Parisian haute couture, and pioneered experiments with the idea of "planned obsolescence". How can you speed up the cultural wear and tear of a product, make it age faster, get tired or tacky? Their methods were later tried out in other commodity fields (see the discussion in Arvastson 2004, Löfgren 2005 and Mattsson 2004). Interestingly enough some objects and phenomena turned out to be more difficult to "obsolesce".

The idea of built-in-obsolescence can act as a kind of burn-out of the new. In the same moment as it is presented on the catwalk, radiating light and energy, it is consumed from within. This double process reminds us that the Latin root of "consume" is destruction. What interests me here is the potential of looking at a cultural process that combines birth and death, making and unmaking. Intensification is linked to destruction: "Consumed by fire" (see the discussion in Wilk 2004).

Material and Mental Burn-out

The concept of burn-out also reminds us of the ways that we create metaphorical translations, as concepts are moved from one context to another. During the 1980s a new diagnosis swept over the Western World, called "burn-out", and it was seen to have originated in the USA. In 1983 the term was first published in Sweden. A newspaper article defined the novel concept as "a long period of emotional overload resulting in emotional short circuit". Two years later another daily paper stated: "Burn-out is the name for mental exhaustion and tedium, that is common among teachers, social workers and hospital staff, a condition that only recently has been given a Swedish name."

But the history of the concept was more complicated. Burn-out turns out to have a long history in the Swedish language. For many centuries it was only used for material objects; a frying pan, a house or a town could be burned out. But in the artistic world of early 19th century Romanticism, the concept took on a new dimension, and it became a metaphor for the death of creativity. Artists and writers started to talk about burned-out hearts or minds. The concept spread rapidly among intellectuals towards the later part of the century. "He is burnt out without ever having burnt for anything but himself", is a writer's description of a colleague. August Strindberg talks about burned out brains, while another author describes himself as "an old burned-out gentleman, with his future behind him". But the condition of burn-out was not applicable to anybody; it was both gendered and class-based. Burn-out was reserved for the male genius, and there was a heroic tone to the concept. You had given the world so much!

In the US the concept was also used for artists, and in the late 20th century rock stars could be described as burned out, because they had been living too intensely, "burning their candle at both ends" with sex and drugs. Then the psychologists and the medical profession moved in, searching for a concept that could describe stressed professionals who suddenly collapsed from overwork and mental fatigue. It re-emerged as a postmodern disease, a new label for problems of exhaustion, disillusion and depression acquired through occupational stress. In the world of the 1980s and 1990s, this concept resonated strongly in some national and occupational settings, while it never caught on in other places.

In Sweden burn-out spread like an epidemic. A consultant who lectured on stress-prevention remembers:

Employees listened to the lecturer who said: 'Have you ever felt a loss of memory? Or problems with sleep? Lack of appetite? Headaches?' People sat with their checklists and thought: 'Oh, My God, I've got burn-out.' The talks had just the opposite effect than intended.

People found that this label fit their own condition to such a degree that doctors were ordered to stop using this magic word, which seemed to attract a wildly diverse set of problems. One of the problems with the metaphor was that it described a state of no return. After a case of burn-out, you were "finished".

The concept, however, lived on both in the media and in people's everyday world. Its immense attraction rested on its metaphorical power. First of all, it was a metaphor of the short circuit. "I have been exposed to mental and physical overload, my whole system has become overheated and now it has collapsed." Secondly, it was a diagnosis that described an active subject: "I have been burning at my job, I have given everything and now I pay an unfairly high price for my strong commitment."

The example of burn-out is interesting because it illustrates how a metaphor for mental wear and tear influences behavior and identity. In a study where we followed a group of middle-managers who had all been given this diagnosis, we could see that the metaphor shaped not only their self-perception, but also reorganized their everyday life (Löfgren & Palm 2005). To be described by others or by yourself as burned-out signaled a special and dramatic transformation, in which you were drained of energy and life, so work seemed meaningless, your body was aching, your memory was gone, and you felt finished. Using this metaphor of fire, problems of both body and soul were seen in a different light, compared to older types of diagnosis like suffering from over-work, depression, or ennui.

Conclusion

The condition of burn-out traveled from the material world into the world of psychology and then to everyday culture. It is striking that so much of the discussion about cultural wear and tear has been borrowed from the material world, so it is always about objects and commodities (Kopytoff 1988; Thompson 1979). When we try talk about the ways in which less tangible cultural phenomena age or change, we still tend to be stuck with metaphors from the material world or with the ageing of organisms from biology. Cultural forms may become vessels, we talk of "empty rituals", no longer meaningful to the participants, or institutions that are "drained of meaning". People can describe themselves as mentally worn-out, an idea grows tired, a cultural symbol fades, an experience turns shallow, a lifestyle feels outdated, and a theoretical perspective carries marks of too much wear and tear. These are not unproblematic translations and on the whole our conceptual framework for understanding these types of cultural changes seems poorly developed. By using the concepts of biological ageing, for example, we give cultural phenomena an irreversible life-course, slowly moving ahead to a certain death. Through this process culture is naturalized, and its real working obscured.

We will always live in a world of metaphors when discussing cultural wear and tear, and we will always have problems trying to evade the moralizing dimensions hidden in such concepts. What kinds of cultural ageing seem threatening or unpleasant, nice, secure, or promising? What kinds of processes result in negative decay, while others just add a pleasant patina, or turn older things into prized antiques or wonderful classics?

References

Arvastson, Gösta 2004: *Slutet på banan. Kulturmöten i bilarnas århundrade*. Stockholm/Stehag: Symposion.

Koolhas, Rem 2003: Junkspace: The Debris of Modernization. In: Chuihua Judy Chung, Jeffrey Inaba, Rem Koolhaas & Sze Tsung Leon, *Harvard Design School Guide to Shopping*. New York: Taschen, pp. 408–421.

Kopytoff, Igor 1988: The Cultural Biography of Things: Commodities in Cultural Perspective. In: Arjun Appadurai (ed.), *The Social Life of Things: Commodities in Cultural Perspective*. Cambridge: Cambridge UP, pp 64–94.

Löfgren, Orvar 2005: Catwalking and Coolhunting: The Production of Newness. In: Orvar Löfgren & Robert Willim 2005 (eds.), *Magic, Culture and the New Economy*. Oxford: Berg, pp. 38–52.

Löfgren, Orvar & Anne-Marie Palm 2005: Att kraschlanda i sjukskrivning. In: Bodil Jönsson & Orvar Löfgren (eds.), *Att utmana stressen*. Lund: Studentlitteratur.

Mattsson, Helena 2004: *Arkitektur och konsumtion. Reyner Banham och utbytbarhetens estetik*. Stockholm/Stehag: Symposion.

Thompson, Michael 1979: *Rubbish Theory: The Creation and Destruction of Value*. London: Oxford UP.

Wilk, Richard 2004: Morals and Metaphors: The Meaning of Consumption. In: Karin Ekström & Helene Brembeck (eds.), *Elusive Consumption*. Oxford: Berg Publishers, pp. 11–26.

Zweig, Stefan 1943: *The World of Yesterday*. New York: Viking Press.

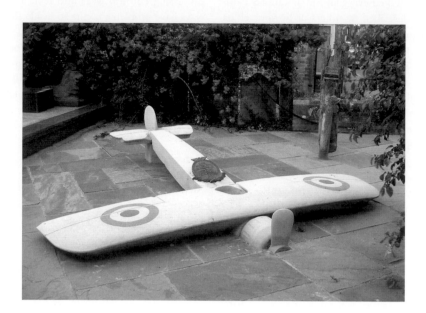

FOSSILISATION*

Elizabeth Shove and Mika Pantzar

In natural history, fossils provide important evidence of past life forms and their activity (Pellant 1990). Things like ammonites, trilobites and graptolites are the tangible remains of what were once living beings. Although their original chemical composition has changed, the physical structure is often perfectly preserved through a process of petrification. Accordingly, there is a sense in which these creatures have a continuing material existence despite being well and truly dead.

In this essay we make the case for appropriating and applying metaphors of fossilisation to the study of social life. We do so in order to correct an astonishing imbalance in analyses of social change. While innovation studies is a recognised area of research and scholarship, and much has been written about the emergence of new social and technical arrangements, there is as yet no equivalent field of socio-palaeontology.

Although we are surrounded by the enduring traces of defunct social practices we know comparatively little about the detailed dynamics of dissolution, obsolescence, partial preservation and occasional resurrection: for the most part, the new is simply assumed to take the place of the old. As with natural history, the systematic study of social fossils promises to shed new light on the missing cultural processes of petrification.

Making and Breaking Links

Where to begin? Ironically, innovation studies is as good a place to start as any. Schumpeter claims that entrepreneurs innovate by combining, relating, integrating and organising pre-existing but previously separate elements in novel ways. We might take issue with aspects of this argument, for example by noticing that consumers and users are innovators too. Yet the notion that innovation is in essence about making new combinations of existing elements can be turned around to generate the parallel suggestion that social-fossilisation is in essence a process of breaking existing combinations of existing elements. This leads to the further proposition that social fossils are materials, ideas or skills that once formed part of an integrated social practice but that have become separated and stranded.

Authors like Giddens (1984), Schatzki (1996, 2002), de Certeau (1998) and Warde (2005) represent practices as relatively enduring entities held together by sets of norms, conventions, ways of doing, know-how and requisite material arrays. In keeping with this approach, Reckwitz defines a practice as "a routinized way in which bodies are moved, objects are handled, subjects are treated, things are described and the world is understood" (Reckwitz 2002: 250). By implication, artifacts, ideas and forms of competence only have meaning and effect (they only live) when integrated into practice. In other words it is through the integrative work of "doing" that elements are animated, sustained and reproduced. When that stops, fossilisation sets in.

These ideas imply that fossils need not only be material: ideas and types of know-how can also be dislocated and left behind as practices evolve. At this point it is useful to introduce an illustrative example.

This object had been abandoned at the back of a cupboard for so long that its function was not immediately obvious. It turns out that it was (is) a press used for extruding biscuit dough to make fancy cookies. Exactly like a trilobite fossil in perfect condition, it clearly existed and yet it was effectively dead. It was defunct because critical links had broken: one with necessary forms of competence, the other with the very idea of investing time and energy in making fancy biscuits at home. It is easy to begin this story with the object. However, one might also say that it is the tacit and embodied competence of dough extrusion (not only the object) that has been petrified through lack of regular reproduction. Few now have the skills, and those few who do are unlikely to pass them on. Alternatively, and equally convincingly, we might start with reference to the mass production of food and the consequent transformation, and in many cases redundancy, of home baking. The point is that the practice is held in place not by the object, the know-how, or the idea but by the active integration of all three. When one link fails, the entire system begins to crumble.

As with fossils in natural history, the soft parts of practice (specifically forms of competence and symbolic meaning) fade quickly from view leaving the material remains behind. In a few years, the press might end up in a museum. If this was a museum of living history, someone might figure out how to make biscuit dough of just the right consistency and on special occasions the requisite know-how would be momentarily resurrected and reproduced. But not the routinised expectation of home baking, and not the equally routinised meaning of what that involves and signifies. Now that the ties have been broken, it is difficult to imagine a situation in which the necessary elements might be reintegrated such that the press could really live again.

Aspects of the (Social) Fossil Record
The social-ecological landscape is changing all the time and it is important to recognise that seemingly stable practices require constant reproduction if

they are to persist. It is surely not the only source of destabilisation, but technological substitution is one of the more visible forces of systemic redundancy. Biros replace the fountain pens that replaced the quill. Three allen wrenches replace the set of spanners previously required to take a bicycle apart. With the ubiquity of camping gas and electric cookers, the craft knowledge of how to light a primus stove evaporates. And so one could go on. There is more to be said about material transformation and extinction but rather than following that route we turn our attention to the fossiliation of redundant images, symbols and embodied knowledge.

Imprints of Practice
The conventional fossil record includes footprints, tracks and burrows along with shells, wings and bones. Can we spot the imprints of practice that are equivalent to the marks of prehistoric activity that have been stamped in rock? As in nature, the conditions are quite demanding; the challenge is to identify preserved traces of elements that exist fleetingly through enactment and embodied performance. Such evidence is often in the highly mediated form of instruction and inscription. We can, for instance, glimpse – but not really reproduce – extinct forms of dance, the skeletal outlines of which are set in the amber of outdated styles of choreographic notation. As Guest (1989) explains, notation systems which served the eighteenth century well fell into disuse as the types of dance for which they were designed went out of fashion. With this, as with so many other forms of codification, writers inevitably "took for granted a certain amount of knowledge on the part of the reader; thus much important information was left out" (1989: 21). The outlines of the steps are there but it is as impossible for the social-ichnologist[1] to do the dance as it is for natural scientists to reproduce the slouch or swagger of a dinosaur from prints left in the mud.

Living Fossils
Another possibility is that the past lives on in the practices of today. If this is so, we might be able to identify what Charles Darwin described as "living

fossils" (1859: 486), the creatures or plants that have remained pretty much unchanged for millions of years. What, then, are the horseshoe crabs[2] of everyday life and what are their trilobite ancestors? Other examples would do as well, but a few comments on Morris dancing allow us to explore this idea. Morris dancing is a type of English folk dancing that was especially popular in the sixteenth century, which is widely believed to have roots in Druidic fertility rituals. Although the ancestry of Morris dancing is subject to much debate, we might nonetheless conclude that it is indeed a kind of "living" fossil. Viewed in this way, contemporary Morris dancing is a lifeless business: a ghostly, zombie like reproduction of an activity no longer embedded in a sustaining network of meaning and purpose.

On the other hand, John Forrest (2000) makes the persuasive argument that Morris dancing has been subject to endless local variation and to a process of evolutionary development that arguably continues today. Since folk dancing only ever exists through enactment, the Morris dancers of the present are engaged in a perfectly lively, perfectly ordinary practice through which concepts of history and tradition (rather than fertility and luck) are maintained and reproduced. In other words, the practice has been transformed but it has not died.

This little excursion into dancing reminds us that practices only exist as long as they are carried on by real people. On reflection we were perhaps too quick to report the (absolute) death of the biscuit press. It might not be as common as it once was but some people still do make biscuits at home and companies making new biscuit presses are still in business.[3] In order to understand the dynamics of social fossilisation we need to take note of the niches in which practices persist and consider the detailed dynamics of recruitment and defection.

Fossilisation in Action

We invited participants to a recent workshop[4] to bring with them items that were once indispensable but that had fallen out of use. The resulting catalogue included a bottle of ink, a spanner, a scalpel, a photocopy card, a child's bicycle seat, an address book, the battery from an electronic device used in training a dog, a diary, a blow lamp, a zip disc, correction fluid and some clothes pegs. Some of the accompanying stories had to do with generic forms of technological obsolescence but others reflected changing personal circumstances and projects.

The bicycle seat is a good example of an item that was momentarily moribund.[5] The seat in question had been outgrown by the child for whom it was acquired but it could still be useful, vital even, to another small person. There are two points to notice here. First, what is a fossil for one person can be indispensable part of another's way of life. Redundancy is situated as well as systemic. Second, and in a way more important, bicycle seats continue to be firmly integrated into contemporary culture even though that integration is sustained by changing cohorts of young children and their parents. When this "normal" turnover of carriers fails and the flow of new recruits dries up, the bicycle seat – as a class of objects and as an experience of riding and being carried – becomes endangered.

The details of case-by-case defection or recruitment are fundamental to and in a sense inseparable from seemingly larger-scale processes that result in the mass extinction of skills, objects and accompanying ideologies. The personal address book provides a fine illustration of this duality and of fossilisation in progress. As described, this particular address book had fallen from use for a number of interconnected reasons. One was that friends (more than family) were moving so often that it was difficult to keep revised entries in proper alphabetic order. Another was that having a permanent record of someone's address was of decreasing significance. Contacts were made and renewed by mobile phone, face-to-face or by email, not by post. Knowing an address matters when paying a visit, but this had become an ephemeral detail: something one would ring up to check when required but that was not worth noting for the future. With phone numbers stored in the phone and emails kept in the computer, who needs an address book?

This case is instructive in that it shows how network-based systems (email, mobile phone) transform and are transformed by personal routines, the net effect of which is to break down the web of social and material arrangements of which the address book was a part.

An Agenda for Socio-palaeontology

In thinking about processes of fossilisation, socio-palaeontologists of the future need to specify how routines and habits (life forms) disappear. How and in what situations do the outlines of practice harden and how are moments of living social interaction turned to metaphorical stone?

As already indicated, there may be scope to borrow conceptual resources from innovation studies and invert them to good effect. If they are to succeed, innovations in practice have to secure resources and capture suitably committed followers. This is often a process of re-alignment and displacement, and there is a sense in which the process of making new links is inevitably one of breaking existing ties. Even so, it may be necessary to think again about the types of agency involved in dismantling rather than engendering new products, ideas and forms of competence.

Although they are likely to deal with the more visible results of fossilisation socio-palaeontologists must not artificially separate the material (or material culture) from the social practices of which it is (or was) a part. To do otherwise would be to confuse the outcome of fossilisation with the processes involved.

In addition, students of social fossilisation should be on the lookout for dormant but not necessarily extinct images, ideas and skills. What are the possibilities of resurrection and in what circumstances might the biscuit press, the address book or the primus stove spring back to life? What if elements return but in new combinations: in what sense can Morris dancing of the sixteenth century be compared with the Morris dancing of the eighteenth century, or of today? Where are the points of no return?

Finally, it will be important to make the most of natural history and the ideas, experience and metaphors it has to offer. There is, for instance, more to learn about sequence and temporality and about incremental and catastrophic change. Does greater interdependence of practices increase the chances of fossilisation? Are more items, ideas and skills subject to social petrification now than in the past? What is the rate of fossilisation in contemporary society? These are just some of the questions that have yet to be addressed.

Notes

* This contribution draws upon "Designing and Consuming: objects practices and processes", a project supported by the ESRC/AHRC Culture of Consumption Programme award number. RES 154 25 0011.
1 Ichnologists are those who study fossilised tracks: http://news.nationalgeographic.com/news/2003/03/0307_030310_dinotracks.html
2 By all accounts, horseshoe crabs have not evolved much in 250 million years.
3 For example, the Italian company Marcato: http://www.marcato.net/mod-ContentExpress-display-ceid-1.phtml (accessed 1.8.05)
4 This was part of the 'Designing and Consuming' project funded by the ESRC Cultures of Consumption programme: see http://www.dur.ac.uk/designing.consuming/ for further details.
5 The clothes pegs and the blow-torch were also temporarily redundant as a result of changing personal circumstances.

References

Certeau, Michel de 1998: *The Practice of Everyday Life*. Volume 2. Minneapolis: University of Minnesota Press.

Darwin, Charles 1859: *On the Origin of Species*. London: John Murray.

Forrest, John 2000: The *History of Morris Dancing 1485–1750*. London: James Clarke and Co.

Giddens, Antony 1984: *The Constitution of Society*. Cambridge: Polity Press.

Guest, Anne Hutchinson 1989: *Choreo-graphics*. New York: Gordon and Breach.

Pellant, Chris 1990: *Rocks, Minerals and Fossils of the World*. London: Pan Books.

Reckwitz, Andreas 2002: Towards a Theory of Social Practices: A Development in Culturalist Theorizing. *European Journal of Social Theory* 2002: 5(2), 243–263.

Schatzki, Theodore 1996: *Social Practices*. Cambridge: Cambridge University Press.

Schatzki, Theodore 2002: *The Site of the Social*. Pennsylvania: Pennsylvania University Press.

Warde, Alan 2005: Consumption and Theories of Practice. *Journal of Consumer Culture* 2005: 5(2),131–153.

COMPOSTING

Katarina Saltzman

In a small bucket underneath the sink in my kitchen I collect valuable stuff. In there goes banana skins, potato peel, soaked tea leaves, the remains of squeezed lemons and faded flowers, overripe tomatoes, wrinkled paprika, slouching lettuce leaves, along with other leftovers and remainders, more or less decayed, moldy and putrid. Every now and then I empty the bucket on my compost heap, and mix my kitchen collection with garden wastes such as dry leaves, weeds, grass cuttings and dead plants. I should probably turn and water my compost pile more regularly in order to achieve an efficient composting process, but I usually have neither the time nor the energy to fulfill these tasks. Nevertheless, after a year or two, when I dig into the pile I might get the spade full of dark brown compost, ready to be used as a first-rate soil amendment in my garden. Quite often each spadeful also contains a number of identifiable remnants of what was once put into the pile, such as peach kernels, corncobs, eggshells and pieces of wood. In addition I might find various worms, millipedes and wood-lice, which show that the process of decomposition is not yet completed.

Besides its practical use, the compost is also good to think with. Processes of composting are present in many shapes and sites, in processes generally defined as natural as well as cultural. Decomposing is simultaneously a process of composing, creating something new out of the worn-out and left-over. As things, structures, ideas and habits become worn, out-dated, replaced, overlooked and forgotten, they often start to wither, putrefy and deteriorate, but in the very same process there is also something new and useful created. By shifting the focus of attention from deterioration to compilation, the compost metaphor provides a tool for an alternative understanding of remains and decay.

I would like to suggest that there are at least three reasons for researchers in the humanities and social sciences to look into processes of composting. First, composting is about revival; it turns the old and deteriorated into something new and fertile. Second, complexity is a key feature of the composting process; in the compost, matter, meanings and unities such as "nature" and "culture" are mixed together and decomposed. And third, composting might offer an alternative, less linear perspective on time. In the following I will take a closer look at each of these three aspects, and give some examples of the metaphorical use of composting.

One could argue that changes, conversions and transformations matching the metaphor of composting might be identified practically anywhere in the world of matter and mind, among humans and non-humans. All material and immaterial structures, things, relations and ideas will sooner or later be reconsidered, outdated and restructured. Ideas are constantly reassessed and habits are modified. In this paper however, my focus is on processes with a clear material dimension, and particularly on the transformation of landscapes and places.

I started to consider the analytical benefits of composting while doing research on transitory landscapes at the rural-urban fringe. In semi-urban

landscapes there are places that "lie fallow" while awaiting future development and quite often such places are, for various reasons, stuck in this state of waiting for many years. This kind of desolate place could stir up feelings of disgust and repugnance in some observers, while others see potential in the indefinite landscape. Most often however, these places are simply overlooked. It is obvious that this indeterminate state attaches uncertainty to people's understanding of the landscape. The main purpose of my research in these areas is to explore what is going on in such landscapes "in the meantime", while awaiting urban development. Because a landscape is never static, even when left over or set aside the landscape is always in transition, through processes and activities of many kinds. As weeds, bushes, unplanned constructions and unscheduled activities get the opportunity to grow and spread in a neglected area, the place is gradually transformed, and as a result the perceptions and valuation of the place are continuously redefined. Objects and activities that are initially regarded as appalling signs of neglect can eventually become essential parts of a landscape with new values.[1]

The 1970s were hard times for the greenhouse business in Sweden. At the eastern edge of Malmö in southernmost Sweden, a large establishment specialized in the cultivation of flowers had to close down after being run by the Gyllin family for about half a century. Changing conditions in the flower market along with the global energy crisis made the oil consuming greenhouse business unprofitable. Hence, the greenhouses, covering 100 000 square meters, were abandoned and demolished, and the whole area was forsaken, as there was at that time no clear strategy for its future use. In the 1980s, municipal planners determined that this abandoned area called *Gyllin's garden* should be turned into a residential district, but for various reasons these plans were not realized. During the time of waiting for this planned but unfulfilled development, the landscape of Gyllins garden has changed, and so has the value of the landscape.

The abandoned greenhouse site has gradually turned into an uncontrolled verdant landscape, nowadays appreciated for its recreational and biological qualities. A period of neglect has created a landscape that is today acknowledged as one of few "wild" places within the urban area of Malmö, frequently used by people in the neighborhood for walking, playing, picnics and school outings. For some people, Gyllin's garden is a refuge, a possible hideout for a very temporary settlement in an old caravan, or an area for activities that do not easily fit into the urban landscape, such as paint ball games. For others it is a good place for walking and training dogs and for yet others it is a place for bird watching, skiing and even hunting. During the last decade, these changing views on and uses of the landscape in Gyllin's garden have been acknowledged in municipal plans, which have actually been altered in accordance with the new values. The plans now say that the abandoned greenhouse industry should be preserved for future generations as a "nature park", while the new residential areas will be built on neighboring fields.[2]

I would argue that Gyllin's garden is a composted place. Through a slow conversion, involving both natural and cultural processes, remnants and leftovers of an outdated business have been turned into a landscape with entirely new value. For me, and I guess also for more qualified gardeners, a truly fascinating fact about the compost is its ability to generate something new and useful out of waste and refuse. It is convenient to be able to get rid of waste by piling it up in a corner of the garden, and then it is interesting to see how the pile shrinks once the process has started, and finally it feels good to uncover and use the earthy-smelling outcome of the process. In Gyllin's garden the "wild nature" that is so much appreciated today has virtually grown out of the ruins a former flower industry. In the present landscape there are still many traces of the former business; trees standing in rows, heaps of dirt, broken glass and pieces of bricks are found here and there, as well as concrete foundations and rusty fences covered by high grass and hedges of lilac. Species such as cypress, forsythia and mahonia add an exotic touch to the wilderness of the garden. The impact of previous activities and the simultaneous processes of decomposing and composing are clearly identifiable in the contemporary landscape.

One theoretical virtue of the composting metaphor is its inherent complexity. The mixing of a diversity of substances is a basic feature of the composting process. Such processes naturally takes place in most terrestrial environments, but a fast and efficient composting of garden and household waste requires certain skills and techniques. Among the many actors involved in the process, psychrophilic, mesophyllic and thermophilic bacteria, fungi, invertebrates, centipedes, millipedes, beetles, and earthworms play their part along with the gardener. All of these actors are seeking and connecting allies to their networks in order to achieve their specific goals. The actions of the gardener, for example turning the compost-heap, will inevitably promote certain networks and restrain others. Composting is hence neither a cultural process, nor a natural process; rather an obvious example of "nature-culture" (Latour 1993, 2004). The analytical act of distinguishing culture from nature does not seem very useful to understand the complexity of the compost. In the compost we also see a mixing and decomposing of "nature" and "culture", and thus composting can be a useful metaphor to approach networks involving humans and non-humans alike.

Gyllin's garden is clearly linked to the origin of the metaphor; the sphere of gardening, but of course no such connection is required for a metaphorical composting to take place. Let us now consider what could happen if a worn-out airport is composted for a few decades. During more than 50 years, 1923–1977, *Torslanda* airport was the point of access for domestic and international flights to and from Gothenburg, the second largest city in Sweden. First established at the dawn of commercial air traffic as a modest establishment next to the mouth of the river, so planes could land on either water or land, Torslanda was gradually developed and extended with the increased importance and amount of air travel. New runways were constructed on former agricultural land and on new landfills along the shoreline. In the early 1970s this was the second largest airport in Sweden, with hundreds of flights every day, carrying more than one million passengers per year. Eventually however, Torslanda could not keep up with constantly expanding traffic. During the second half of the 1970s the airport was abandoned for the new, larger and more up to date Landvetter airport, located further away from the city. Hence, all the activities connected to the airport moved away, and left behind a deserted structure of runways, hangars, terminal buildings and parking lots, and a stunning silence. Since then, the future of the former airport has been debated. Situated close to large industries, oil depots, refuse dumps and a major harbor, but also very near the attractive coastline and archipelago, Torslanda is caught between conflicting interests. In the meanwhile, a multitude of formal and informal activities and land uses have developed on the former airfield.

The same research project mentioned in connection with Gyllin's garden has also studied the current uses and perceptions of the landscape at Torslanda. In these studies in progress, ethnologists Lennart Zintchenko, Barbro Johansson and I approach this landscape through the eyes and practices of people currently using the area for different purposes. At present, parts of the former airport have been converted to residential, industrial, commercial and recreational purposes, but there are still vast areas on the former airstrips used temporarily as storage areas for containers and brand new cars, tracks for motorcycle driving practice, and the activities of Gothenburg model airplane club. A plentitude of small businesses, industries, shops, garages, etc. reside in the airport buildings. In between the more or less well-defined places, there is room for many kinds of casual activities and active contesting of space. Among our informants are young members of the local riding club that uses a hangar as their stables and parts of the former airfield as pastures, bird watchers who are lobbying for the protection of a former ocean bay that houses a rich bird fauna despite its location in-between the former airport and an oil port, and inhabitants of a neighboring summer house colony that have for decades endured the noise within a stone's throw of one of the runways of the airport, which is now partly covered by an expanding golf course.

Composting requires just the right combination

of factors such as temperature, moisture, supply of oxygen and a multitude of microorganisms. In the case of Torslanda, a combination of factors such as economic interests, legal regulations, natural and manmade topography and infrastructure together with human and non-human micro-actors (including, for example, animals, machines and organizations) constitute the basic circumstances for composting. A large number of networks have been co-existing, interacting and competing in the processes of decomposing and "re-composing" the former airport.

If Torslanda is to be regarded as a place that has gone through a composting process, what would be the positive outcome, the fertile "soil" produced in this compost? Could the cacophonic plentitude of more or less organized activities and land uses that have developed in the area while awaiting decisions concerning the future use of the area be a potential model of the future? What kind of values have developed in this compost? Is there, for example, social value in a space where particular groups can freely exercise particular activities? Zintchenko has noted that the flat ground has been used by for example Pakistani cricket players and blind people practicing walking. Could aesthetic values also be defined, for example in the colorful towers of stored containers, in the tire marks on the remaining runways, or maybe in the very decay of a former international airport? Within contemporary art, this kind of transitory and contradictory landscape may well be acknowledged or deliberately created.

During the last year, parts of the former airport have been converted into a new residential area called *Amhult* after a former village in the area, including single houses, apartment buildings and a new commercial centre. This project has caught a lot of attention, because in August 2005 Amhult was presented as one of the three sites of a large housing exhibition in Gothenburg. Studying the material in which the new area is presented and marketed, one could notice that the current uses of the remaining parts of the former airport are virtually overlooked. Computer animated pictures of the view from the new and exclusive houses next to the former control tower do not include any of the container and car storage areas on old runways, or small scale businesses in old terminals. That area is simply depicted as green, maybe to match the descriptions of "fantastic views towards the river mouth, the sea, the archipelago and the golf course". The temporary landscape that has evolved while awaiting decisions and transformations has clearly not been considered an asset in the development of the new housing. These images are fully in line with the conventions used in spatial planning, where a customary understanding of urban development basically recognizes only two stages: before and after the transformation. The values that develop during or while awaiting the process of transformation are seldom acknowledged (Qviström & Saltzman 2006).

In my own garden I quite often find myself carrying heavy plastic bags of compost from the garden shop, instead of using my own. This sometimes leaves me with a trace of bad conscience; being an environmentally conscious gardener I should use soil amendment produced in my own garden, from my own organic waste. I recognized these feelings while reading the garden essayist Michael Pollan's thoughts about the moral imperative of the compost (Pollan 1991). So, why don't I always use my compost, even though I appreciate the principles of composting? Maybe because the plastic bag alternative seems easier and quicker; I don't have to dig into the heap and screen its content. I don't have to worry about the fact that I might have put some weeds in there, whose seeds will probably spread with the compost. And I don't have to be reminded that I really ought to turn the whole heap. So instead I put my effort and money into buying and carrying plastic bags all the way from the shop. Perhaps the same kind of awkward priorities are active in the case of Torslanda? Perhaps it seems easier and quicker to transform the landscape through values and structures brought in from somewhere else, rather than examining and working with the complex processes developing in the forsaken airport?

Composting is based on a different kind of logic than the commercial logics of contemporary society. Composting requires time, oxygen and mixing,

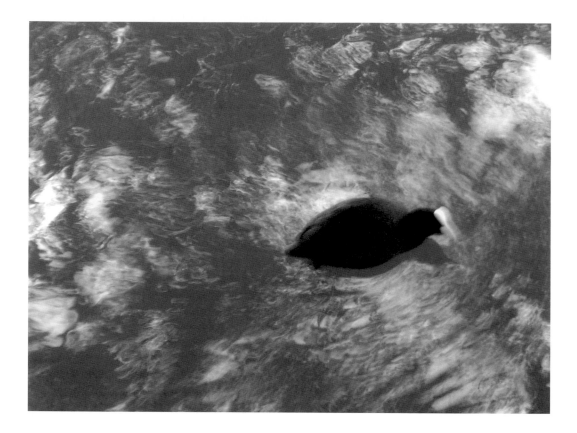

THE DOPPLER EFFECT

Ella Johansson

At the last page of the first book Laura Ingalls Wilder wrote on her childhood *Little house in the big woods* she is lying in bed, while her father plays "Shall Auld Acquaintance be Forgot" on his violin.

> When the fiddle had stopped singing Laura called out softly, 'What are days of auld lang syne, Pa?' 'They are the days of a long time ago, Laura' Pa said 'Go to sleep, now'.

The other books on and by Ingalls Wilder depict a journey into modernity. The prairie, onto which they will set off in the next book, will be the stage for a drama about this isolated but loving and hard-working nuclear family. As we read on, this prairie landscape is filled up by railways, general stores, iron stoves, schoolhouses and printed calico. *Little house in the big woods* deals with another, less transparent landscape, representing Laura's early childhood, as well as the childhood memories of her parents and grandparents. The book is a retrospection into a timeless, innocent place before Fall, departure, movement and history. Not a narrative in itself, it consist of fragments representing a landscape of wilderness, kinship, traditional crafts, log houses, open fires and strange beasts, the Eden which was to be left for the West.

> But Laura laid awake a little while, listening to Pa's fiddle softly playing and to the lonely sound of the wind in the Big Woods. She looked at Pa sitting on the bench by the hearth, the firelight gleam-ing on his brown hair and beard and glistening on the honey-brown fiddle. She looked at Ma, gently rocking and knitting. She thought to herself, 'This is now.' She was glad that the cosy house, and Pa and Ma and the firelight and the music, were now. They could not be forgotten, she thought, because now is now. It can never be a long time ago.

Writing in the early 1930s, aged 65, Wilder deals with the early 1870s. But time references in the text "more than eighty years ago," indicate that the book was reedited in the early 1950s, making it one of the last things she wrote. This certainly brings out my sentimentality. As a child it thrilled me when I found out that the writer lived until 1957, one year before I was born; that our life spans almost touched each other in time. Laura's concluding statement is what Ernst Bloch would call "das Fall ins Jetzt" or "Durchbruch des Hierseins". It constitutes a sudden break through, or fall from distant fictive storytelling into the present and presence of the reader or listener. Wilder makes a reference to the *memento mori* "what you are, I have been, what I am, you shall be". This is not just sentimentality; there is a witty and playful cynicism in these concluding sentences. It is a sovereign commentary from beyond the grave, a final joke, addressing the vanity and naivety of our conception of time. The point is that we all, just like young Laura, uplift and celebrate the present – that limited span of time that we experience – as something more authentic than the time of lives of a long time ago.

their neighbors uninvited. Nowadays this is no longer polite and everywhere people are sitting alone in front of their screens." In the 2000s, television can be discussed as a historical phenomenon, a device for creating community and slowness: "When television was introduced you would be invited to those who had a set, to sit by their dining table and eat fancy cakes while watching."

When listening to Americans getting together and getting to know each other it is striking that they often chat about old television shows from their childhood. They seem to use this conversation to create community and consensus, based in a shared history. Television has become tradition, and a stable, secure key symbol that embraces and provides the aura of a particular era.

From innovation studies we know how the Doppler effect makes historical sense of the density of a certain time span. A Swedish documentation project in the 1940s looked into "the new era coming to our local community," understood then as a study of the mechanization and industrialization of rural Sweden in the past century. People were asked about new technology or new consumers' products. When did they appear in the village and who bought them? One outcome was that everybody remembered that their own farm or household was the first in the village to buy those particular machines or home equipment that were crucial to modernity.

The study did not result in a very accurate map of the time and place where modernity arrived, but it said something important about the reception of change, of how the experience of being at the edge of time and history is processed. Surely, every daughter has heard form her mother (and every mother has told her daughter) about how *she* was always the first in town to wear spectacular new fashions. Even Laura Ingalls did this, for example when she writes about the sisters daringly adopting a hairstyle with fringe.

Sound as Metaphor

The Doppler metaphor, in the case of the ambulance's siren, shows us that the relativity of time is hard to integrate with social theories that stress the importance of rational agency, or of reflexive subjects planning for the future. Instead we get this confused figure on a sidewalk, trying to look civil and composed in spite of all the sensory impressions the ambulance produces. The dopplered ambulance is a social metaphor which does emphasize and explain the heightened experience of presence and life which pervades the observer's viewpoint.

Our observer on the sidewalk may be worried about what is happening, what made somebody need an ambulance, but is no doubt feeling slightly content about being out in the street instead of inside the ambulance. The siren metaphor also tells us that the observer's feeling of alarm is imaginary. It contradicts any idea of the uniqueness of the present. The siren is alarming and potentially disastrous (and it probably is for the passenger in the ambulance[2]). Yet those disturbed by the dopplering ambulance will then carry on with their lives as before.

Metaphors are often visual. The concepts "image" and "picture" are even used as synonyms for "metaphor". Thinking in terms of sound and soundscapes could be a productive way of creating metaphors for time and temporal processes, especially for the experiences and subjective aspects of time. First, sound has no stability in time. It is not possible to "keep" or maintain sound as a thing or a visual object. Second, we are easily influenced by, or vulnerable to sounds. It is difficult to escape from, defend oneself from, or objectify a sound.

Sound is a good metaphor for time experiences because it does not have an immediate extension in space. The act of listening to sounds places us in the dimension of time. The Doppler effect, however, shows us that there are other spatial dimensions. There is a place, a moving point, which locates the listener. These other dimensions are usually unintelligible or misinterpreted by social scientists. The Doppler sound, a siren, or the sound from cars passing by on a highway, is therefore also a good metaphor for presence in the present. This feeling of presence involves the phenomenological aspect of "being there" as well as socio-psychological aspect of either discontent (the alarmist attitude to events which are close in time) or enchantment (putting hope in the present as a decisive moment).

An indication that Doppler effects have a subconscious significance in the culture of late modernity is the prevalent use of American police sirens in films and other sound media and the excitement they produce. These sirens' tones heighten the importance of the present. Important things are at stake, and the outcome of the moment is uncertain. American sirens are audible icons of speed, excitement, metropolitan ambience and also of presence, of things happening *now*, of *now* being a decisive moment for an otherwise arbitrary future. The efficiency of this sound makes the Doppler effect completely tangible. This perception is strengthened by a trick that improves the effect.

The sound American sirens really make is not constant, so it is itself imitating the Doppler effect. They have a simulacra of the effect built into each pulse. The heightening of the tone in the singular pulses can be compared to the hectic and threatening sound of passing cars, if one stands close to a highway.

Presentism

One popular explanation why trains become slower, social relations are diminished, and innovations get less exciting over the years, is that time is going relatively quicker, or that events and innovations happen more frequently. Time is said to be more densely packed with action, thus feeling faster, so people are accordingly getting blasé and harder to impress or stimulate. The chapter on "slow motion" in this volume has several good examples of ways that contemporary life can be represented as a problem of increased speed and density. The Doppler effect shows that this escalation is not necessarily inevitable. It might be an illusion caused by a belief in the uniqueness of the present. The Doppler effect also explains how we can continue to be shaken up by important news, as well as why we so quickly forget our reactions, so that we are soon ready again to declare that nothing can really impress and shake up people who live *now*.

The everyday forms of this *presentism* are not the only ones molded by the Doppler effect. Presentism in social theory used to be about the uniqueness of the era expressed with figures about the density of social conflicts, the pace of technological progress,

the amount of discontent and alienation. In postmodern and post-structuralist theory this density has accelerated even more, and has become the focus for many social theories. We read that we live under "conditions of post-modernity" which increase the density of everything, the speed of time itself.[3] The uniqueness of the present gets, in this urge to catch up with and explain the contemporary, represented as an implosion and a collapse of time and history, the death of history.

The cultural Doppler effect is a process that positively addresses the important, but difficult, project of analyzing the past and the present on equal terms, using the same methods and based on the same ethics. This task is at the core of the important contributions European ethnology and anthropology can make to complex societies. These disciplines have a role to balance other, less comparative, branches of the social sciences, and above all to contradict the many forms of cultural critique which are dedicated to "contemporalism", to the fetishization of the present present.

Notes

1 Historicism in the sense Sir Karl Popper uses it.
2 As a contrasting statement to the point of the Doppler metaphor for how time is *experienced*, one might add Walter Benjamin's text on the Angelus Novus, which points out the weight of the past. He states that all of history, which the backward looking angel of history looks upon, is an enormous tragedy, which piles "wreckage upon wreckage".
3 Above all in the writings of Paul Virilio.

References

Benjamin, Walter 2003: *Selected Writings*, Vol. 4: 1938–1940. Cambridge: Harvard University Press, p. 392–393.
Bloch, Ernst 1969: *Spuren*. Gesamtausgabe Bd. 1. Frankfurt am Main: Suhrkamp, p. 98.
Donald, Merlin 1991: *The Origin of the Modern Mind: Three Stages in the Evolution of Culture and Cognition*. Harvard University Press.
Popper, Karl 1957: *The Poverty of Historicism*. London: Routledge.
Schneider, Reto U. 2004: *Das Buch der verrückten Experimente*. München: Bertelsmann, p. 43–47.
Virilio, Paul 1986: *Speed and Politics: An Essay on Dromology*. New York: Semiotext(e).
Virilio, Paul 1997: *Open sky*. London: Verso.

leisure time. When the boundaries between working hours and leisure time appear to be more and more difficult to maintain, it seems that we find the differences between high and low speed at the boundary between weekdays and weekends, when time off is separated from working hours. In the talk of increased speed and the need for slowness we can discern an invocation as well as a diagnosis. When sun-bathing on the beach, strolling in the woods, relaxing in the summer cottage or driving the camper, we leave the watch behind to sense a feeling of being out of time or at least to get a notion of time passing a little bit slower, as it perhaps did in the past.

Thus slow motion appears as a cultural phenomenon in its own right; a phenomenon surrounded by speech, intentions and values. But as an ethnologist I am also interested in slow motions that are quiet and hard to discover, motions that are so slow that they hardly appear at all as motions, and instead seem to be solid or even invisible.

In some research performed a few years ago on the history of psychiatry between 1850 and 1970 (Jönsson 1998), I noticed that incarcerated patients, whose conditions seemed permanent and who repeated their behaviors day after day, quenched the interest of psychiatrists. The notes in the case records tended to be more and more sparse and monotonous. "Same as before", "condition unchanged", "status quo" were dutifully noted every six or twelve months. Facing the unchanged condition, the production of psychiatric knowledge was as silent and still as the condition of the patients appeared to be. Confronting this condition, the observer was blind. Only motion and resistance activated the machinery of observation and the apparatus of therapy. Slow motion in this sense and context might be considered as an action of resistance. To do nothing or to do something very slowly are well-known methods of resistance, especially in institutional contexts.

The stillness and quietness that surrounded the patient in permanent conditions gave me detailed information on the conditions of the production of psychiatric knowledge. The quietness stood in sharp contrast to the speech of change and scientific evolution that characterized psychiatry and its identity and self-understanding.

I found signs and experiences of slowness not only in patient records. Time ticked differently in different spaces of the hospital. Where change was obvious, in the open wards of treatment and hope, time was straight, aimed at the certain goal of recovery, health and discharge. The place for illness, permanence or change in the wrong direction was the cell, the closed space for the singular inmate. In this room, closed not only for the inmate but also for the observer's gaze, no hope was in sight. Rather than being therapeutic, the function of the cell was to contain bodily secretions, untidiness, noise and the violence of the patient. In this room, time rather than moving straight forward, was cyclic if it was even noticeable. When recovery and change could not be envisioned, the psychiatric interest faded. In the cell psychiatric time slowed down or even stopped. Its stillness was a sharp contrast to the "open" wards of therapy and hope.

My point is that notions of time and motion are very much dependent on different perspectives and methods of examination and investigation. Psychiatry had its methods, which resulted in a certain kind of knowledge; methods with different sensibilities for motion and change on one hand, and for slowness and chronic condition on the other.

But how do we as ethnologists study slow motion or slow processes, especially slow motions that border on permanence? To what extent are we dependent on motion and change to record phenomena? Let me approach these questions through the system of concrete bunkers that once marked and defended the westerly and northerly limits of the Third Reich.

A walk on the beach of northern Jylland, Denmark, gives the visitor several examples of how time and space work together as a slow but intractable force. These bunkers were constructed by the engineer Fritz Todt (1891–1942) and form part of the Atlantic Wall with its approximately 15,000 bunkers. The aerostatic form of the bunkers not only let projectiles slip off its surface, but did the same for the gaze. The bunker was prematured as worn, and was smoothed to avoid all impact. While a regular house is anchored and placed in the terrain by its foundation, the bunker was placed on the ground to allow limited movement when the earth is struck by projectiles (Virilio 1994: 37). The bunker floats on the ground. Because of this, many bunkers are tilted without any signs of serious damage. As Paul Virilio notices, these "steles" are the result of a world of fast moving objects (Virilio 1994: 39). But they are characterized by, if not immobility, very slow motion.

On the coast of Jylland, like other parts of the Atlantic northern coast, these concrete, streamlined lumps have moved at irregular speeds and directions towards the sea. Of course, the movement itself cannot be noted by the eye. The capsized objects themselves, their tilt and distorted position, give the observer not only an understanding of the idea behind this defensive architecture, but also a notion of slow motion that can only be discerned from the leaning, tilting and sloping.

The bunkers of the Atlantic Wall teach us to be aware of distortion, and show us that distortion and irregularities can be signs of motions that are discernable only through studies of long sequences and close readings of distortion itself. The defensive and almost stationary bunkers also emphasize the ways that fast and slow motion often come together hand in hand. The slow bunker had, as its opposite and enemy, missiles moving so fast that they could barely be seen in real time.

Long historical perspectives are one way to get hold of slow processes. Like a long film compressed to a few minutes, studies of the past allow us to identify and analyze slow processes. This is a well-known historical method. However, here I have also argued that by focusing on and searching for slowness, quietness and stillness we can find ways to explore cultural processes that at a first glance seem absent or invisible. What perspectives on the inmates were illustrated by case records which repeated expressions like "status quo", "no change", etc.? What information was to be derived from the quietness of the slow or non-existent motion of a "permanent" condition? By focusing on slowness and phenomena of permanence one could analyze elements that were of great significance to the inner life of the institution, the foundations of the psychiatric production of knowledge, and the construction of patienthood.

My second example, the Atlantic Wall bunkers, makes a different point. The tilted bunkers of the beach express motions manifest for the eye only through deviance and irregularities. They show us that irregularities should not necessarily be seen as only anomalies but also as the result of long term slow motion. Together with close views and readings, the concentrated search for distortion and deviation, the concept of slow motion leads us to a sort of analytical technique which allows us to explore landscapes and contexts of stillness and silence.

A question for all researchers in the anthropological field is how we can find a multitude of points of observations, so that we can identify and construct scientific problems. Sometimes I feel that we have made ourselves dependent on the daily reports of mass media in the search for research problems with public relevance. We do have a well developed and trained seismographic instrument to discover the manifest processes of cultural significance. However, this positive ability ought to be combined more often with an eye or an ear that aims for slow processes that are not necessarily followed or surrounded by words but by serenity and silence, phenomena and processes that are not shaped by fast and/or clear manifest change but by their slow change and culturally reserved silence.

My quest for slow motion assumes that the world is not, in every respect, fast changing. On the contrary, I propose that quiet traditions, repetitions, and habits are still crucial – but more invisible – parts of society and of the everyday life of human beings.

References

Amin, Ash & Nigel Thrift 2002: *Cities: Reimagining the Urban*. Cambridge, UK: Polity Press.

Banham, Reyner 1980: *Theory and Design in the First Machine Age*. Cambridge, MA: MIT Press.

http://www.google.com/search?client=safari&rls=sv-se&q=l%C3%A5ngsamhet&ie=UTF-8&oe=UTF-8 (2005 08 22).

Jönsson, Lars-Eric 1998: *Det terapeutiska rummet. Rum och kropp i svensk sinnessjukvård 1850–1970*. Stockholm: Carlssons.

Virilio, Paul 1994: *Bunker Archeology*. New York: Princeton Architectural Press.

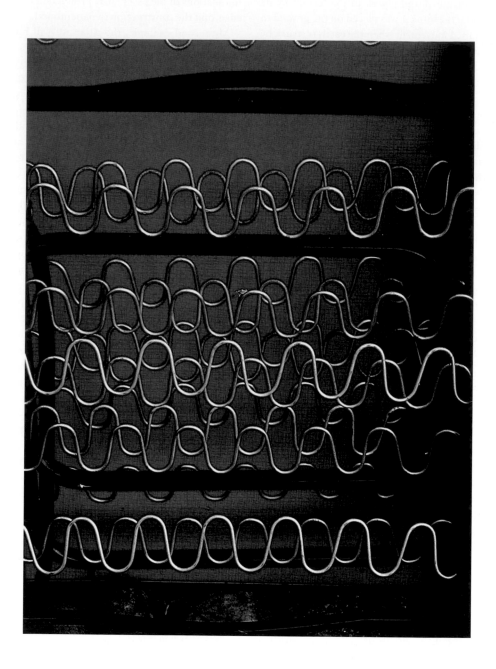

SYNCH/UNSYNCH

Sven-Erik Klinkmann

In the thriller *Collateral* (2004), Tom Cruise is a contract killer called Vincent. There is a scene depicting a shoot-out in a Korean night club in East Los Angeles. Filmed with hand-held cameras and accompanied by the noise of shooting and relentless disco music, the space of the night club shoot-out collapses as in a major catastrophe (or catastrophe movie) as we watch the scene. Bodies are thrown towards each other and onto the floor. But as much as the scene depicts a powerful eruption of entropy, chaos, and cultural kinesthesis (see O'Dell 2004), the scene can also be understood as an example of cultural synchronization. At the same time as everything crumbles, the relentless and intoxicating rhythms of the dance music played in the night club actually seem to gather kinesthetic energy from the shoot-out (Klinkmann 2005). This kind of cultural synchronization, here seen on a relatively small scale, is the theme of this chapter. More specifically I want to examine the concept of cultural synchronization ("synch") by way of its negation, cultural desynchronization ("unsynch"), with examples taken from a broad field of practices, mainly through popular music.

The scholarly interest in timescapes, temporal semantics, anachronisms and the like is a rising area of cultural research today. I will not go into these broader theoretical frames more than simply mentioning a couple of comprehensive efforts to theorize time, timescapes and cultural understandings of the meaning of time. Two notable efforts in this research on time concepts, which have informed my understanding of the concept of synchronization, are the work done by Adam (1990, 2004) and Grosz (1999, 2004). Time can of course be understood from several different angles. Time can be seen from the point of view of compression, durability, movement, pointedness, recurrence, speed, situatedness, etc.

A central proposition here is that the concept of digital real time has proven to be something of an Archimedean fixation point, at the same time absolute and relative, both fixed and forever flowing into the becoming, into future. The "absolute real time" of digitality has enforced the concept of now and at the same time given cultural synchronization a boost. As Gere (2004) has noted, 'real time' also stands for the more general trend towards instantaneity in contemporary culture, involving increasing demand for instant feedback and response, one result of which is that technologies themselves are beginning to evolve faster. The increasing complexity and speed of contemporary technology is the cause of both euphoria and anxiety, Gere writes.

As I will show, the concepts of synch and unsynch are closely related to a powerful emergence of a constantly narrowing, ever more abstract point of *now*. At the same time this focus on the now-moment seems to lead to emergences of action, not least bodily action, because there seems to be quite a strong linkage between these three basic concepts (now, action, body; cf. Grosz 2004; Hassan 2005).

A cultural understanding of the synch/unsynch phenomenon stems, I think, mainly from two separate semantic terrains. On one hand is the concept of the organic, i.e. that which belongs to nature, the sphere of ecology, with its order and its flow. On the other hand there is the sphere of the machine, or a mechanistic logic, in which the various parts of a larger whole, an engine, a cultural aggregate, or some other complex man-made thing (e.g. a computer), works by ordering timely flows within the machinery.

If the idea of cultural synchronization seems to stem from two different, but related terrains, those of the ecological and of the mechanistic orderings of things, I also look into its opposite, the lack of synchronization. It could be argued that you only are able to spot the synchrony when you see the things which do not fit. Things out of step can be the best guide to the steps. I will proceed by discussing different conceptions of the unsynch-phenomenon, in the following order: (1) cool/uncool, (2) sung/unsung and (3) fashionable/unfashionable. I do not regard these three aspects of the synch/unsynch phenomenon to be comprehensive. Other important dualities might be the untimely, the prophetic and the timeless. But in this analysis I will concentrate upon these three aspects of time.

Cool/Uncool

The concept of cool has a cultural background in the urban jazz scene in Harlem, New York in the 1930s and its movement into the American youth culture of the 50s as a general emblem of both rebellion and group connectedness. Cool is a semiotic marker of style related to the special cultural formations – youth subcultures for example – which emerged in the sociocultural context of modern Western industrialized and urbanized society (Danesi 1994). Cool's relevance to popular culture and music has something to do with phenomena such as marginalization, liminality and reflexivity (Klinkmann 2002: 121ff.). In the realm of popular culture, these concepts are strongly connected to an experience of a fleeting now, passing into an immediate future. Or, to put it in Löfgren's phrase, in the contemporary world of a catwalk economy, or an experience economy, the trick is to be able to "communicate the fact that you are a fast, innovative and creative ac-

tor on the market, one who already has a claim into the future". As Löfgren notes, the crucial questions concern this short temporal span, when one is a step ahead, capitalizing on the short time span, identifying the absolute new, and staging, exploiting and controlling this fragile capital called "newness" or "being ahead" (Löfgren 2005: 57ff.).

An example of the cool hunter is Swedish pop music critic Andres Lokko, who has been described as the most interesting music critic in Sweden, with a postmodern sensibility (Lindberg et al. 2000: 375–377). In his own words, he wants to be "childish" with curiosity and enthusiasm intact. At the same time he is a socialist for whom uncool (sic!) words such as engagement and empathy are important. Lokko believes in an emphatic, passionate form of writing. Lokko's idiom includes a preoccupation with temporality, and marking out cultural capital in the form of a distanced, or slightly ambivalent, position with regard to popular, widely held tastes in youth communities.

Lokko's world of coolness is related to the many markers of the critic's positions regarding taste and tastemaking (cf. Bjurström 1997). His preferences are often described as "falling in love" with particular music. His sympathies and antipathies are frequently constructed through mini-stories. Writing about a new CD by British pop group Prefab Sprout, which he sees as idiosyncratic and unfashionable, he calls the cowboy theme of the CD "a perfect and almost deliriously unfashionable theme." Obviously to underline the impression of uncoolness in this case, he tells a story about an old friend of his, a rabid Prefab Sprout fan, who works today as a journalist on a home fashion magazine and writes about classical music and opera in a Swedish evening paper. This describes an almost total drop out from the popular music orbit, the ultimate of uncool in this case.

Lokko's columns and reviews can be read as stories of his own positioning in relation to his relevant cultural milieu – the Swedish and metropolitan pop music world – involving highly complex temporal transformations, displacements and juxtapositions. He tells stories of his musical yesterday, of his now, and of pockets of timelessness in his life of listening to pop music. He often shows how something he didn't understand at one point has now become clear to him (the unsung/sung phenomenon). A case in point is the female singer/songwriter Margo Guryan and her sole record *Take a Picture* (1968), which was, he writes, "a completely forgotten pearl which nobody would have had the chance of hearing had it not been for Siesta" (a Spanish indie record company) (Gradvall 2002: 97).

Lokko's time framing frequently uses the phrase "in this instant", a magic substance giving life to the music in question. In a column in *Svenska Dagbladet* (10.12. 2005) he notes that pop music is about seizing the second: "For us who love it (pop music) as much as we love life itself it is all that matters. When the song has faded we can go about with our ordinary chores without giving it a thought afterwards again."

If he has listened to a record for a week it's a long time, since the pace of taste is fast in the world of pop. But he also invites achronism as his confidant. Listening to British singer and guitarist Matt Deighton is for him an act of timelessness comparable to angling (Gradvall 2002: 247) (at least since Izaak Walton's seventeenth century classic, *The Compleat Angler, or the Contemplative Man's Recreation*, the themes of angling and timelessness are closely intertwined in the popular imagination). Lokko's world is centered on modernism of the 1960s (ibid.: 264–265) and "ultramodernism", for example the Japanese "pop-noise savant" Cornelius (ibid.: 457–458).

In a key text about a record collection including 50s jazz, 60s soul, old blues and British mod bands, he meditates upon the modernism of the 60s, in his view the cornerstone of all that he values in pop music. To Lokko, modernism is "to forever be one step ahead, to always search around the corner where no one else has had the idea to look, to build his/her own world of unreachable ideals in music, clothes and politics, a world which no one ever gets access to" (ibid.: 264). Lokko's rhetoric is oddly reminiscent of the "utopian" science-fiction series *Star Trek*.

Lokko seems to be drawn to a temporal positioning that could be called an "instant future" or a "miniature utopia", existing just out of reach or a step from the buzzing and chaotic mess of the

cultural, overcrowded *now* and culturally overdetermined popular music history. Being cool is for Lokko "to refuse to step into line" (ibid.: 69). Being uncool in his scheme would indicate that the person in question moves in the cultural mainstream, follows trends and behaves as a cultural copycat.

As Swedish journalist Karin Ström notes in *Svenska Dagbladet* (3.12.2004), café culture is a cultural domain even more trendy than design or music. The impetus to be cool is even more important in the café than in other areas, because the rate of change is so fast. Tomorrow a café coretto might be just as uncool as café au lait. The trendiness of the café world leads to new emerging niches, such as the borderless café, which can be a café in the grocery store, in the little record shop, or the cafés with an expanding agenda, a coffee shop with bulgur salad and Turkish coffee, chocolate tasting, readings of fairy tales, or dance exhibitions (Ström 2004).

Margins between the extreme positions of the cool/uncool dichotomy shrink, the question of a blurring of the borders of the whole concept of coolness is gaining currency. One could speak of the cool/uncool paradox, where in the light of the speeding up of the forward moving and narrowing now moment, all things tend to become uncool in an instant. An example of this paradox is the reportage by Karrie Jacobs, writing in *Metropolis magazine* on the retro-stylings of Ironworks Lofts, a community in Frederick, Colorado. There she found "stand-alone" loft houses and single family subdivision houses tricked out in industrial brick and steel with names like the Firehouse and the Cannery. Jacobs has become interested in this kind of place and design simply because she is an "uncool hunter" (as she calls herself), and her talent is "discovering the places where hipness goes to die. I drive around the country and stumble on phenomena that make me realize that something I once valued is about to be eaten alive by mindless commerce."

The loft is a monument to the disappearance of industry, she notes. The borders of fake and real, of innovation and nostalgia tends to become blurred as a dichotomy and simply turned upside down in the kind of temporal organization which the cool/

uncool dichotomy represents. According to Jacobs, a good place to seek out the uncool is the point where style is pried loose from any semblance of meaning.

Sung/Unsung

Another type of anachronism is the unsung person or phenomenon, often the unsung hero. I will give some examples of this temporal mode and discuss one of these unsung heroes, and explain why they are important to more general temporal semantics. What is remarkable about unsung heroes such as country soul singer and guitarist Eddie Hinton, country singer Keith Whitley, post punk chanteuse (cum ex model) Marianne Faithfull, pop music producer and musical visionary David Axelrod, and jazz bassist Henry Grimes, is that their life stories seem to be taken directly from one of the bleaker Dickens novels, with their enormous upheavals of personal and professional fame and fortune. The common denominator of these unsung heroes is that they have had an initial success not quite extraordinary, still healthy. Then their life and career went into a tailspin of the most intense sort. Thus, Marianne Faithfull, the top model of the swinging London scene of the 1960s and ex girl friend of Mick Jagger, experienced a serious downfall in the 1970s when heavy drug and alcohol abuse transformed her into a homeless and tragic figure living on the edge of society. Eddie Hinton, guitar ace in the glory days of southern soul, was busy recording in Muscle Shoals, Alabama in the 1960s and early 1970s, but personal turmoil left him on the street, penniless and heartbroken. Heavy drug abuse also left visionary producer David Axelrod living a life as a bum in LA. Keith Whitley, one of Nashville's chief contenders for the title of "country star of the 80's", couldn't cope with alcohol and ended his days dead, drunk on a carpet at the age of 34.

Henry Grimes was a busy and highly respected bass player in the world of swing and free jazz in the 1950s and 60s. He recorded with both "the King of Swing" Benny Goodman and with the free jazz prophet Albert Ayler. The remarkable story of his fall and redemption is told in plain, unadorned prose on the music site *All Music Guide*:

In 1967 when he was just 31, Henry Grimes disappeared completely from the jazz scene. Decades passed and he became one of jazz's most prominent missing persons. He was long presumed dead because no one in jazz heard a word from him. So in 2002 it was a major surprise when Grimes was discovered living in a hotel in South Central Los Angeles, where he had resided for the past 20 years. Grimes, who had become frustrated with the music world and suffered from some ambiguous mental problems, had spontaneously quit music and worked odd jobs for years.

Grimes was discovered by Marshall Marrotte, a social worker and writer, and was soon interviewed by *Sound to Noise* magazine. William Parker, a fellow jazz bassist, sent him a bass in December 2002 and since then Grimes is back in the cultural economy, has regained his form and has played with a combo led by avant-garde guitarist Marc Ribot, a group dedicated to the revitalization and reimagination of the music of free jazz visionary Albert Ayler.

Henry Grimes', who was "lost" for three decades and then made a remarkable comeback, life story follows a pattern which is also *mutatis mutandis* applicable to narratives about many other "unsung heroes'" lives. The basic element is that of the fall from success or grace, the long wasted years, and then the peripetia or recasting of fortunes, with an anagnorisis, a recognition and rediscovery of who the person "really" is, and his/her re-establishment in the "right" position in the cultural landscape. The classical storytelling of these unsung heroes resonates with the stories of Ulysses, Don Quixote, Robinson Crusoe, Edmund Dantes and other such heroes/heroines of (melo)dramatic fiction (Watt 1996; Brooks 1976/1995). The crucial point of these stories is the moment of peripetia (reversal of fortunes) and anagnorisis (recognition) which have elements of rediscovery and reimagination. Not even death can prevent magical anachronism from taking place. Some unsung heroes are celebrated and deeply missed by many fans only after their untimely death. This is the case with both Keith Whitley and Eddie Hinton. What the unsung heroes seem to be telling us is that the fleeting moment of synch can appear at any time, even after physical demise. Even death is not an obstacle to being in synch!

Fashionable/Unfashionable

I find the fashionable/unfashionable duality especially intriguing in relation to the concept of synch/unsynch, because it has an important connection to matters of cultural capital, including the highbrow/lowbrow dichotomy. Bourdieu's influential work on cultural and symbolic capital is spatially oriented, and time concepts are strongly underplayed.

Examples of the lowbrow unfashionable mode would be the German budget supermarket chain Lidl with its downsized design, and flea markets and old-time dance bands and singers. The unfashionable aspect of these examples is in no way one dimensional. What one person describes as unfashionable another can view as exciting, nostalgic, exotic and the like. The unfashionable quality of a certain product or representation is above all connected to its low cultural or symbolic status, and the low budget nature of the enterprise. There seems to be no consensus about what is fashionable and what is not. The cultural positioning of those who make this distinction is crucial, just as with the cool/uncool dichotomy. There is now a surge in the fashion of cultural value of being unfashionable. This is clearly about the highbrow variety of the unfashionable. British crooner and guitarist Richard Hawley is a case in point. An internet site calls his second solo CD, *Lowedges* (2003) "an out-of-its-time curio that likely woulda won more hearts 40 years ago than it'll probably win in this here and now" (Gravitygirl). About his latest offering, *Coles Corner* (2005), *All Music Guide*, notes:

> Reveries, nostalgia, longed-for wishes, regret, sadness, and the bittersweet mark of the beloved left on the heart of the left and lost. Early rock & roll and rockabilly, country, traces of the vintage-'40s pop, jazz, and even some blues, fall together in a seamless, nearly rapturous whole. Hawley's guitar sound, ringing like a voice from another present era, steps beyond dimension to underscore the emotion and story in his voice.

Here the unfashionable has clearly become ultra-fashionable.

A couple of examples may further illustrate this tendency. The first concerns Pope John Paul II. Shortly after his death Swedish journalist Maciej Zaremba wrote in *Dagens Nyheter* (6.4.2005) about "an unfashionable pope who was ahead of his time". The illustration to Zaremba's article is highly appropriate: a young male break dancer flying through the air head down and feet high up in the air, and in the background of the picture the old and sick Pope on a stool with his head characteristically slightly bowed. The picture was taken on the 25th of January 2004, a little more than a year before the Pope's demise.

Zaremba claims that the reputation of Pope John Paul II will not rest on his stance on contraceptives, nor even on his views on abortion or Opus Dei, which were the same as his predecessors. Zaremba adds, citing cultural critic Slavoj Žižek, that John Paul II remains hopelessly old fashion, and his mark in history will rest on the extent to which he has changed the established order of things, and widened human beings' freedom and dignity.

A decidedly positive appreciation of the unfashionable is served by the Swedish Academy's permanent secretary Horace Engdahl who in a speech on the Academy's yearly celebration on 20th December 2003 (Svenska Akademiens årshögtid, 2003), remarked that poets hate the notion of being driven forward by the pike of time at their neck. An evening at the Academy in the beginning of the same year was dedicated to Swedish 19th Century writer Daniel Amadeus Atterbom's fairy tale drama *Lycksalighetens ö* (The Island of Bliss), a play which Engdahl notes has never been in synch with the spirit of the day and has been eternally overlooked as national drama. During that night in the Academy this bad luck was, according to Engdahl, broken. Actors and musicians unfolded the world of princess Felicia (protagonist of the drama), a world which strangely had fooled time by never being topical. And, remarks Engdahl, nobody really knows how old the unfashionable can become.

Apropos of the presumed unfashionableness of the Academy itself, he compares the Academy to a crocodile, one of the most ancient animal species. The academies are, in Engdahl's words, the crocodiles of cultural life, predestined to survive most of the social phenomena they confront during each epoch. Their chronology is outside the usual, which in his view may lead to misunderstandings between them and the rest of the world.

Concluding Remarks

I have discussed the concept of synch/unsynch by way of three different, but related temporal dualities. The concept of cool/uncool is closest to *now*, and also to new media. The sung/unsung dichotomy forms part of a historical, transmedial narrative while fashionable/unfashionable is the widest in temporal and mental scope and scale.

So what then is cultural synchronization really about? Is it a matter of degree, a scheme with a center of sorts, a moving center which takes the form of a *now* moment, a digital real or absolute time around which secondary temporal patterns are established, or is it a cultural resonance built of something more out of step, out of time, but still in synch with something else? And how can we measure cultural synchronization?

There are no easy answers to these questions. Synch and unsynch are about patterning and rhythm. Though the synch/unsynch dichotomy seems to form a strictly technical concept – this duality is as absolute as digital zeroes and ones – it actually shapes our cultural and social understanding about central concepts like the positive "development", "progress", "evolution", "harmony", and "utopia" and the negative "discord", "backlash", "dystopia", and "Armageddon". It therefore has normative and teleological qualities. Therefore, and also because it seems so "objective" and technical, the synch/unsynch distinction is basic to other distinctions. It forms, at least today, the main temporal taxonomy of rhythm on which the other related distinctions (cool/uncool etc.) can play. As pointed out by Wilk (2005), synchronism manipulates the ordering of events to create an impression of commonality and contemporaneity, and it can also be seen as a means of creating objects in the past which can be manipu-

lated for the purposes of mystification and demystification, distancing and control. Or to put it the other way around, the uncoupled, unsynchronized diversity of different times, seems to challenge our society (Brose 2004).

In a world said to be characterized by fragmentation and acceleration, we could predict that the demand for cultural synchronization will rise. Critics of contemporary social and technological developments see such a development in the form of standardization, globalization, digitalization and temporal compression (see Harvey 1989: 240ff.).

Psychiatrist Thomas Fuchs (2001) blames a lack of psychosocial synchronization for psychological melancholia. Fuchs says melancholia results from desynchronization, an uncoupling in the temporal relation of organism and environment, or individual and society. The triggering of melancholic episodes is thus understood as having a basis in time. When resynchronization fails, the person falls out of common environmental time. This kind of anomalous temporality closely resembles that of the unsung heroes above.

The discussion about synchronization raises the need for an ecological-temporal archeology, to use a slightly tautological phrase. Following Adam (2004: 143–148), one could begin to draw the lines of a preliminary map of the cultural semantics of different timescapes, involving aspects of the synch/unsynch continuum. Those discussed here could then be condensed in the following way:

1. *Uncool* seen as forgotten time pieces, gems, or pearls (Margo Guryan). A temporality close to now, the category of the unsung; involves time travelers, discoverers.
2. *Uncool* seen as culturally produced time effects (Loft houses in Colorado, Prefab Sprout). A temporality related to now, involving "retro", uncool hunters.
3. *Unsung* seen as the preferred mode of storytelling of anachronisms, which could also be described by way of various meteorological metaphors such as up-winds, fall winds, wind changes, turbulence, and pressure changes (Eddie Hinton, Henry Grimes, Marianne Faithfull).

4. *Unfashionable* seen as cultural crocodiles or dinosaurs, relics, often involving stubbornness, steadfastness (the Pope, *Lycksalighetens ö*, the Swedish Academy). A temporality close to timelessness: the now or almost now, which in some cases also can be experienced as a form of timelessness, an eternal present, *kairos*, etc.

5. *Unfashionable* as cultural leftovers, trash (flea markets, Lidl, café au lait). Things that should have been wiped out, forgotten a long time ago.

This short scheme is by no means comprehensive or clear cut. There is always complex border crossing, transgressive representations, that often are of uncertain or ambiguous artistic merit and relevance, in this text Richard Hawley, the Pope, Prefab Sprout, and *Lycksalighetens ö*.

References

Adam, Barbara 1990: *Time & Social Theory*. London: Polity Press.

Adam, Barbara 2004: *Time*. London: Polity Press.

All Music Guide 2005: Henry Grimes, Biography. http://www.allmusic.com/cg/amg.dll?p=amg&sql=11:wya9kezt7q7x~T1 Accessed 10.6. 2005.

All Music Guide 2005: Richard Hawley, *Coles Corner*. http://www.allmusic.com/cg/amg.dll?p=amg&token=ADFEAE E47818D94FAC7E20D7843A4A84B161FB029048F68710 2B4754D2BB114688197FEA57F4C79BE8B608E33BC8A B70A31943D2C8F157FEC3643D3D88A2A06A3B3B4107 0E3534FD&sql=10:6fkpu3esan7k~T1.

Bjurström, Erling 1997: *Högt & lågt. Smak och stil i ungdomskulturen*. Umeå: Boréa.

Brooks, Peter 1976/1995: *The Melodramatic Imagination: Balzac, Henry James, Melodrama, and the Mode of Excess*. New Haven and London: Yale University Press.

Brose, Hanns-Georg 2004: An Introduction towards a Culture of Non-simultaneity? *Time & Society*, vol. 13, no. 1 (2004), pp. 5–26. London, Thousand Oaks, CA and New Delhi: Sage.

Danesi, Marcel 1994: *Cool: The Signs and Meanings of Adolescence*. Toronto: University of Toronto Press.

Fuchs, Thomas 2001: Melancholia as a Desynchronization: Towards a Psychopathology of Interpersonal Time. *Psychopathology: International Journal of Descriptive and Experimental Psychopathology, Phenomenology and Psychiatric Diagnosis*, vol. 34, no. 4, 2001.

Gere, Charlie 2004: New Media Art and the Gallery in the Digital Age. *Tate Papers*, Autumn 2004.

http://www.tate.org.uk/research/tateresearch/tatepapers/04autumn/gere.htm Accessed 10.6.2005.

Gradvall, Jan, Andres Lokko, Mats Olsson & Lennart Persson 2002: *Feber*. Stockholm: Modernista.

Gravitygirl: – richard hawley – *lowedges* (http://gravitygirl.shafted.com.au/0703/020.html. Accessed 12.12.2005.

Grosz, Elizabeth (ed.) 1999: *Becomings: Explorations in Time, Memory, and Futures*. Ithaca and London: Cornell University Press.

Grosz, Elizabeth 2004: *The Nick of Time: Politics, Evolution, and the Untimely*. Durham: Duke University Press.

Harvey, David 1989: *The Condition of Postmodernity: An Enquiry into the Origins of Cultural Change*. London: Blackwell.

Hassan, Robert 2005: Timescapes of the Network Society. Fast Capitalism 1.1 2005. http://www.fastcapitalism.com/ Accessed 10.6.2005.

Jacobs, Carrie 2004: I am the Uncool Hunter. *Metropolis Magazine* 5.1.2004.

Klinkmann, Sven-Erik 2002: *Elvis, coolness och maskulinitet i femtiotalets USA. Populära fantasier från Diana till Bayou Country*. Vasa: Scriptum.

Klinkmann, Sven-Erik 2005: Cultural Kinesthesis in Mediascapes: A Comment. *Ethnologia Scandinavica. A Journal for Nordic Ethnology*, 2005.

Klinkmann, Sven-Erik, 2006: *På drömmarnas marknad*. Hedemora: Gidlunds.

Lilliestam, Lars 1998: *Svensk Rock. Musik, Lyrik, Historik*. Gothenburg: Bo Ejeby Förlag.

Lindberg, Ulf, Gestur Gudmundsson, Morten Michelsen & Hans Weisethaunet 2000: *Amusers, Bruisers & Cool-Headed Cruisers: The Fields of Anglo-Saxon and Nordic Rock Criticism*. Århus: University of Århus.

Löfgren, Orvar 2005: Catwalking and Coolhunting: The Production of Newness. In: Löfgren, Orvar & Robert Willim (eds.), *Magic, Culture and the New Economy*. Oxford & New York: Berg.

O'Dell, Tom 2004: Cultural Kinesthesis. *Ethnologia Scandinavica. A Journal for Nordic Ethnology*, 2004.

Ström, Karin 2004: Kaffeterror. *Svenska Dagbladet* 3.12.2004. http://www.svd.se/dynamiskt/kultur/did_8663138.asp Accessed 9.6.2005.

Svenska Akademiens årshögtid. 2003. Accessed 9.6.2005. http://www.svenskaakademien.se/SVE/hogtidsdag/2003/

Watt, Ian 1996: *Myths of Modern Individualism: Faust, Don Quixote, Don Juan, Robinson Crusoe*. Cambridge: Cambridge University Press.

Wilk, Rick 2005: Time for "the Maya". Speech prepared for Wenner-Gren Symposium: "The Public Meanings of the Archaelogical Past: Sociological Archaeology and Archaeological Ethnography".

Zaremba, Maciej 2005: En otidsenlig påve som var före sin tid. *Dagens Nyheter* 6.4.2005. http://www.dn.se/DNet/jsp/polopoly.jsp?d=1058&a=399564 Accessed 9.6.2005.

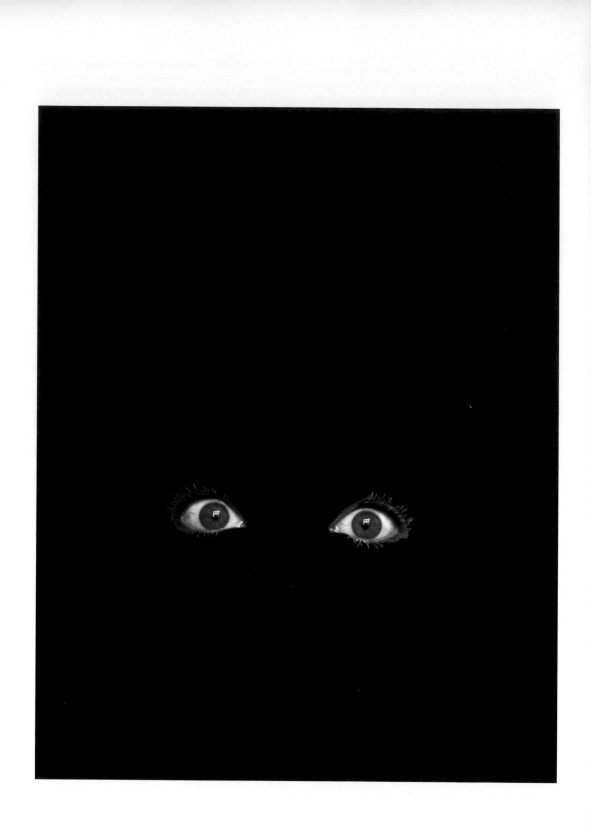

STEALTH

Per-Markku Ristilammi

We have a situation where cities and large companies are competing for investments on a global market. Prestige projects are built in order to draw attention to locality. Every city wants its own Gehry-Guggenheim museum in what could be called "The Bilbao-effect" (Foster 2002). In this case architecture can be seen as sites of spectacular spectatorship. One example of this would be the award-winning Turning Torso apartment tower project in Malmö.

But in contrast to this focus on visibility the events of September 11th may have led to a reconfiguration of the relationship between visibility and non-visibility that has been one of the fields of tension within modernity. Being invisible has come to mean being secure. But if security becomes ever more important these forms of spectacular buildings also become potential targets. If we connect this fear of visibility (cultural scopophobia) to event marketing practices connected to place, we can question if the current trend for constant visibility through branding is viable. Maybe we can find other analytic metaphors, in order to better understand identity formation connected to place, and *stealth* could be one of them.

> *Stealth* – any military technology intended to make vehicles or missiles nearly invisible to enemy radar or other electronic detection.[1]

Military strategy has, at least since the end of the 19th century, become an art of knowing when to be invisible and when to emerge into visibility. The development of weapons technology has meant that everything that is visible is a potential target. Dwarfing and extending fields of vision has been at the core of modern warfare. Stealth has also been one way of dealing with the consequences of the need for disciplining organization. Being under the "perruque" has always been an art of the weak (de Certeau 1984; Scott 1985), but has also strategically been a technique deployed by those in power.

One could tentatively argue that the events of September 11th have released a renewed interest in the art of cloaking, considering that exposure seems to be a threat, regardless of location. Will we see an opening for a new set of performative practices, practices that return and use the (modern) technique of camouflage? These dystopic renderings point to the need for meaningful camouflage techniques (see Hansson in this volume).

Stealth obviously requires an element of camouflage, but stealth has the additional feature of being an offensive technology. Stealth could then be defined as camouflage used in order to reach operative goals. The logical ending of a stealth process is a surprise attack where the victim/enemy is either destroyed "before they knew what hit them" or rendered incapable of effective defense by the sheer force of the attack.

Hostile takeovers on the stock market are preceded by stealth processes where information is being kept at a minimum and only a small number of people are involved in the decision making process. Stealth is therefore not primarily about being hidden from visibility. It is more about finding the right moment in time/space to become visible. These kairos processes can be seen in the corporate world, increasingly in national and international politics, but also on a smaller scale in informal economies.

> And then I thought that if I was ugly, I would turn into something new, something dark and slippery like a stealth bomber or a manta ray, and I'd go wherever I wanted and nobody would know, and I'd be happy like I could never be happy before (Ivy in *Savage Girl* by Alex Shakar).

The character Ivy in Alex Shakar's 2001 novel *Savage Girl* is a schizophrenic fashion model who cuts herself in order to gain anonymity. As the story continues the effect is quite the opposite. She becomes a super model in a world where marketing is everything and where she has her own website with a camera that records everything she does in her apartment. This is a world with, what Baudrillard would call *obscene visibility,* where the reality of the former world, where it was possible to step off the scene, no longer exists. But as Ivy's attempt to gain anonymity shows, *like a stealth bomber or a manta ray,* visibility is not meaningful without its contrast.

One way of identifying stealth is to look at various informal economies and the ways companies try to blur the edges of their enterprises. If the new economy was about clear and visible brands, branding can now be seen as a tactic of diversion, of blurring around the edges of the immediately visible.

It is an often noted, but seldom analyzed fact that if everyone in a system would strictly abide by the rules, the system would cease to function. Therefore a formal system, in order to function, must create safety valves of informality and stealth. Invisibility cannot be defined in an essentialist mood. Invisibility must be constructed in relation to visibility. That is why stealth activities always take place in a symbiosis with the visible society.

The most vulnerable moment in stealth processes is the moment of visibility. If this takes place in the wrong time or place, the entire goal of the operation is threatened. Stealth processes therefore require knowledge about cultural geography. Spaces in

themselves are not visible or invisible. The relation between the visibility and the invisibility is always a social one, defined by relations between people, therefore also defining the space of stealth. And if informal space is a social construction, it is also political. Formal, and thus visible, space is often created through the political sphere and since informal space is intertwined with the formal, informal space is deeply political.

The fact that the informal is a social construction also leads to recognition of the fact that informal is processual. People are always located in different stages in the process of moving in or out of the formal, being visible or invisible, in cultural stealth mode or not. Since stealth processes are tools of power, they also give rise to new forms of inequality. This might be a time where the demand for constant visibility in various branding ideologies, paradoxically is turning into a deep fear of visibility, and where this fear is being turned into an increasing demand for control of the visibility of the other. This ultimate visibility can be exemplified by Giorgio Agamben's notion of the "camp" (Agamben 1998), where Homo Sacer, the prisoner outside the law, but inside the power of the sovereign, lives in constant visibility, without any access to the power of cloaking.

Note

1 Stealth. Encyclopædia Britannica. 2004. Encyclopædia Britannica Online. 18 Nov. 2004 http://search.eb.com/eb/article?tocId=9069503.

References

Agamben, Giorgio 1998: *Homo Sacer: Sovereign Power and Bare Life.* Stanford, California: Stanford University Press.

Certeau, Michel de 1984: *The Practice of Everyday Life.* Berkeley and Los Angeles: University of California Press.

Foster, Hal 2002: *Design and Crime and Other Diatribes.* New York: Verso.

Scott, James C. 1985: *Weapons of the Weak: Everyday Forms of Peasant Resistance.* New Haven: Yale University Press.

STILL LIFE

Kathleen Stewart

A still is a state of calm, a lull in the action. But it is also the machine hidden in the woods that distills spirits into potency through heat, vapor and condensation.

In painting, a still life is a genre that captures the liveliness of inanimate objects (fruit, flowers, bowls) by suspending their sensory beauty in an intimate scene charged with the textures of paint, experience, and desire.

Hitchcock was a master of the still in film production. A simple pause of the moving camera to focus on a door or a telephone could produce powerful suspense.

Ordinary life, too, draws its charge from rhythms of flow and arrest. Still lives of pleasure and pain collect like marbles to bear witness to a life: the living room strewn with ribbons and wine glasses after a party, the kids or dogs asleep in the back seat of the car after a great (or not so great) day at the lake, the collection of sticks and rocks resting on the dashboard after a hike in the mountains, the old love letters stuffed in a box in the closet, the moments of humiliation or shock that suddenly lurch into view without warning, the odd moments of spacing out when a strange malaise comes over you, the fragments of dream and experience that pull at ordinary awareness but rarely come into full frame.

A still life is a machine that distills events and scenes into a liquid potency. A static state filled with vibratory motion, or resonance, it is the intensity born when the urge to react, the progress of a narrative, or the stability of a category is momentarily suspended in a sink of what Deleuze might call "passion" (Massumi 2002: 26–28).

It gives the ordinary the charge of a suspension and an unfolding. Something happens to give pause. It could be something big and dramatic or a literal stoppage that arrests the flow of the projects we call things like the self, agency, home, a life. It can prompt the expectation that something might emerge out of the ordinary. Or it can make a fetish of the charged, open disguise of ordinary things.

Fragments

For years now her early childhood has been coming back to her as fragments of trauma and beauty.

She remembers her kindergarten class walking back from Woolworth's, carrying a box of furry yellow chicks; the look of red tulips standing upright in her mother's garden married to the taste of found raspberries and tart rhubarb ripped out of the ground when no one is looking and eaten with a spoonful of dirt.

The scene of her mother dressing to go out in a beautiful black dress and red lipstick cuts to the brilliant blood exploding from the face of the boy next door when he falls from a cliff and lands face down on the cement in front of her. Then the scene cuts to the rhythm of shocks, days later, as her father and the other men tear the cliff apart boulder by boulder. Each time one hits the ground, it shakes the glasses in the quiet, shaded pantry with an impact that seems to her transformative.

There is a spectral scene of her little brother

hunched over something in the row of pine trees that hug the house as she passes him on her way to school and then, on her way back for lunch, the sight of the house in flames and the driveway full of fire trucks with flashing red lights. The phrase "playing with matches" seems written across the blue sky in huge, white, cloud letters.

Or there is the day all of her grandparents come to visit and they are floating up the treacherous driveway in a big wide car. Then the wheels are sliding off the icy edge and the big car lurches to the verge of the cliff and hangs suspended. The white heads in the back seat sit very still while she runs, yelling for help.

There are fingers crushed in doors, the screams stifled in a panic to keep the secret of the rabbits we have captured. The rabbits are in the cellar, now running around in their wild confinement.

Sunday drives are ice cream cones dripping down sticky fingers in the back seat and the wordless theft of the baby's cone, silent tears running down fat cheeks. There is a terrible weight of complicity when no one alerts the front seat.

There are dreamy performances like the one at the VFW hall. Her sister is the "can can" girl covered in clanking cans and she is the "balloon girl" dancing in floating plastic spheres to the lyrics of "the itsy bitsy, teeny-weeny, yellow polka dot bikini" while everyone laughs.

Later, there are Saturday mornings spent fidgeting at her grandmother's table while her mother and all her aunts tell graphic stories of alcoholism, accidents, violence, and cancers. Stories prompted by the seemingly simple work of remembering kinship ties and married names. And there are the nights walking the streets with her mother, peering into picture windows to catch a dreamy glimpse of scenes at rest or a telltale detail out of place. A lamp by a reading chair or a shelf of knickknacks on the wall, a chair overturned.

So still, like a postcard.

Scenes of Life

Sometimes a scene of a finished life appears like a beautiful figure on the horizon. For a minute, it's like a snapshot hangs suspended in the air while we watch, wide-eyed. It becomes something to chase or something to use as a screen. And it's hard not to look for the telling little detail that will give it all away.

Her mother's painting class has become a support group. She says it really *is* because there are really interesting people in it, meaning they have interesting lives, meaning they all have their problems.

Mary is the quiet one who never says a word and everything is always fine with her. But one day she lets something slip about a first husband and they are all over it. To make a long story short, she married the guy who helped her get away from her first husband and now they're so happy they eat low fat, vegetarian food, take all kinds of pills, and measure and weigh everything so they can go on living forever.

Sue's first husband was cheap; he wouldn't spend a dime. He took to his bed on their wedding day and never got up again. He finally committed suicide on the day of her second marriage. The others notice that she talks fast and never seems to sit down.

They suspect Betty comes from money. She's more of the garden club crowd. But her family isn't exactly what you'd call good to her and she lost her only son in a car wreck. She paints too fast; she is just happy to get one done and get on to the next one. Her husband makes the little boxes and plaques to keep her busy. She's nice talking but once in a while she'll swear – "that son of a bitch."

Carol's husband quit working because he couldn't take the stress. He roamed around the house all day. Then he decided that most of his stress came from her. He started following her around the house, writing down everything she did that stressed him out in a little leather notebook.

Donna's husband left her and their four kids for a younger woman. She finally found another man but the others are suspicious of him because he told her that she was *soooo* beautiful and he said she was going to turn his life around. (The eyes roll.) She has his ring and he's moved in with her and right away he's quit his job and he wants her to sell her house and buy another one because he doesn't want to have any reminders of her former husband. And it looks like he drinks. She's counting. It looks like it's four cocktails a night, at least.

Her mother, Claire, is the good listener. She doesn't like to air her problems. So the others think she's the one with the perfect life. When she gave them all a copy of Nicholas Sparks's romantic novel, *The Notebook*, they decided that was what Claire and her husband were like. One day when one of them was talking about a woman who did something daring she said, "Well I would never do that, but I bet Claire would."

Intensities

We carry around shifting impressions of scenes spied and stories overheard. The cultural landscape vibrates with rogue intensities. There are lived, yet unassimilated, impacts of stress, loss, happiness, bitterness, longing, fear, rage, pleasure. There are fragments of experience unframed by the known stories of a life. There are bodies out of place. There are plenty of people in free fall. Resentment simmers up at the least provocation. But then a tiny act of human kindness, or a moment of shared sardonic humor in public, can set things right again as if any sign of human contact releases an unwanted tension.

She's driving onto campus early one morning. The pickup in front of her stops in the middle of the road to let an older, heavy-set woman cross the street. The woman scampers across, too fast. Then she looks back, first at the man and then all around, with a big smile, vaguely waving. Too grateful.

Sunday mornings, homeless men line up for breakfast at the Jehovah's Witness church down the street. Men of all colors, but this is no utopia of racial mixing. They look hot, tired, out of place. They come on buses or walk cross town carrying all their belongings in dirty backpacks.

She's walking in her neighborhood with Ariana. White woman, brown baby. Some teenage boys pass them, scowling. Brown boys, dressed tough, showing attitude. But as they pass, one of them turns to the others, sweetly, "Did you see that *cute* baby?"

She knows a woman in her 40s who lives alone, never married. Her life is full of good work, good friends and family, all kinds of pleasures, passions and forms of self-knowledge. But it's like there's no frame to announce that her life has begun. She knows this is ridiculous, but she swims against a constant undertow.

It's the 4th of July and the roads are gridlocked after the fireworks. Her friend Danny and his girlfriend are sitting in traffic when they notice that the guy in the car in front of them is starting to lose it. He backs up as far as he can, touching their bumper, and then surges forward to the car in front of him. Then a big space opens in front of him. My friends watch, as if in slow motion, as he pulls his car forward as far as he can and then floors it in reverse, ramming them hard. As he pulls his car forward again, they jump out of their car. This time when he rams their car he rides up over the bumper right onto the hood of their car. His wheels spin and smoke while he dislodges his car and then he just sits there. Danny sees him reach for something on the floor of the car and imagines a gun. A traffic cop is now staring at the guy but he doesn't make a move toward him. Danny goes over and tells the cop about the something reached for on the floor. He points out that there are all kinds of people on the sidewalk. Then Danny goes over and pulls the guy out of the car and brings him over to the cop. The cop arrests him.

She pulls up to a tollbooth in New Hampshire. The attendant says the guy in the car in front of her has paid for the next car in line. It takes her a minute to process what she's hearing. Oh! They both gaze at the car ahead pulling into traffic.

She gets called to jury duty. A young African American man is facing five years minimum sentence for breaking and entering. At the jury selection, the lawyers ask a room of four hundred people if anyone has a problem with that. She says she does. She tells hypothetical stories of injustice. The lawyers are bored. They focus their attention on the only four black people in the room, all women. They are dismissed for the day. She walks back to her car behind the four black women. They are saying that they have no problem with punishment. If this man did what they say he did, he should be punished. But it isn't their place to judge. That's the Lord's place. The next morning, the four women go up to the judge. He dismisses them. The man's lawyers immediately enter a guilty plea. The man gets 25 years because it's a repeat offense. She is amazed at the whole thing.

One day in Walgreens she sees a young, handsome, tan man waiting in line. He wears a mechanic's uniform with his name stenciled on the pocket. When he talks or smiles he holds his hand up over his mouth but everyone stares anyway. His teeth are grossly misshapen. A few stick straight out of his mouth. There is a double row on one side. Like he has never been to a dentist – not as a child, not now.

Sometimes she shops at a poor people's supermarket called Foodland. Everyone calls it "food stamps land". Homeless people walk up from the river for cheap beer and bread. People live in the parking lot in cars and vans. She begins to notice one woman who lives with her two kids in a truck. She notices her, especially, because she has long, black, dyed hair but there is always a big circle of white hair on the crown of her head. One night there is a jumpy, red-faced man with her. He runs up to her, excited by his discovery that they have six-packs for two dollars. She gives him a hard stare. He says "What? Coke! I'm talking about coke! I found a good deal on coke for the kids!" He tries to act outraged, as if he thinks he's an unsung hero, but it's like he's not quite up for it.

A few days later, she sees the jumpy, red-faced man on campus. He is on foot, crossing the street at the entrance to campus with three other men – two Latinos, one African American. They are carrying big yellow street signs and the red-faced guy is saying "Isn't this great? What did I tell you? MAN!" They are moving fast, nervous and excited. But the minute they hit the campus sidewalk they hesitate, gathering in a loose circle. The black man says something about security... the cops. "What the fuck! Oh, SHIT!" A cop car pulls up to the curb in front of them. The black man bravely goes over and sticks his head in the window. Then the red-faced guy slowly sidles up to the car. They haven't been on campus more than 60 seconds.

A stranger shows up at her door in the middle of the afternoon. She and her husband are thinking of buying the big house across the street. She wants to know if anyone in the neighborhood uses chemicals on their lawns, or drier sheets. At first, she has to ask the woman what a drier sheet *is*. But then images pop into her head: the sweet smell of drier sheets coming in with the breeze on a cloudless day, the bright blue sky and the flowers in the yards, the little orange flags sticking up out of the grass at the schoolyard, warning that chemicals have been sprayed, the ChemLawn trucks parked up on widows' hill in front of the places with the big lawns.

She mutters a short-hand version of all these things to the woman standing at her door, but really all it takes is a look and the woman is gone, leaving little seeds of anxiety to bloom.

Public Specters

Public specters have grown intimate. There are all those bodies lined up on the talk shows, outing their loved ones for this or that monstrous act. Or the reality TV shows where the camera busts in on intimate dramas of whole families addicted to sniffing paint right out of the can. We zoom in to linger, almost lovingly, on the gallon-sized lids of paint cans scattered around on the living room carpet. Then the camera pans out to focus on the faces of the parents, and even the little kids, with rings of white paint encircling cheeks and chins like some kind of self-inflicted stigmata.

The ordinary can at any moment morph into shock or a dragging undertow. It can feel strange and unwelcoming, full of unpracticed habits and unknown knowledge. Little details out of place can feel like a tell-tale sign charged with meaning.

Day Tripping

There was a time when the two women would go on day trips, traipsing around small Texas towns in various states of preservation and faded beauty. There were town squares rimmed with ornate, stone-cut German buildings from the nineteenth century that now host antique shops or a local campaign headquarters. There were serendipitous scenes like the café that featured pies piled high with whipped cream and butter icing where the waitress described every ingredient in each of the pies in supple, loving detail. Or the auction house where a woman with big hair and a big accent described last night's auction. People came from all around and left with ancient armoires and gilded doll carriages. Or the little police station where the two women went to find a public bathroom. A group of men in uniform talking about fishing stopped and stared at them for a long minute before a woman kindly took them behind the desk. There was the weeping icon in a monastery on a dusty hill where the women had to choose wrap-around skirts and head-scarves from a big box by the door before they could be ushered into the chapel. And the time they saw two teenage girls ride bareback into town, leaving their horses untethered behind the dry goods store while they got ice cream.

The day tripping had struck other people's fancy too. There was a day trips column in the weekly entertainment paper. There were local travel books you could carry with you to make sure you didn't forget the name of the fabulous barbeque place with the great pork chops or the authentic Mexican cantina tucked away on a side street. The New York Times had started a weekly section of the paper called "escapes".

But the two women's traipsing seemed like an intensely private thing, and special. They could rest their eyes on the scenes they happened into. They would pick up little tidbits to bring home: Czech pastries, some peanut brittle, a butter dish in the shape of a sleeping cat. They would imagine themselves inhabiting a town where cabins covered in creeping vines took on the solid ephemerality of an inhabited place and local characters flickered in and out of view like dream figures. They would drift into a free-floating state feeling of possibility and rest. It was not small town values or clean living they were after but the way the synesthetic web of fabulated sights and tastes made objects resonant. It was as if they could dwell in the ongoing vibrance of the ordinary.

The imaginary still lives they carried home from their forays held the promise of contact. Their charged particularity framed an active process of desire. This can become a simple and basic pleasure – a way of making implicit things matter.

The practice of day-tripping keeps the dream of a private life alive by way of its pleasures and compulsion, its rhythms, its timing, its stopping to contemplate still lives.

Reference

Massumi, Brian 2002: *Parables for the Virtual*. Chapel Hill, N.C.: Duke University Press.

TRANSFORMING

ZERO-MAKING

Gösta Arvastson

Zero is generally understood as indicating equilibrium, an initial point or origin. *Zero-making* is the action directed towards elements of cultures where the meaning of an object is set to zero. A. [Industrial] Zero-making was introduced in the 1990s in terms of new production concepts, human resource management, flat organizing, *zero defects* in production, multi-skilling and new management techniques emphasizing total employer loyalty.

Zero-making is defined as a revolutionary theme. It is the setting of time to zero in order to organize a fresh start, erasing history, wiping the slate clean and promoting the idea of late modern corporate revolutions with labels like: Japanization, The New Economy, ICT Society, The Third Industrial Revolution and The Velvet Revolution. B. [Sports] [Synonymously] Sudden death: Extra play in a situation of equal score after a game to determine the winner.

INFLECTED FORMS [Union politics] *Hammer blow. Redundancies to zero.* [Theatrically] *A boring performance. A display that stupefied all onlookers.* [Transports/Zero visions] *No accidents at all.* C. [Economy] The system or range of zero activity in a country, region, or community. a. Call for a higher level of civilization: *Effects of a new era were felt at every level of the corporation.* b. A specific type of calculation of zero growth: *A sustainable development.* c. The cheapest class of accommodations, especially on an airplane. D. [Religious] The interpretation of God's will within the world.

Zero-makers: The term generally refers to the ability to paralyze the mental capacities with references to compelling circumstances [Ozone layer]. The professional skill of zero-making is generally held by *zero-makers, de-programmers* and *dead-enders.*

Zero-making Process: The information of nothing taking place. Everything is perceived in a zero time, in the same way as the Freudian tradition suggests that words such as "near" and "far" would be the same, pronounced with different emphasis. Another interpretation is the revolutionary theme, the spiral movement of zero making, and the atmospheric impression of opportunities that it conveys. Zero could have been accidental but it is hard to eliminate, it includes the pleasure of playing with high markers or hidden aces with a calculated risk of zero benefit as in the activities of what is called "black dog opportunities" on the stock market.

Zero-making consequences: The evolutionary models of the past will no longer provide a series of achievements. Zero-making wipes out the Grand Narrative of modern times: the movement toward collectively defined goals, the visions bringing people together and the impact of collective efforts. In this classical narrative there was always a higher level of civilization to be reached even when the conditions of work seemed hard and hostile, sometimes with the dreams of a work-free society. From generation to generation the liberation came closer. In, for example, the rational management of motor industries it included set of values, stressing loyalty and collective involvement. There was also the importance of visions – a world of dreams that were something other than everyday work, as Henry Ford pointed out, when he concluded that his leadership in Detroit had nothing to do with cars. His target was the creation of the New Man. Visions seemed to forge the imaginary road to the future. Making visions reminds one of the *politics of desire*, coined by Zygmunt Bauman (1992). Places such as the shop floor were crossroads of desires. Emerging zero time in late modernity instead concentrated all desires on an ongoing present, a constant roundabout of cultural meaning. The present was the name of the game.

Setting time to zero, the degeneration of time and space, invokes a detour from the inscription of modern visions. The new temporal diversity, the collision between speeds and directions found in the hyperpotential point of car plants, cities, hospitals, shopping streets, and migrant blocks circles around a personal and cyclical time of the present, or as Londoner's sometimes put it: "diarizing the day". The centre of gravity is steadily working toward the subject itself. No models of technological advancement will be found in the past and no models are possible to find in the future.

Something happens when the credibility of technological visions collapses. The canon of modernistic *mouvement*, as we learned from the nineteenth-century debates, the small death of departure, as coined by Paul Virilio (1991) will no longer be part of the story. Zero-making is like an appeal to the randomness of the future in the way the surrealist André Breton expressed it: "There is nothing I love so much as that which stretches away before me and out of sight."

Zero-making as the invention of anomalies: Zero-making is likely to infect the equilibrium of symbols and values. Zero-making signifies the double moment of cultural presence in terms of either/or. Everything is to be played out as the doublings of culture. Sign against sign, symbols against symbols, all that which is no longer related to each other, the end of beginnings, the acceleration of traditions, the gravity of newness, and the consumption of signs. In this perspective zero-making is a "way of life".

E. [Radical disillusion] Zero-making is the appraisal of change and the rejection of progress. It is the promotion of traditional zero-makers (the priest, the soldier, the medicine man, diviners of the future). Earlier the public image was clarified as social institutions through rituals and in dress, gestures and characters. The late modern version is transparent, beyond the terrain of social institutions and economy. Instead we are talking about the place-less laboratories of zero-making, the terrain of advertising; the magnetism of optional bodies and cultures.

F. [Meteorology] The concept of Zulu time goes back to the poetry of Z in the American alphabet. It has been used in many professional areas, broadcasting, aviation and meteorology, as Coordinated Universal Time (UTC). a. [War technologies] Zero factors, coined during the Gulf War by Western media, followed the illusion of breaking points of global development. b. Zero-making was the operation that aimed for the fabric of a new era, while setting time equal to nil. c. Zero defect: Complete perfection. d. The failure of waypoints, the turning away from a track; Zero-making implies under specific conditions a search for the original focus of attention: a ritual, a passage, a transition-level [aviation] of perceptions [altitudes]. e. The making of zero is about the levelling out of rising curves, progress, and evolution. f. The seduction of our times, taking it all over again, a touch [and go] of events. g. The theatricality of cultural destruction. h. The miracle of reset buttons. i. The non-entity of nothing. It is the collapse back into the nativeness of human relations.

G. [Human sciences] The making of no influence or importance; the making of nonentity. a. [Personal attitudes] *A professor who was a total zero.* b. [Ranking and careers] *A paper of zero knowledge.* c. Traces of zero-making are generally conceived as the obsession of finding non-functional values [zero-making invokes a detour from the inscription of modern visions] in the flow of apparently functional information: *His prospects were approaching zero.*

INFORMAL: *Today I accomplished zero.* a. Informal zero-making: The call for absent friends, inoperative, or material objects being irrelevant in specified circumstances: *The town has practically no opportunities for amusement, zero culture.* OR: *Today we have all zeroed around.* The condition of nothing, nihility, nothingness.

TRANSITIVE VERB: Inflected forms: ze·roed, ze·ro·ing, ze·roes, zulu-ing, zulu-ed.
To adjust a material object (like an instrument or a device) to zero value.

PHRASAL VERBS: [Zero in…]: *The ethnologists zeroed in on the display of toys in the store window.* [Zero out…]: To zero out a cultural understanding of nothing by cutting off funding.

References

Arvastson, Gösta 2005: The Zulu Dimension. *Cultural Studies, Critical Methodologies*, Vol. 5, No. 3, 402–410.

Baudrillard, Jean 1988: *The Ecstasy of Communication.* New York: Semiotext(e).

Bauman, Zygmunt 1992: A Sociological Theory of Postmodernity. In: Peter Beilharz, Gillian Robinson & John Rundell (eds.), *Between Totalitarianism and Postmodernity: A Thesis Eleven Reader.* Cambridge, Mass.: MIT Press.

Virilio, Paul 1991: *The Aesthetics of Disappearance*, translated by Philip Beitchman. New York: Semiotext(e).

ARTIFICIALIZATION

Russell Belk

Apart from a small wealthy elite segment of the world that craves natural foods, natural fibers, natural childbirth, organic gardening, feng shui, human powered sports, environmentalism, deep ecology, natural death, and preserves for nature, wildlife, nudity, and aboriginal peoples, what the mass of humanity clearly prefers is an artificial, sanitized, synthetic environment. Through our consumption choices we clearly signal a preference for synthetic foods, artificial additives, genetic modification, pesticides, herbicides, atomic energy, surrogate motherhood, artificial intelligence, Disneyfication, and McDonaldization. This is not mere passive acceptance of conditions foisted upon us by conniving marketers or totalitarian governments. Rather it reveals an active desire for the artificial over the natural, the "real." Consider the popular computer game *The Sims* and its many spin-offs. In these games, players acquire artificial houses, artificial furnishings, artificial bodies, artificial partners, artificial children, artificial pets, and artificial lives. What is more, dedicated Sims players delight in and obsess over these surrogate objects in a way that seldom attends the consumption of their real counterparts. We delight in the artificial, even when it simulates a real world to which we seem to have become alienated, jaded, or indifferent.

Admittedly, the distinction between the real and the artificial is often a somewhat arbitrary one. As Zerubavel reminds us, "The proverbial Martian cannot see the mental partitions separating Catholics from Protestants, classical from popular music, or the funny from the crude" (1991: 80). But the fact that boundary between the artificial and the real is itself artificial does not mean that it doesn't exist; merely that it is socially constructed. What is of most concern here is why it is that we seem to increasingly prefer things on the "artificial" side of this divide rather than where precisely we draw this line.

For all intents and purposes humankind mastered the real by the mid-twentieth century. We can transform, build, or destroy our landscape at will, rapidly transport people and things to new locations, build dizzyingly tall skyscrapers, and alter the human body so that even death is cheated. In the modern account, such mastery of the real along with increasingly scientized explanations of the once inexplicable represents progress. But the postmodern account has a much more playful take on the real and unreal. In this view Marx's complaint that "All that is solid melts into air," should have been intoned in a much more celebratory voice. For the real is too much with us. What we crave, and increasingly what we get, is more artificialization.

Although Walter Benjamin lamented the loss of the aura of the artist and the fate of "The Work of Art in an Age of Mechanical Reproduction," it is more the current situation that the mastery of the real and the over-rationalization of our existence threaten the sacred aura of the wondrous. Rather than further elitist rationalist criticisms of Disney, computer games, Las Vegas, plastic surgery, McDonald's, cybersex, and megachurches (of the sort offered by Baudrillard and Eco in their critiques of hyperreality), we need a greater appreciation of the attractive side of such artificialization.

Let us take as examples three related artificial sources of pleasure: *pachinko* parlors, gambling, and that Mecca of the artificial, Las Vegas. Each offers a seemingly mind-numbing artificial world that is all too easy and tempting to ridicule. Yet each of these artificial enclaves offers a haven from the even more mind-numbing reality of the world outside its confines.

It is estimated that one out of every four Japanese people plays *pachinko* regularly. The steel balls placed into these vertical pinball-like machines garner an expenditure of $300 billion a year, or considerably more than the annual Japanese defense budget. Despite rumored ties to the Mafia-like *Yakuza*, playing *pachinko* is a legal form of gambling. But more than this, *pachinko* offers an escape from purposefulness, an escape from self. As Richie (2003: 121) observes:

> The various pressures of city life are … felt strongly in Japan, and *pachinko* is a big city phenomenon… Although originally the patrons may have been the jobless and the hopeless, now it is those for whom the job is not enough. These repair to the *pachinko* parlour as do others to further areas of addiction – bars for example. Like people in bars, those in the *pachinko* halls feel no pain. Instead, it might be argued, they are experiencing a sort of bliss. This is because they are in the pleasant state of being occupied, with none of the consequences of thinking about what they are doing or considering what any of it means. They have learned the art of turning off. In this attainment boredom is requisite. Yet some kind of activity – the droning of prayers or the clicking of the balls – is also necessary. The ritual may seem empty but it is not. It is filled with nothing. Oblivion is achieved.

We begin to see in this analysis a willing absorption by the artificial. If this seems irrational, this is a distanced judgment that misses the phenomenological point of such activity.

Allen's (1995) observations of the irrationality of his own gambling addiction may offer the missing phenomenological perspective on the pursuit of the non-self through mindless absorption in an artificial world:

> Gambling invites me to take an hour's recess from adulthood, to play in a well-demarked sandbox of irrationality and to look at the world as a magical place, which of course it is when the light hits it at the right angle. Those people who stubbornly remain adults and who look upon gambling's happy meaninglessness from within will see a phalanx of games that from an adult's wintry perspective you cannot hope to master. Those adults will see me, and the people sitting next to me, giving our money away week after week to people who do not love us (1995: 315).

But we must go further into the belly of the gambling beast – to Las Vegas – in order to more fully appreciate what is going with such artificial and "irrational" pursuits.

Calling Las Vegas the place "…where the death of God is staged as the spectacle of the Kingdom of God on Earth" (1999: 170), Taylor (1999) observes the pleasurable nothingness of the city:

> In the hot sands of Vegas's silicon lights, the transcendence of the real vanishes, leaving nothing in its wake. In the dark light of this nothingness, it appears that what is is what ought to be. When this word of acceptance is actively embraced, the Holy Land ceases to be a distant dream and the Kingdom becomes virtually real (1999: 201).

In other words, nothingness comes to be realized as the utopia we seek.

We see a similar celebration of artificiality and nothingness in such diverse contexts as Andy Warhol's brand art, Disneyland (e.g. Doctorow 2003), and Disneyfied religion (Lyon 2000). Warhol called his atelier "The Factory" and proclaimed that everyone should be a machine. He also said, "Some critics called me Nothingness Himself and that didn't really help my sense of existence any. Then I realized that existence itself is nothing and I felt better" (Warhol 1975: 7).

Here too we see the annihilation of self as a kind of freedom, but a freedom obtained without any of the dedicated meditation of the Buddhist monk, the self abnegation of Hindu or Muslim fakir, or the discipline of the cross-legged *zazen* practitioner. And while Warhol's art may seem to celebrate the real thing (whether Brillo pads, Campbell's Soup cans, or celebrities), it only produced an *image* of these things and ultimately, through repetition, it desensitizes and anesthetizes us to reality.

That Disneyland is quintessentially artificial is hardly a surprise. It was, after all, the primary target of both Baudrillard and Eco in their critiques of the hyperreal – the more than real, better than real, hyped reality. But while its production may be hyperreal, Disneyland's consumption is instead hyporeal – less than real. To the people queuing to glide through "It's a Small World," this is less of an engaging magic kingdom than a small passive world whose consumption by park visitors barely differs from that of couch potatoes watching television or zombie-like denizens milling through the shopping mall. And in each of these hyporeal cases of consumption, these are our choices rather than something imposed upon us. We choose to veg-out or zone-out in these places, much as we choose to "get stupid" or "get wasted" on mind-numbing drugs. We do so to seek a non-self not all that different from the non-self of Buddhism.

Disneyfied religion should not be surprising either. As Lyon (2000) points out, by any account religion is all about transcending mundane reality. It's just that in this purportedly postmodern age, people want from religion what Henry Maier called "an easier, faster, no-fuss, microwaveable God" (Lyon 2000: 136). What is striking about both Disneyland and Disneyfied religion is the easy pleasure found in the empty rituals of participating in the nothingness of their artificiality. They offer predictability, reassurance, and thus the chance to detach the self from the demands of what we take to be reality. While producing Disneyland or McDonald's may require active employee management of emotions

(e.g. Hochschild 1983; Van Maanen & Kunda 1989; Ritzer 1993), consuming them is a much easier and less thoughtful experience.

In the *pachinko* parlor, gambling, Las Vegas, Warhol, Disney, Disneyfied religion, television watching, mall shopping, and McDonald's patronage, we can sense the exquisite contradiction of the artificial. By providing an alternative to the all too real world (RW for short in VR [Virtual Reality] parlance), what remains is nothing, or as Boyle described it, "There's nothing there. Nothing contained in nothing. Nothing at all" (1998: 691). At the same time, this nothingness can provide a pleasing escape from somethingness; from, in paraphrase of William Wordsworth, the world that is too much with us. To be sure, this is not the intense pleasure of ecstasy or the transcendence of epiphany. Nor is it the non-materialistic existence that Wordsworth had in mind. But on the other hand, neither is it the nothingness of hopelessness, despondency, nihilism, cynicism, or numbness that Ritzer (2004) sees in imposed corporate globalization or that Postman (1993) sees in the march of "technopoly." It is rather a small state of mindless bliss that we freely choose and that acts as an interlude between harsh acts of reality.

Two novels that best capture this state of mild pleasure and mindless bliss are Julian Barnes' (1990) *History of the World in 10 ½ Chapters* and Haruki Murakami's (1993) *Hardboiled Wonderland and the End of the World*. The two books offer different scenarios in which the lead character opts for nothingness or artificiality over a real world with real pleasures. In the last half chapter of Barnes' imaginative book, the lead character awakes to find himself in heaven. There he learns that he is corporeally intact and can have anything he wishes or else he can choose to have his consciousness killed off forever now or later. After experiencing all the pleasures he can envision, including getting his golf game down to 18, meeting the world's most famous people (both living and dead), shopping for anything and everything, winning at Wimbledon, setting a world record in the marathon, excelling at various other sports, making love to the world's most beautiful women, and eating and drinking the world's most exotic concoctions, he eventually becomes bored and opts to be annihilated as have all those who preceded him. In Murakami's postmodern tale the split-brain narrator is instead offered a choice between living in one half of his mind in an imaginary world of unicorns, a library, meaningless tasks, and a walled-in city and living in the other half of his mind in a real world in which he faces eventual death. He chooses the artificially constructed world over the real world. He has succeeded at nothing less than overcoming the reality of living in the material world. That is, he has succeeded in achieving a nothing existence.

Both of these tales are metaphors for the choices we make daily, for example in watching television rather than doing something more active and less artificial. We – especially, but not exclusively, those of us in the more affluent world – live in a world of post-abundance, in which we can pretty much have it all. But it all seems less and less appealing. In recognizing that the world is too much with us, we reveal a craving for a less materialistic, less burdensome, less imperfect, and less demanding world. The only way we are likely to find such a life is by embracing artificiality. There is a definite irony in rejecting nature worship in favor of the worship of the artificial as a source of release from other artificial parts of our life. But Thoreau's Walden is full of mosquitoes, hard work, and precious few creature comforts. There is further irony in the fact that we willingly pay for the privilege of a less materialistic world in places like Esalen (a spa). Simplicity does not come cheaply these days. And yet another irony is the tyranny of the machine and possession maintenance in the prosthetic iPods, computers, televisions, and other artificial devices needed to temporarily free us from reality. But to instead rely on our own imaginations is increasingly perceived as too much work. It puts us too much in touch with our selves rather than offering purposeless escape from the self.

Clearly our growing preference for artificiality, and the nothingness and anesthetization it offers,

represents a significant cultural phenomenon. There are likely some important cultural differences in this preference as well. Cultures differ in their seriousness versus playfulness, their independence versus interdependence, their religiosity versus agnosticism, their affluence versus post-affluence, and in other ways that will likely influence choices involving sources of artificiality and the manner in which it is pursued. But our expanding embrace of artificialization is very real.

References

Allen, Edward 1995: Penny Ante. In: Mike Tronnes (ed.), *Literary Las Vegas*. New York: Henry Holt & Company, pp. 313–324.

Barnes, Julian 1990: *A History of the World in 10 ½ Chapters*. New York: Vintage.

Boyle, T. Coraghessan 1998: Filthy with Things. In: *T. C. Boyle Stories*. London: Penguin, pp. 675–691.

Doctorow, Cory 2003: *Down and Out in the Magic Kingdom*. New York: Tor.

Hochschild, Arlie 1983: *The Managed Heart*. Berkeley: University of California Press.

Lyon, David 2000: *Jesus in Disneyland: Religion in Postmodern Times*. Cambridge: Polity Press.

Murukami, Haruki 1993: *Hardboiled Wonderland and the End of the World*. New York: Vintage.

Postman, Neal 1993: *Technopoly: The Surrender of Culture to Technology*. New York: Vintage.

Richie, Donald 2003: *The Image Factory: Fads & Fashions in Japan*. London: Reaktion Books.

Ritzer, George 1993: *The McDonaldization of Society*. Newbury Park, CA: Pine Forge Press.

Ritzer, George 2004: *The Globalization of Nothing*. Thousand Oaks, CA: Pine Forge Press.

Taylor, Mark C. 1999: *About Religion*. Chicago: University of Chicago Press.

Van Maanen, John & Gideon Kunda 1989: Real Feelings: Emotional Expression and Organizational Culture. In: L.L. Cummings & Barry M. Staw (eds.), *Research in Organizational Behavior*, Vol. 11. Greenwich, CT: JAI Press, pp. 43–104.

Warhol, Andy 1975: *The Philosophy of Andy Warhol*. New York: Harcourt Brace.

Zerubavel, Eviatar 1991: *The Fine Line: Making Distinctions in Everyday Life*. New York: Free Press.

BACKLASH

Kirsti Mathiesen Hjemdahl and Nevena Škrbić Alempijević

Commie Junk

Once a year the streets of Zagreb are filled with piles of junk, old stuff that the inhabitants of the town centre no longer need or want, cleaned out of attics, cellars, drawers and closets. It is carried out of front doors or thrown out of windows. And as the days proceed, the pavements and doorsteps become more and more difficult to pass through. Sometimes one gets a glimpse of previously well-known, but now long and often deliberately forgotten images. May 2004, an email dumped into the inbox, with three photos attached. It is a rather short, but precise, message: "Here you can find some pictures related to the huge junk on the Zagreb's streets these days. Enjoy. P.S. some of those images are really HUGE junk :-)."

The first picture is a bright red conference paper decorated with the star, the sickle and the hammer and the acronyms SKJ (meaning Savez komunista Jugoslavije – the Association of the Communists of Yugoslavia), lying on some worn-out car tires. The second picture shows a book titled *Priče i legende* (Stories and Legends), by Maksim Gorki, a Russian author whose works on the social injustice, the sorrows and pride of workers and peasants, was an obligatory reading in Yugoslav schools during the communist period. The third picture is of an envelope with the seal saying "Republički odbor, Zagreb" (the Republic's Committee, Zagreb) and a stamp of 1 jugoslavenski dinar, Yugoslavian dinar).

The reason the mail-sender considers these items HUGE junk is not because they are worn out, or just old and useless material. It is because they belong to an era, a political system, a country and a society that no longer exists, and to a past that somehow seems to have vanished into thin air. It is so-called "commie junk."

Rewriting History

It is almost surprising that such junk can still be seen in the streets of Zagreb, since there has been an effective cleaning process going on in the country for quite some time. Although such objects, once priceless and now worthless, have never been publicly thrown onto huge public bonfires, a radically new perspective on THE Croatian history emerged in many spheres of public life, influencing every pore of people's everyday routine. This brand new, but still presented-as-absolute truth, was concretized in urban toponymy, in changing names of town streets and squares, and in the removal of monuments and memorial plates glorifying nameless WW II warriors and communist legends, and in memorials to the new heroes of the nation (Rihtman Augustin 2000: 35–60).

The libraries were purged of anything "inadequate", books written by Serbian authors, those in Cyrillic alphabet or containing "Yugoslav spirit". The museum presentations of Croatian culture and history simply left out some "undesirable" historical chapters. The same void was created in education: "This past is too recent, and therefore too problematic and difficult for us to deal with", as a professor of history put it, when explaining to his students why the communist area of the twentieth century is

still considered a tricky topic, and is therefore also left out of the curriculum (Birt, in print).

The Croatian War of Independence in the 1990s was not only waged against the aggressor, the once heroic Yugoslav People's Army, as celebrated in popular songs, and the Serbian troops in the trenches; it was echoed in each household, in every town street. All the material culture symbolizing the former political formation and its communist regime became the enemy of the newly established state. They simply had to be removed, out of sight and out of mind.

This removal was done with little fuss and noise; instead the objects have just sunk into dead silence and oblivion. There were rarely any official proclamations about which images should be ostracized and which ones should be reinvented and placed in the centre of the symbolic scene. Still, people knew what was considered to be *pro* and *con* in the Croatian nation-state. This silent ban was only felt when one happened to go against the tide.

Pure Croatian Air?

One of the first to speak out about this way of removing the "Yugoslav" and introducing the "Croatian" was the author Dubravka Ugrešić. In articles in *Die Zeit* (23 October, 1992) and *Independent on Sunday* (6 December, 1992), she argued that the tin cans on sale in Zagreb kiosks, decorated with the red and white Croatian coat of arms, bearing the message "Clean Croatian Air", are not just innocent souvenirs, but rather metaphors of the whole cleaning process taking place in the independent Croatia (Ugrešić 1999: 60).

Ugrešić gives a whole range of examples of whom, how and what "this magic spray-formula" is opposed to. She claims that in the new system of values, which is based on the polarity of clean–dirty, "Byzantine blood" is the most dangerous polluting substance. This is simply another, and more refined word for *Serb* and *Orthodox*. Other dirty enemies include insufficiently pure Croats, saboteurs, traitors, anti-Tuđman commandos, commies, Yugonostalgics, and like-thinkers (Ugrešić 1999: 61). After publishing this text, the author herself was more or less *cleaned* out of the country. In a postscript, in the prize winning book *The Culture of Lies: Antipolitical Essays*, she tells what happened:

> Although the text was not published in the local press, everyone immediately knew what was in it and the author was suddenly cast into the role of isolated target of frenzied attacks by her compatriots: the new political elite, newspapers, television, radio, fellow writers, colleagues at the Arts Faculty in Zagreb, friends, anonymous writers of threatening letters, unnamed righteous telephone callers … Her furious compatriots – proclaiming the author a liar, traitor, public enemy and a witch – fuelled a pyre and the author, consumed by fire in her own homeland, left to continue her life in exile. During a brief Christmas visit to Zagreb in 1996, the author was greeted by an anonymous message on her phone: *Rats, you've been hiding! So you're still here! You're still breathing under the wonderful Croatian sky? Get out of Croatia!!* (Ugrešić 1999: 63–64).

Kumrovec May 22nd 2004

It is early morning hours, but along Josipa Broza street people have been up and busy for a long time already. They are hammering the last nails into the stage and making sure the "Day of Youth" banner is hanging properly over the road, raising the blue, red and white Croatian flags, placing obstacles on the streets, marking the arena of the celebration and cutting it off from the rest of Kumrovec, which will try to continue its everyday, mundane routine. To put it in Johan Huizinga's terms (1992), the spatial frame of the play is being defined.

The museum stands are taken out of the barn and filled with souvenirs that are not usually found in the museum souvenir shop, and are ordered especially for this occasion: T-shirts claiming that Tito is "a man of peace", caps with Tito's signature, cups, decorative plates, and ashtrays with his image or a picture of the house where he was born. Along the road other stands, more diverse in shape, are about to emerge as well. One guy is decorating a tree by hanging Tito's framed portrait on its trunk, a picture once found in almost every classroom and office in the former Yugoslavia, and others are putting old partisan uniforms, helmets, and military decorations on the lawn. A couple is spreading cassettes, books, and pictures of similar subjects all over a car, a display of goods for sale. The displays are enormously creative, and the quantity and variety of things on display almost unbelievable. In Kumrovec on this particular day, the market for old commie stuff is so large that you will even find new reproductions on sale. Truly, this is all small-scale craft production, but it is slowly growing into a major business (Jurković, in print).

It is the Day of Youth! In this little village where Marshall Tito was born, some five thousand people from all over the former Yugoslavia have gathered to celebrate, relive, pay respect to, and remember Tito's birthday. Or rather, the Day of Youth is celebrated three days before the actual date. As people are travelling long hours in order to attend, and May 25th is no longer a public holiday in any of the new nations in southeastern Europe, the only practical possibility was to move the celebration to the nearest weekend.

People are all moving towards the hot spot of Kumrovec: the birthplace of Josip Broz Tito, and his life-size statue in the front garden. Photos are being taken, greetings delivered, people are bowing to the statue, and bouquets and wreaths, mostly of red flowers, are being placed in front of Him. One woman came running into the garden and shouldered her way to the statue, obviously very excited. She stroked it several times, and at every stroke she would say, "This is for Radenković, this is for Majda... – and so on." Obviously she was fulfilling her commitment to her friends, as well as their joint commitment to the statue. This kind of behaviour makes one question whether people are approaching Tito's representation, or Tito himself (Belaj, in print).

One delegation after the other fills the street of Kumrovec, carrying neatly designed flower decorations and waving old Yugoslavian flags along with huge red flags with golden stars. Comrades are catching up with old acquaintances, hugging and greeting one another. Visitors are spontaneously breaking out in song, accompanied by accordions: "Comrade Tito, We Swear to You", "Over Forests and Mountains", and "Comrade Tito, a White Violet". Tears are falling as people are singing at the top of their voices, not only because of hearing these long-forgotten songs, but because of the memories they awake (Petrović & Rubić, in print). People are also affected by seeing people dressed in the old uniforms of partisans and pioneers, proudly exhibiting badges with Tito's picture, both from this year's and previous celebrations, and holding huge posters of Him, and signs saying "Tito in Our Heart" and "Yesterday, Today, Always Tito" high in the air.

Are you "The Birds of the Feather"?

At the tables in front of the pub "By the Old Mate", a group of young people is preparing for the day. They separate themselves from the rest of the people attending the celebration of Tito's 112th birthday in Kumrovec, 24 years after his death. They approach individuals in this crowd, "armed" with recording equipment and questions about why and how visitors are marking this Day of Youth, but they are often met with counter questions: Are you one of us? Where do you come from? Oh, there were a lot of partisans from that island! Is that a Tito-friendly place? Are we "the birds of the feather"? Are you "believers"?

We are part of this group of young people: nineteen ethnologists from the University of Zagreb, and one Norwegian from the University of Bergen.[1] We have been preparing for this event for months, through lectures on phenomenologically-inspired cultural research, on multisited fieldwork, and, on a personal level, by facing and personally dealing with this particular past – which despite being recent seems so distant and long-gone.

The Croatian co-author of this paper explained to the Norwegian researcher that "We can't make this research project an obligatory course. Forcing students to go to Kumrovec on the Day of Youth would be like yet another assault. Participation in this project has to be a totally voluntary choice". For the majority of students the main attraction of the project was initially wanting to learn more about phenomenologically-inspired fieldwork. As preparations continued, however, the participants reported increasingly about the reactions and interest they received from outside the classroom.

Several said that for the first time their university studies managed to engage their whole family back home, and that the project prompted lively discussion around dinner tables. Parents and grandparents told about their own experiences and memories of Tito, and about living in a communist society. "I thought that I was the only one in Croatia actually remembering Tito", a grandmother put it. Others said that for the first time in their lives they had thought about this part of their own past, much less discussed it in a public sphere.

All the participants had different approaches[2] to the Day of Youth celebrations in Kumrovec and the many mutual questions we were exploring. What happens when the past we are remembering turns infamous and the memories we cherished become stigmatised and tabooed? How do we remember then, and more importantly, how do we express this changed attitude? What happens to the places declared the central topos of socialist ideology in the new ideology, since it so strongly represents the cradle in which "the greatest son of our nations and nationalities" was rocked?

Being there, focusing on how the Day of Youth is experienced by those in the celebration, seems even more important because the whole event is still stigmatized in contemporary Croatia. It provides researchers with an alternative path towards understanding a society, and it enables them to explore cultural processes of change and continuity, and to see the effects of power relations that are often inaccessible.

Backlash or Voicing of "Other" Truths when One Least Expects Them

In many ways Kumrovec celebration may be viewed through the term "deviance": it is performed by people generally regarded as "marginal", at an "infamous" place that has disappeared from the nation's mental maps, on the date of the former national holiday of a dissolved country, including a ceremony commemorating the birthday of a person whose historical role is highly controversial. Still, it

does not deviate from the way memory of the recent past has been treated in contemporary Croatia. The celebration itself is an uncalled-for reaction to official silence, an expression of alternative truths not voiced in the mainstream public sphere, which can only happen in "forgotten" places and "forbidden" forms.

This kind of backlash can also be seen in the other diverse expressions of attitudes towards the common past in other countries which were part of the former Yugoslavia. So for instance, in his article on the so-called Balkan culture, the Slovene sociologist Mitja Velikonja discusses parallel patterns that emerged in Slovenia during the 1990s (Velikonja 2002: 189–207). One is "balkanophobia", a political and media discourse which tries to define cultural distance from the so-called "non-Slovenes", a popular term for members of the other ex-Yugoslav nations. The other is a rapidly growing "Balkan culture" which is inspired by old Yugoslav symbols, myths and stories. This "Balkan culture" is not based on the previous generations' Yugonostalgia, but is instead a challenge to and subversion of dominant discourses. It is an innovation, a new kind of cultural reception and production, and mode of self-identification among young people – even teenagers who never actually lived in the times of Yugoslavia.

Thus, although the narratives generally cherished during the communist regime have been suppressed from all the visible strata of collective memory, recognizable topos, dates and figures still remain important in personal life histories, and the experience of individual remembrance. They are stubborn spots that deliberately resist or accidentally hide from the efficient spray of Mr. Clean that blanketed Croatia in the early 1990s. It is a kind of backlash: an attempt to erase a stigmatised imagery which leads to the unintended consequence of its reinvention. The failure to discuss things and give them a "proper" burial creates energy that preserves the very things that are supposed to vanish, giving them a new lease on life. There are always cracks in the seemingly impeccable surface of the dominant public narrative, through which alternative truths are ready to burst out into the open: the more pressure one applies to cover them, the more eagerly they strive to come forward.

Backlash is a way of voicing alternative truths before there is a possibility of "refreezing" tabooed and difficult segments of the past. As Vesna Teršelić, a lecturer at the Peace Studies in Zagreb, puts it:

> I believe that all can be processed, but it is an ongoing process of dialogue, additional research, it is ongoing process of cultural projects, more theatre performances, more books, and more films. (…) There have been so much talk about history textbooks in Croatia, increasingly they are getting better, and it is not such a horror as it was, although history curriculum is a problem. But then, you know, what will take us very many years is getting rid of this notion of one truth (in Škrbić Alempijević & Hjemdahl 2006).

It will probably also take some years before Balkan Culture, as seen in Slovenia, emerges in Croatia. There were at least not many signs of an "easy-going-pop-art"-relationship in the Day of Youth celebrations in Kumrovec 2004, neither for the participants or the researchers studying them. Even for the young ones, this past seems still too close.

Notes

1 Marijana Belaj, Danijela Birt, Toni Blagaić, Koraljka Bogdanović, Jasna Dasović, Kirsti Mathiesen Hjemdahl, Jasmina Jurković, Petra Kelemen, Iva Končurat, Nenad Kovačić, Anamarija Kučan, Marija Kulišić, Tihana Lovrić, Tihana Petrović Leš, Željka Petrović, Marijeta Rajković, Tihana Rubić, Robert Šešerko, Nevena Škrbić Alempijević, Tanja Štignjedec.

2 While some were focusing on the music, the design, the rhetoric, the dressing, the souvenirs, the guest book, the things taking place around the statue, at Villa Kumrovec and at The Political School, others were following in the footsteps of school classes, people dressed as pioneers, different age groups attending the celebration, participants from different regions within ex-Yugoslavian countries, and local ones from Kumrovec. Some also followed the celebration on a distance, focusing on the media coverage, film productions, and the national archives.

References

Belaj, Marijana: Tito poslije Tita. Kip Josipa Broza kao žarište obrednog ponašanja. In: Nevena Škrbić Alempijević & Kirsti Mathiesen Hjemdahl (eds.), *O Titu kao mitu: Proslava Dana mladosti u Kumrovcu.* Zagreb: FF Press and Srednja Europa, in preparation for publishing.

Birt, Danijela: O važnosti mjesta. Odakle svi ti ljudi na Danu mladosti? In: Nevena Škrbić Alempijević & Kirsti Mathiesen Hjemdahl (eds.), *O Titu kao mitu: Proslava Dana mladosti u Kumrovcu.* Zagreb: FF Press and Sredjna Europa, in preparation for publishing.

Huizinga, Johan 1992: *Homo ludens: o podrijetlu kulture u igri.* Zagreb: Naprijed.

Jurković, Jasmina: Trgovanje Titom. Od "komunističkog otpada" do suvenira. In: Nevena Škrbić Alempijević & Kirsti Mathiesen Hjemdahl (eds.), *O Titu kao mitu: Proslava Dana mladosti u Kumrovcu.* Zagreb: FF Press and Sredjna Europa, in preparation for publishing.

Petrović, Željka & Tihana Rubić: "Druže Tito, mi ti se kunemo." Uloga glazbe na proslavi Dana mladosti. In: Nevena Škrbić Alempijević & Kirsti Mathiesen Hjemdahl (eds.), *O Titu kao mitu: Proslava Dana mladosti u Kumrovcu.* Zagreb: FF Press and Sredjna Europa, in preparation for publishing.

Rihtman Auguštin, Dunja 2000: *Ulice moga grada.* Beograd: Biblioteka XX vek.

Škrbić Alempijević, Nevena & Kirsti Mathiesen Hjemdahl 2006: "Jesi li jedna od nas?" S proslave Titova 112. rođendana. In: Lada Čale Feldman & Ines Prica (eds.), *Devijacije i promašaji.* Zagreb, in print.

Velikonja, Mitja 2002: Ex-Home: "Balkan Culture" in Slovenia after 1991. In: Sanimir Resić & Barbara Törnquist-Plewa (eds.), *The Balkans in Focus: Cultural Boundaries in Europe.* Lund: Nordic Academic Press, pp. 189–208.

Ugrešić, Dubravka 1999: The Culture of Lies: Antipolitical Essays. London: Phoenix.

BACKDRAFTS*

Tom O'Dell

In November of 1989 I received a letter from Prague that was sent to me by a friend, Renata. As I opened the envelope I was surprised to find that in addition to a letter, Renata had included a bell, about the size of a thimble, hung from a thin red ribbon. It was made out of a simple ceramic material and lacked any sort of ornamentation. As bells go, this was a modest object.

However, what I held in my hands was more than a cheap bell, it was the materialization of a *cultural backdraft* that had swept through Prague, Czechoslovakia, and much of Eastern Europe over the course of that fall. Amongst firefighters, *backdraft* is known as an explosive phenomenon that derives its energy from a longer process of accumulation in which the power of partially un-burnt gases and other combustibles are suddenly released when presented with a new source of fuel. The fuel that ignites backdrafts and causes the pursuant deflagration is oxygen – something that might otherwise seem benign.[1]

As Renata explained in her letter, hundreds of thousands, maybe millions of Czechs were taking to the streets in the evenings ringing these little unassuming ceramic bells. It was, she explained, part of a growing protest, a call for change. For the communist government in power, the call for change had been an ever present and ongoing annoyance that seemed to bloom periodically. It had always been controlled, but it nonetheless always lurked in the background.

The bell was interesting as a physical manifestation of a cultural backdraft because it metonymical-ly bore witness to several parallel processes leading up to the 1989 demonstrations. In part, it resonated with an awareness of similar ongoing events in other Eastern European countries that helped to strengthen the protest movement in Prague. However, beyond this, it also spoke of the existence of an invisible power that compelled hundreds of thousands of people to come together and agree upon the use of the bell as a symbol. And it clearly exemplified how years of accumulated (and routinized) dissatisfaction with the existing regime and the conditions of daily life could be channeled through a simple object and given a new collective focus and energy. In this context, it is a revealing reminder of how even the most trivial of actions (including the small movements of the wrist leading to the ringing of a bell) can cause backdrafts to ignite existing fuel in an irreversible manner.

In what follows, I shall more closely examine the cultural anatomy of backdrafts and the processes fueling them. I argue that we need to more closely examine the repetitive activities and routines of daily life. Backdrafts are interesting because they do not just suddenly occur; their potential develops over time as tensions build under a facade of stability and continuity.

Unnoticed Signs

For the anthropologist, the challenge is to identify the processes leading to backdrafts before they explode. But this requires an appreciation of things that are inconspicuous. Unfortunately, the current trends in

cultural research tend to be moving in the opposite direction, towards a predominant focus upon that which is turbulent, vividly problematic, and palpably present (see the discussion in Shove 2003: 1). We find a predilection for the study of such phenomena as disciplining powers, acts of resistance, arenas of cultural contestation, and forces of fragmentation, atomization, and hybridity (see for example Pile & Keith 1997; Rojek 1995; Young 1995). This is a world of scholarly interest that emphasizes visible signs of change over continuity, regularly invoking metaphors of liquidity, fluidity, flexibility, and speed (see Bauman 2000; Sennett 1998; Urry 2000, 2003; Virilio 2000). And while much of this work has significantly contributed to our understanding of the problems facing contemporary society, it does little to explain the processes that keep daily life from becoming unglued, spinning completely out of control for many people.

In some ways the invocation of the backdraft metaphor could be understood as yet another sign of the scholarly preoccupation with highly visible and dramatic phenomena. To be sure, cultural backdrafts often have defining moments that mark the point when they coalesce into a recognizable force: the tearing down of the Berlin Wall, the destruction of the Twin Towers in New York on September 11th, or the revelation of the poisoning of Ukrainian presidential candidate Viktor Yushchenko in the late fall of 2004. These are the big events, the "conspicuous moments", that tend to be remembered in history books and heritage celebrations, but they are only a very small portion of the "cultural biography" of any backdraft (Appadurai 1986). Behind these highly visible events there is a long period when daily life seemed to follow a normal course. This point might be easier to illustrate with examples that are less dramatic than the orange revolution or the fall of communism.

Backdrafts do not always make the news. Within academia there is a rich flora of stories about departments that, at least from the perspective of outsiders, suddenly seem to implode or disintegrate. The defining moment may be a heated exchange of words that suddenly polarizes a department or even a larger community of scholars. However, signs of a coming tempest can be found nestled unpresumptuously in such things as a footnote in a leading journal, a snide comment at a conference, or an intentionally (?) omitted reference. They can also be more obvious; a professor's choice to leave one department for another, or increasingly vigorous debates in journals. In part, the pressures driving these processes may stem from competing theoretical perspectives and political positions, but emotions should not be overlooked as an important source of power for backdrafts. Indignation, hurt pride, the need to be right and respected, these are just a few of the emotional energies driving backdrafts through university corridors (Ehn & Löfgren 2004).

However, university settings are not unique. Emotions are an important source of cultural energy in many other backdraft contexts, but emotions have to be understood as more than isolated phenomena internally bound to the psyche of individuals. As Arlie Russell Hochschild has argued, "emotions always involve the body, but they are not sealed biological events" (2003: 125). The question is, how do they accumulate cultural resonance over longer periods of time, creating a mood (or atmosphere) that transcends the individual?

Accumulating Energy

Perhaps a small part of the answer can be found in homes around the world. In popular discourse, western homes are often likened to castles and cocoons isolated from the trials, tribulations, and pressures of public life. However, within the confines of their homes, people conduct some of the most emotionally charged discussions and negotiations they will face during their lives. Homes are places in which love and affection can find a focus and source of confirmation, but they are also places in which people work to synchronize slightly different values, and perceptions of "normality" over longer and shorter periods of time (Morley 2000: 57).

Homes are a cultural arena in which small things can make big differences. A sock that did not quite make it into the hamper (again), a dinner that was not ready on time, a load of laundry that included the wrong mix of garments or an inappropriate water temperature; any of these small events may be individually insignificant. Nonetheless, in the gendered context of serial domestic lapses, past oversights and warnings can prepare the ground for reactions on an unexpected scale as ideals about how the home should be organized come into conflict with the reality of actual events. The problem here is not simply that people forget to perform their domestic chores in an "appropriate" or "agreed upon" manner, but that old habits, and dominant social structures have a way of repeatedly making themselves felt. As a result, as Jean-Claude Kaufmann has demonstrated in a study of domestic role sharing amongst French couples,

> the most trivial gestures take on awesome dimensions... Taken separately, each action – the neatly ironed underpants, the sock left lying around – appear (sic!) unimportant. Yet society is present in each of them transformed into social objects, determining the individual who thinks he or she controls them (1998: 211).

In this context, small repetitive acts like those linked to the mundane routines of daily life can work as key sources of cultural energy capable of continuously re-stoking an emotionally charged atmosphere – causing temperatures to rise and tensions to build until a breaking point is reached.

Signs of an impending conflagration often exist long before anything dramatic actually happens, but they tend to be either overlooked, or regarded as insignificant. The cultural energy generated by backdrafts seems to be compressed and accelerated by processes of denial in which the warning signals of an imminent pyrolysis are observed, but dismissed. Unfortunately we know very little about how denial is culturally organized and sustained. In contrast, cultural theorists have devoted a great deal of time and space to emphasizing the role played by reflexivity in late modernity (Beck 1992; Giddens 1991). We need to turn the tables to reconsider some of the limits of this reflexivity. We also need to contemplate the ways breaches in reflexivity, as well as other forms of non-recognition and denial, can facilitate the development of backdrafts.

Bodily Practice and Pre-reflexivity

Many of the seemingly trivial activities people carry out on a daily basis are pre-reflexive. Rather than being strategically planned out, or organized by conscious design, they are simply done out of habit, for reasons that can be hard to explain (Kaufmann 1998: 138). They might include a daily compulsion to wipe-off the kitchen countertop just before leaving for work, or a desire to listen to music while dusting. But in the long run, even small shifts in these types of practices can have a bearing upon the way in which we view ourselves, and understand the world around us. This is a point that has been emphasized by Henrietta Moore:

> Shifts in meaning can result from a reordering of practical activities. If meaning is given to the organization of space through practice, it follows that small changes in procedure can provide new interpretations of spatial layout... Shifting the grounds of meaning, reading against the grain, is often something done through practice that is, through the day-to-day activities that take place within symbolically structured space (1994: 83).

Understood in this way, small shifts in practice can generate new experiences that challenge existing norms, values and structures. The stimulus for change in this case comes, at least in part, from corporally bound impressions that produce a sense of "business as usual". As small changes in the performance of daily practices become routinized they have the potential to produce new interpretations of the surrounding world.

The subtleties of this process have been partially illuminated by Sarah Pink in a recent study she conducted of the relationship people have with their homes and housework in England and Spain (Pink 2004). Among other things, she discovered that men tended to attribute a degree of agency to their homes and the dirty surfaces and textures within them. Activities traditionally associated with housewives, such as cleaning, were often recast in the minds of men as adventurous endeavors of conquest. Men pitted themselves against "menaces" such as dust, mould, and smelly carpets, and in the process unconsciously reframed the "feminine activity" of housecleaning as a masculine project which they had to fight day after day (Pink 2004: 135f.).

The shifts in meaning that Pink describes are not dramatic, but they open the way for a reevaluation of the understanding of specific gendered activities associated with the home. As an aspect of backdraft, the processes involved in these types of minute changes in meaning and understanding are an important field of study that require further empirical and analytical study. The question is, in what ways do repetition and routine have the capability to produce a strong sense of continuity and stability, while simultaneously incorporating moments of change that go unnoticed, or at least unregistered as people live their daily lives? And in what ways can these changes be seen as a precondition for other changes?[2]

Burning Out

Having asked this question, I do not mean to imply that small changes always lead to larger cultural transformations. Some backdrafts lose energy or disappear before they ever have the chance to explode. In Eastern European politics, overwhelming force was repeatedly used to smother backdrafts in the process of deflagration. But brutal force is not always the most effective means of extinguishing backdrafts; while having short-term effects, it also reveals a loss of power and control. It is a sure sign that something else will be smoldering in the background.

Other backdrafts seem to lose energy through the introduction of new routines. This is a standard tactic that has long been used to quell growing tensions in domestic settings, and it is the strategy around which the industry of marriage counseling has developed. In this case, the production of new routines may be a very active and conscious endeavor or to make compromises, but it may also be an unconscious move – resulting from "gut feelings" that

help people "tip-toe" around sensitive issues and problems (cf. Kaufmann 1998: 26). Whatever the case, the end result may be the establishment of new routines that alleviate past tensions. In this sense, some backdrafts, rather than resulting in dramatic change, may actually work to hinder it. The question is, how do these processes work in other contexts beyond the home as well as within it?

Backdrafts are interesting, as I am arguing, because they are around us all the time, but they have the tendency to develop and affect us in ways that are often nearly imperceptible. Sometimes they lead to dramatic cultural, political, and social changes. However, more often than not, they simply lie there in the background working in contradictory ways and contributing to the production of something people loosely refer to as the "spirit of our times" (cf. Svensson 1997).

Backdrafts challenge ethnology to focus more explicitly upon the small, at times seemingly trivial and banal activities and practices of daily life and to understand how these work to drive larger cultural changes. At the same time, as the example from Prague that this article opened with illustrates, the study of backdrafts also requires a sensitive understanding of how transnational cultural processes affect local settings. To paraphrase a quote from Marianne Gullestad (1989), an appreciation of the role backdrafts play as cultural processes requires a renewed sensitivity to the manner in which "small facts" and "large issues" continuously speak to one another, simultaneously perpetuating conditions of both continuity and change in everyday life.

Notes

* This article is part of a project, *Home-made: The cultural dynamics of the inconspicuous*, funded by The Swedish Research Council.

1 See Bengtsson, L.G. & Karlsson, B. (1997) *Fenomenen övertändning, backdraft och brandgas-explosion*, Räddningsverket, rapport P21-185/97.

2 Non-recognition, as it turns out, can take many forms. In some cases – like that of the misplaced sock – it contributes to a pressure cooker like atmosphere in which people slowly become aware of the tensions developing around them. Indeed, it is perhaps not surprising to

note that many of the backdrafts I have described here seem to include a hard to define point at which actors increasingly become cognizant of their own interests in relation to those of others. Reflexivity may work as a catalyst of change in this context, focusing people's attention, helping to define a goal, problem, or source of emotional discontent, and facilitating a recognition of the manner in which seemingly disparate processes and activities in everyday life may be linked.

References

Appadurai, Arjun 1986: Introduction: Commodities and the Politics of Value. In: Arjun Appadurai (ed.), *The Social Life of Things: Commodities in Cultural Perspective*. London: Cambridge University Press, pp. 3–63.

Bauman, Zygmunt 2000: *Liquid Modernity*. Cambridge: Polity Press.

Beck, Ulrich 1992: *Risk Society: Towards a New Modernity*. London: Sage.

Bengtsson, L.G. & B. Karlsson 1997: *Fenomenen övertändning, backdraft och brandgasexplosion*. Räddningsverket, rapport P21-185/97.

Ehn, Billy & Orvar Löfgren 2004: *Hur blir man klok på universitetet?* Lund: Studentlitteratur.

Giddens, Anthony 1991: *Modernity and Self-Identity: Self and Society in the Late Modern Age*. Stanford: Stanford University Press.

Gullestad, Marianne 1989: Small Facts and Large Issues: The Anthropology of Contemporary Scandinavian Society. *Annual Review of Anthropology*. Vol. 18, 71–93.

Hochschild, Arlie Russell 2003: *The Commercialization of Intimate Life: Notes from Home and Work*. Berkeley: University of California Press.

Kaufmann, Jean-Claude 1998: *Dirty Linen: Couples and Their Laundry*. London: Middlesex University Press.

Moore, Henrietta 1994: *A Passion for Difference: Essays in Anthropology and Gender*. Cambridge: Polity Press.

Morley, David 2000: *Home Territories: Media, Mobility and Identity*. London: Routledge.

Pile, Steve & Michael Keith 1997: *Geographies of Resistance*. London: Routledge.

Pink, Sarah 2004: *Home Truths: Gender, Domestic Objects and Everyday Life*. Oxford: Berg.

Rojek, Chris 1995: *Decentering Leisure: Rethinking Leisure Theory*. London: Sage Publications.

Sennett, Richard 1998: *The Corrosion of Character: The Personal Consequences of Work in the New Capitalism*. New York: W.W. Norton & Company.

Shove, Elizabeth 2003: *Comfort, Cleanliness & Convenience: The Social Organization of Normality*. Oxford: Berg.

Svensson, Birgitta 1997: Livstid. In: Gunnar Alsmark (ed.), *Skjorta eller själ? Kulturella identiteter i tid och rum*. Lund: Studentlitteratur, pp. 38–61.

Urry, John 2000: *Sociology Beyond Societies: Mobilities for the Twenty-first Century*. London: Routledge.

Urry, John 2003: *Global Complexity*. Cambridge: Polity Press.

Virilio, Paul 2000: *Polar Inertia*. London: Sage Publications.

Young, Robert 1995: *Colonial Desire: Hybridity in Theory, Culture and Race*. London: Routledge.

CUSTOMIZING

Birgitta Svensson

Ebba is a "customer experience designer" though she sometimes calls herself a "strategy consultant". She works with social innovation, hybrid creation and social software. "The meaning of my job is to explain how we can build our identity together," she says. Her company designs services, environments and interactions. She is a young Swedish woman who started her career in San Francisco and London. Now she is working in Stockholm in her own company. Talking to her is like talking to one of my ethnography colleagues; her vocabulary is filled with culture analysis buzz words. We seem to use the same concepts, but to very different ends. Here we may follow how concepts from academia are translated into market practices.

In a world of hyper-competition and high speed in brutal markets, the packaging of messages through design and branding is crucial. The ideal of a strong brand governs a great deal of thinking in the new economy. It concerns both commodities and people. The concept of identity is used to market goods and, conversely, business terms such as trademarks and logotypes are applied to people. The process through which a strong brand or trademark is established can be conceptualised as a customizing process. All concepts used in this process make you think of a kind of utopia where everything is changeable, possible to remake and improve. Concepts used in this process sound like a utopian dream of immense flexibility – anything can be totally changed. The words are also catchwords in something that seems to be the mantra of our time – competitiveness – a kind of me-chanical utopianism within the new economy. This utopianism is very powerful, and has a strong influence, on everything else in business. Being competitive makes you successful. It is the way politics is run and it is also a way of homogenizing the nation, the city, the population and making it part of the global society. To be a part of this wonderful world you have to customize yourself to be competitive.

As soon as you have bought a new product today, especially if it is digital and network based, you get information about how to customize it to fit your personal needs. This process is also applied to people. Several different professionals like Ebba, work with customizing people to chosen identities, by designing interactions between people, places and information. Others work with styling and extreme makeovers to completely transform your looks and your life. Customizing is a highly individualized process and the customizers use expressions like "I want to give people instructions on how to create their own customs. In the end, your most successful customizing process is the one you develop yourself". In the world of consultants customizing is a cultural process that enables you to create a unique look and feeling, even a new way of life, a new ethnicity, sexuality or economy, by converting tradition, convention, norm, routine, practice, habit and ritual into "self-expression". In constantly customizing yourself you establish the unique creative identity that is required in the post-Fordist entrepreneurial society. In this process it is love, not sense of duty, that makes you successful.

There is a close relationship between cultural and economic factors in this process. Customizing as an elite project has, of course, a long history. Here I am interested in the mode of customizing that emerged in the 1980s, when new elites started to gain power by customizing themselves constantly, while at the same time it became their job to customize other people. People who make this process a cumulative one are constantly on the move, transgressing normative borders, constantly creating fresh acquaintances, information and contacts. The customizing process depends on people with no fixed conventions, sexual habits, everyday market routines or other ways of life. On the contrary the process is essentially adapting to new rituals while also participating in formulating these rituals and practices by organizing new conventions and tailoring and modifying people to new roles.

The process as such is rather silent, however strong in its makeovers, since it remodels and fundamentally changes people. It is not a cultural process that just implies life styling but also aims for permanent changes to body and mind, though it is ostensibly adapting people to casual fashions and changing market values. At the same time it is very personal, modifying clients, shoppers and consumers according to individual requirements. To understand what is going on in this process I will focus on the work of customizers.

Customizers Customizing in the Customizing Process

The professionals that work with customizing are interesting because they act as a kind of "applied" cultural analysts. Their competence is multifocal. They customize others at the same time as they customize themselves and homogenize the market according to the customs accustomed by them. By studying them we can observe how identities are produced or maintained. They decide at least something about which identities can pass in the market today, since they form an important part of the moulding and creation of public opinion. There is a continuous interplay between customizing and being customized.

In the customizing process the customizers shape identities by the dialectical movement between fixed and non-fixed identifications. Parts in the process are changeable while others remain permanent. It is a question of a process where you have to be aware of ambivalence, complexity and be the creator of new norms and rituals. This is possible if you admit that there are no traditions, no conventions, no routines to be followed or practices to adapt to.

Urban Fashion

When I first met Ebba she was dressed in clothes from We, a brand that I had never seen before. She did not look as conventional as could be expected from a business consultant, but rather like a hip hop youngster. I soon got to know that the clothing company We does not use commercial advertising but is given to certain people who themselves work as the advertising space. On their website you can read:

We Clothing is an urban fashion company with a base in snowboarding and skateboarding. There were never any questions about what We Clothing wanted to create: a clothes company based on personal engagement and conviction; a theme of shared ideas and common values; and friendship, trust and honesty among equals. With a network of contacts among artists, athletes, companies and media, the priority was always to create a feeling of solidarity. The term "Superlative Conspiracy" symbolizes what We Clothing as a clothes brand and company represents: a group, a family of good and competent people working toward the same ideal.

In these four sentences they say something about what is important about the customizing process and in the subsequent discussion I will use their words as headings and catchwords.

One of the main features in the customizing process is creating and configuring auto-alert and self-correcting processes within a new elite of young market oriented people that see themselves as the "fast, innovative and creative actor(s) on the market" (Löfgren 2005). In some ways this ties in with the fashionable research on "creative cities", found for example in Richard Florida's work (Florida 2002, 2005). He has pointed out that the fastest growing economies are located in cities with open-minded mixes of alternative and bohemian life styles, gays, artists, minorities etc. The idea of "the creative class" has opened up new avenues of advancement for women and members of ethnic minorities. In my ongoing study on the customizing elite in Stockholm, I have also found that many of the consultants have another ethnic background than Swedish and that when they become successful their ethnic categories are subordinated. Many of these consultants are women or homosexual men, with backgrounds that often used to be seen as hindrances in traditional business life. However the diversity is, as Florida (2005) says, not diversity in all aspects and manifestations, but a diversity of elites. The consultants in the customizing process are nomadic people, migrants moving between places and positions. As newcomers they get a cultural double vision that also make them suited to hybridise and customize others to new cultural patterns and identities.

At the same time as the customizers are moving around the world, they seem to gather in and create certain places. Place is playing an important role in organizing this process. It is a key economic and social organizing unit. Saskia Sassen (2002) conceptualises the global economy as depending on a network of what she calls "urban glamour zones" like Stureplan in Stockholm. They are characterized by world-market orientations and significant concentrations of company headquarters, specialized corporate services, and asset-management institutions. She also points out how this new elite of consultants creates its opposite in all the service jobs needed to support them. Places they go tend to be what she calls the "sunken plazas", like Sergels torg in Stockholm (cf. Franzén 2004).

Superlative Conspiracy

The company We shows what is important among the customizers in the customizing process. A company shall be a decent buddy and give you a feeling of "trust and honesty among equals". They do not use commercial advertising but get publicity through activists. The message of how to dress and other identity rules and codes are transmitted among the appropriate people. Customizing is a hidden process that is active among people in a new elite, while it is rather silent to others. Magazines like *Connoisseur*, a Swedish product aimed at affluent people, are customizing journals that have marketing goals to organize events among successful people as platforms for bringing out new brands and messages on the market. Some of the actors in this world also play an important role in public opinion since they are the ones who give comments in media – not only on what is going on for the moment but also what will come in the future. Oscar is a well known man in Sweden. He appears on TV either as the presenter of a program or as a guest in other shows. He cooks, discusses important political issues, health matters, etcetera. He is also considered to have the most appropriate clothing outfit for any given occasion. One year he was elected the most well dressed man in Sweden. The day after his recognition, Oscar congratulated himself to the appointment in the Swedish daily papers. He is witty, funny and customizes himself ironically with attributes like braids and eye shadow.

Limited Edition

Ebba emphasizes that customizing is all about making differences. This is also what the business gurus Nordström and Ridderstråle state with the concept of "karaoke capitalism" (Nordström & Ridderstråle 2003). They argue that there is a karaoke reality within business, which they describe as

> a cosmopolitan club with endless individual choice but also a paltry place for institutionalized imitation. The dirty little secret of management theory and practice is that business schools, benchmarking and best practice have transformed the entire world of commerce into a super-group of karaoke copying companies. And imitating someone else will never get you to the top – merely to the middle.

Instead of doing karaoke business, they believe that you have to be an original – not a copy. All of our identities should be unique limited editions. To customize a unique talent is, according to them, the only sustainable and successful strategy for the future.

Beyond Money

Lina is a customizing consultant that emphasizes how important it is "to do your own thing", which she considers as doing the things that you want, regardless of what you gain from it. A customizing consultant job is something "beyond money", she says. She explains it as a world of partnering, shortcutting and networking. You exchange services, codes and customs. Partnering builds relations and confidence between consultants, entrepreneurs and customers which all have the same interest in common – to transform themselves and others into different identities at different occasions. You are simply customers to each other and have to co-operate to be able to trust each other's competence and your mutual economic interests. They use expressions like: "We are like chameleons, we love to dress up and disguise ourselves even for everyday use. Sometimes we change clothes several times a day to customize ourselves to our customers."

Short cutting and networking is a question of being able to locate, adapt and customize the right people with each other in as short a time as possible. One of the most important aspects is fitting into different business nodes. It is a question of exchange, of knowledge beyond money. Lina depicts herself as linking together people and countries – a global citizen. Then she stresses how important it is to be full of nuances, innovative, many-sided, transformable, multicultural, to be witty, have humour, knowledge and a strong message. Her customizing projects are located in Sao Paolo, Kairo, New York and Shanghai.

Customizing as Control Process

This process makes you aware of the cultural competence found in cultural double vision and being able to quickly decipher codes that make you formable and successful. To cultivate a unique talent is the only sustainable success strategy. The uniqueness in

turn is used on the market to further strengthen this talent. When for instance Virgin Atlantic Airways explain why it is important that each of their flights has a unique name, the airline is looking for the best of what it has dubbed "jetrosexuals" or the "new jetsetters". Ignoring borders and time zones, these people make the world smaller with each journey, the company says, and it is these travellers that have made the airline a successful venture (CNN/Money August 9, 2005, PM EDT). The names that Virgin uses correspond to the cultural codes in the customizing process, like "the networker", "the islander" etc.

Part of the success for those practicing this process is that rituals rapidly change according to their values. As a contemporary phenomenon it shows in all its obscurity some of the cultural qualifications that govern conduct and behaviour in the business world. Here is a competitiveness that demands unique talents, individuals and identities.

But what is the customizing process really about? Are values and identities rapidly changing while new multicultural, diversified and complex identities are taking shape? Or does it show people customizing to old reliable identities? What sometimes looks like freedom to transform your self can in fact be seen as a form of extraordinary control. It controls the actors in the networks in customizing others while it is also a process that makes use of the mutual relationship between customer and customizer in intricate systems of favours and favours in return.

What kind of metamorphoses and cultural transformations do we meet in the customizing process? Does it simply answer to new political imperatives of competition and competitiveness? In that case it is not newer than the modern society itself. As Patrick Joyce shows in his book *The Rule of Freedom* (2003), it was already in the cities of the nineteenth century that the citizens were made governable in the name of freedom. Even if the ambitions have been intensified the result is the same. When you create all these originals, they also form a distinct category – the customer experience designer and a customized market.

The agenda or action programs within the customizing process show us both the old modern utopian dream of everything being transformable and transgressable and how these programs tend to homogenize people into new categories and identities.

References

CNN/Money. August 9, 2005, PM EDT.

Florida, Richard 2002: *The Rise of the Creative Class: and how it's Transforming Work, Leisure, Community and Everyday Life*. New York: Basic books.

Florida, Richard 2005: *The Flight of the Creative Class: the New Global Competition for Talent*. New York: Harper Business.

Franzén, Mats 2004: Between Stigma and Charisma: Towards a Politics of Place. Paper to the ENHR-conference, Cambridge July, 2–6, 2004, Housing and Social Theory Workshop.

Joyce, Patrick 2003: *The Rule of Freedom: Liberalism and the Modern City*. London: Verso.

Kantola, Anu 2005: The Power of Competition Transforming Political Imaginaries. Paper at the CRESC Conference in Manchester.

Lund, Kristina & Birgitta Svensson 2005: Att designa sig själv. In: *Formgivare: folket. Fataburen*. Nordiska museets och Skansens årsbok.

Lund Hansen, Anders 2003: Urban Space Wars in 'Wonderful' Copenhagen: Uneven Development in the Age of Vagabond Capitalism. In: Petersson, Bo & Eric Clark (eds.), *Identity Dynamics and the Construction of Boundaries*. Lund: Nordic Academic Press.

Löfgren, Orvar 2005: Catwalking and Coolhunting. The Production of Newness. In: Löfgren, Orvar & Robert Willim (eds.), *Magic, Culture and the New Economy*. New York: Berg.

Nordström, Kjell A. & Jonas Ridderstråle 2003: Karaoke Capitalism: Management for Mankind. Stockholm: Bookhouse Publishing AB.

Sassen, Saskia 2002: *Global Networks, Linked Cities*. New York: Taylor & Francis Ltd.

Thrift, Nigel 2001: 'It's the romance, not the finance, that makes business worth pursuing': Disclosing a New Market Culture. *Economy and Society*, vol. 30, no. 4, 412–432.

MENUING

Robert Willim

On a daily basis people make many choices from different assortments, menus and databases. These choices are made among the garments in their favourite stores, just as in the cutting and pasting functions of the software they use to work and create. Are there any common denominator for these situations and activities? They may all be examples of the cultural process of *menuing*.

There are two sides of menuing. First is choosing and making decisions with the help of menus and preconfigured assortments or databases. Second, menuing is also the activity of designing menus; sorting out, categorizing and arranging. These two sides of menuing are fundamental in any industrialized consumption society, rooted in systems of standardization and the systematics of handling assorted materials that emerged with industrialism.

The menu has a mediating function and works as a kind of prosthesis. It helps people make choices through prior categorizing, sorting and packaging. At the same time it restrains and controls. This restraint can be both a liberty and a burden. It may free the mind by letting people choose with less effort. At the same time it limits the possible choices they can make. The full range of choices has been limited to those included in the menu.

Menuing may cover a wide range of activities. It would be possible to include everything from the choices made by shoppers from the spring collection at H&M, to the ways that different filters and effects are used in computer software like Microsoft Word or Photoshop. Menuing is a trait of industri-

alized societies during the twentieth century, and it is now becoming even more pervasive when menus and selection from databases characterize digital media. Let me give two brief examples to outline the concept.

Two Examples

1. Choosing a living space. In Sweden, during the early twentieth century, a national program to build domestic houses was started. Owning one's own home became a symbol of liberty, and it also became a financial possibility for many Swedish families. Several factories offered houses made from prefabricated modules. This prefab industry was possible because wooden building material was abundant, and it was easy to assemble prefabricated wooden modules. Soon similar looking houses were popping up like mushrooms all over Sweden. Families could look in catalogues from firms like Borohus and Myresjöhus to choose the combinations of modules for their own individual houses (Edlund 2004). This way to offer, buy and build houses was cheap, convenient and allowed limited individualized variability from the assortments in the catalogues.

Catalogue houses illustrate how housing became part of the standardized systems of industrialism. Author and journalist Per Svensson has written about Swedish twentieth century living, and mentions the book *Sweden Speaks* which was launched at the World Fair of 1939 in New York. The book, an initiative by the government, marketed Sweden as a country of the future, and told the world about

examples like the prefab houses: "The foundation has been cast in concrete, and now the ready-made walls, complete with window frames and other fixtures, are being raised. With the help of friends and good neighbors the job is done in a few hours some evening" (Svensson 2002: 55). According to the marketing rhetoric, building a house was a combination of the DIY (do it yourself) spirit needed to assemble the prefabricated elements, and the modern industrial knowledge outsourced to the prefab industry. In between these two parts we find the selection practises of menuing.

The menuing activities involved in the choices of Swedish prefab catalogue houses are still very much alive. Nowadays it is possible to buy catalogue houses in a wider range of different styles. The company Arkitekthus, for example, offers prefab houses designed by famous Swedish architects. The variety of catalogue houses track the rise of menuing as a cultural practice, and show how it is closely linked to the rise of industrialized consumer society. But menuing is not just about choosing what to buy from a catalogue.

2. Menus on the computer screen. Let us move to today's computerized world. Consider your situation in front of the computer screen. Hands on keyboard, the illuminated window shows an image in some graphic program like Photoshop. A flick of the wrist, the cursor moves up, a menu appears. You pick a filter and apply it to the image. The image is transformed. Move the cursor to another menu, choose another function. And so the work goes on. This type of environment and this interface dominate most software today. It is prefab, multiple choice, cut and paste, drag and drop. As media researcher Lev Manovich has pointed out, new digital media are the best expression of the logic of identity in advanced industrial and post-industrial societies, because computer interaction is about choosing values from a number of predefined menus (Manovich 2001: 128).

Digital Habits and Imaginations

Digital media offer clear examples of the dynamics of menuing. Let's therefore elaborate a bit on the role of digital media when it comes to this concept, and when it comes to design. Menus are examples of interface design. But menuing does not just entail material or textual organization. It is also about the way structures and order trickle down into the cultural (sub)conscious. Menus shape people's imaginations of the everyday. Menus are vehicles in the formation of habits. This is especially clear in the world of computer practices. Within the graphical user interfaces that have prevailed in software for around twenty years, the menu has been a widely used design concept.

In what ways can menuing be connected to the use of everyday things and the processes of habit formation? Design theorist Donald A. Norman made a distinction that can be used to expand the discussion on these connections. He talks about *knowledge in the head and in the world.* He uses these concepts to explain how precise behaviour can emerge from imprecise knowledge (Norman 1998: 55). Whenever the information needed to do a task is readily available in the world, the need for us to learn it diminishes. He goes on:

…consider typing. Many typists have not memorized the keyboard. Usually each letter is labeled, so nontypists can hunt and peck letter by letter, relying in knowledge in the world and minimizing the time required for learning. The problem is that such typing is slow and difficult. With experience, of course, hunt-and-peck typists learn the positions of many of the letters on the keyboard, even without instruction, and typing speed increases notably, quickly surpassing handwriting speeds and, for some, reaching quite respectable rates. Peripheral vision and the feel of the keyboard provide some information about key locations. Frequently used keys become completely learned, infrequently used keys are not learned well, and the other keys are partially learned. But as long as the typist needs to watch the keyboard, the speed is limited. The knowledge is still mostly in the world, not in the head (ibid.: 56).

When a person types frequently, a habit is formed. The knowledge of how the keys are placed move from the world to the head. Menuing is about the relations between these two different kinds of knowledge. People rely on "knowledge-prothesises" in the world. When choosing from a menu we experience a sort of comfort that things are familiar, as usual. Everything is in its "right" place. "This is one reason people can function well in their environment and still be unable to describe what they do. For example, a person can travel accurately through a city without being able to describe the route precisely" (ibid.: 57).

People do many things without being attentive to their actions at the moment. Menuing is located in this twilight zone between attention and non-attention. We'll now go on to use a computer related situation to illustrate the workings of menuing, order, and habits.

Let's Switch!
Dr X has bought a new computer. After some minutes of breaking seals and wrappings the smell of new electronics reaches her or his nostrils. The smell is exactly like that of the last computer. But this time something is different. The new computer is an Apple. The last one was a Dell. The new operating system is Mac OSX. The last one was Microsoft Windows XP.

After more minutes of seal breaking, manual browsing, and plugging in cords, it's time to configure the preinstalled software. And a familiar looking desktop emerges on the screen. At least when it comes to the conceptual mapping and basic layout. But then Dr X recognises the menus. The menus! They are similar to some degree. But then they are not. When she or he place the cursor over them, and clicks, they are rolled out as usual. But their content is different. Ok, no big deal. Much is familiar. However, Dr X can now look forward to a near future, filled with unlearning and learning all the kinds of inconspicuous practices that fill a life characterized by menuing.

This is an illustration of some of the aspects of switching menus. When people encounter new systems, orderings, menus and environments, a great deal of what have appeared to be inconspicuous activities require reflection. What has earlier been nearly automatic has to be unlearned and revised. This occurs when switching computer systems, and it also happens in many other situations. For example, when people move their homes they have to change many everyday practices (Schaffer 2001). Menuing is an essential part of habit formation, which is a central feature of human behaviour. As interface and system design consultant Jef Raskin points out:

> …humans cannot avoid developing automatic responses. This idea is important enough to bear repetition: No amount of training can teach a user *not* to develop habits when she uses an interface repeatedly (…) If you have ever unintentionally driven toward your normal workplace on a Saturday morning when you intended to go somewhere else, you've been had by a habit that formed through repetition of a fixed sequence of actions. (…) Thus, after you take the wrong turn on Saturday, you may suddenly realize that you intended to drive in the opposite direction; this realization makes your navigation your locus of attention, and you can interrupt the automatic sequence of actions that would have led you to your workplace.
>
> When you repeat a sequence of operations, making *and keeping* what you are doing your locus of attention is the only way to keep a habit from forming. This is very difficult to do. As expressed in a common phrase, our attention wanders (Raskin 2000: 21f.).

What's on the Menu, and what's not?
Menuing takes people through their everyday lives in late modern society. It is, as mentioned, intimately coupled to habit formation and routines. And habits are sometimes visible and reflected upon, but often they are the unreflected grease of the everyday machinery. This makes menus and menuing inconspicuous but important phenomena.

So, what's on the menu, what's being served today?

Please make your (individual) choice. There is a conceptual congruity among different choice situations in menu and assortment based societies (Willim 2003). There are for example similarities between the way houses were bought and sold in early and mid twentieth century Sweden and the ways that we interact today with computers. Of course, there are also differences. The routinized behaviours of interacting with computers differ quite a lot from the conscious choices made from catalogues. Menuing can foster different kinds of behaviours and cultural processes depending on context. However, an important common denominator is that complexity is hidden and packaged in standardized menus characterized by a limited number of choices. Therefore, a juxtaposition of these different examples can be fruitful.

But there must be some cracks among these processes. What is not on the menu? What things which are *off* have the potential to become *on*? The absent becomes something energizing (Hertz 1999: 400). Absent menu options may be things wanted, but unavailable, which expose the shortages of an assortment. This condition was condensed by the TV show Saturday Night Live into the phrase "cheeseburger, cheeseburger, cheeseburger…" which was a famous parody of a restaurant which offered many choices of the same cheeseburgers. What's on the menu? A lot of cheeseburgers. This is a failure of the provider and the selector.

Other shadow sides of the processes of menuing are people's more or less conscious desire to use things that are outside the given menu assortments. This can be seen as a search for otherness and self-chosen exile. It allows one to be no part of "it", but still to remain in some way connected. During the years these endeavours of revulsion have been labelled sub cultural, underground, alternative or avant-garde movements. The analytical point is to relate the desire to be an outsider, or "to be no part of

it" to the process of menuing. How is something that has been outside a set assortment to be commodified and included in a collection? Here we find the familiar process of garbage turning into vintage, or the worthless and revolting becoming the cool and fashionable. And while we are here, why not also see how items are removed from menus?

Menuing tells us how the range of processes between choice and routine work in several contexts. It helps us understand the creative processes of digital media, and it captures some major aspects of consumerism. With the spread of menuing, knowledge about menu psychology as well as menu and assortment design have become important skills. A cultural analysis of this phenomenon should be an important contribution. It can be worthwhile to analyze the congruities of different situations of menuing, and also to search for variations. It is also crucial to take into account the double-edged nature of menuing, providing both a relief from frequent choice situations, and a major constraint on freedom.

References

Edlund, Rickard 2004: *Kataloghuset – Det egna hemmet i byggsats*. Stockholm: Byggförlaget.
Hertz, Paul 1999: Synesthetic Art – An imaginary Number? *Leonardo* 5/1999.
Manovich, Lev 2001: *The Language of New Media*. Massachusetts: MIT Press.
Norman, Donald A. 1998: *The Design of Everyday Things*. Massachusetts: MIT Press.
Raskin, Jef 2000: *The Humane Interface: New Directions for Designing Interactive Systems*. Boston: Addison-Wesley.
Schaffer, Scott 2001: Social Change and Everyday Life. *Journal of Mundane Behavior*, vol. 2, no. 2 (June 2001).
Svensson, Per 2002: *Svenska hem. En bok om hur vi bor och varför*. Stockholm: Bonnier fakta.
Willim, Robert 2003: Claiming the Future: Speed, Business Rhetoric and Computer Practice in a Swedish IT Company. In: Christina Garsten & Helena Wulff (eds.), *New Technologies at Work: People, Screens and Social Virtuality*. Oxford: Berg.

MYSTIFYING

SELF-MYSTIFICATION

Billy Ehn

It has been said that when strangers begin to accept each other because they experience themselves as strange, they start a promising development. This is a rather surprising thought. If I do not understand myself, how should I be able to understand other people? But since understanding and acceptance are not necessarily intertwined, social life may work anyway, in spite of the value and function that "understanding" has for the definition of cultures. Non-understanding is often perceived as one of the ways to demarcate the boundaries between different cultures. The Other is not regarded as of the same kind as you, since his or her behaviour is unintelligible. But this is too simple. Maybe it is also possible to see non-understanding as an essential part of every society, even among friends and relatives, and in that case what we call "culture" could be analysed as a universal way of disguising strangeness and make it endurable.

Many people have of course noticed that the mysterious Other is actually present in each person. When you confront the experience of non-understanding in relation to yourself, in the form of confusion, misbelieve or mystification, you are enacting on a personal level the same cultural processes of social estrangement. Feelings of shame and guilt are also, as personal expressions of self-critical view-points, confronting the individual with public norms.

In everyday life most people probably want to be like other people, i.e. "normal" and not conspicuous. In other situations they wish to be seen as unique individuals and receive positive social attention for being different. Normality and uniqueness are two social poles in the everyday search for a meaningful self, hard work that may be analysed from social, cultural and psychological view-points. This is a well-known human paradox, which takes varying form in different settings.

But the paradox has a dimension that is not so obvious. There seems to be a point of intersection in which people look at themselves with wonder, as if they were somebody else. Who the hell am I? Why do I think and act in this way? They just do not understand the person they are used to. This intersection is an ongoing *dilemma of self-mystification*, a well known experience in everyday life, but perhaps not as a cultural process. On the surface the dilemma looks like a psychological phenomenon of little interest for cultural analysis, but that is quite mistaken.

Self-mystification is really as cultural as any elaborated rituals or meaning-loaded symbols, despite its individualistic appearance. The secrets we keep about our inner life are more common than we fear. When you open your eyes and shake your head because of your own unintelligible behaviour, you are not as alone as you feel. It is of course not unusual to smoke cigarettes and at the same time know perfectly well how dangerous it is, or to drink too much alcohol or eat junk food. Lots of things that people do they know perfectly well is not good for them. They act irrationally and sometimes ask themselves why. I include myself among these people. They have sexual and other fantasies that they do not dare to tell anybody else about (see Pyburn, this volume).

If you could get inside people around you, you would most likely hear the same confused questions again and again, at least in our times and in our Western countries. Why do I do, feel, and think this way? What is wrong with me? Silently or loudly, people are having discussions with themselves that are as full of conflicts and misunderstandings as public debates. If that is a general human condition, or if it is a circumscribed tendency, depending on time and place, I do not know, but I think that it would be interesting to analyse self-mystification as a cultural process in varying symbolic and expressive forms.

Self-mystification is not only ignored as cultural work in everyday life, it is also a social arena for inner debates on practical morality and borders of decency. There you communicate with yourself, in a language and with arguments that you have learned from others – and what is communication if not cultural? The experience of being in conspiracy with your worst aspects of self is far from uncommon.

During a lecture for five hundred students, I dared to ask them in what way they see themselves as odd or strange. I asked them to write the answer anonymously on a slip of paper, which I later collected. Some of the answers I read out loud and commented upon. At an earlier lecture I had put the same question in a more open manner, and then almost all the students mentioned other people as strange, not themselves. They thought that other people behaved like idiots, in traffic and other public places, as parents or work mates, as bosses or customers. The answers often started with a "why?". Why have so many car drivers stopped using their signal when they turn? Why are young girls carrying water bottles everywhere? Why do dog owners want other people to play with their animals? Weird, is it not? The way I put the question evidently directed the answers away from self-reflection.

But when I asked them about themselves, I was surprised to find that these young men and women frankly admitted that they do not understand a lot of the things that they do, think, and feel. They ap-peared as strangers to themselves. I cannot tell if that is promising. But there was an evident touch of relief in the disclosure of personal secrets that may be interpreted as a wish to unmask oneself. Confessions, however intimate they are, function as symbolic messages of belonging.

These self-critical revelations demonstrated a great variety of human weaknesses that create a kind of symbolic bond between anonymous writers. The students wrote among other things that they do not understand what they do to themselves or other people, why they keep on smoking and drinking too much alcohol, why they are jealous without reason, unnecessarily greedy or too suspicious. They are dominated by strange habits, in constant fright and worry, having feelings that they do not recognise.

The students are evidently mystified by their inability to do what they know is best, to learn from their mistakes, to know what they really want and to make clear decisions. They seem to be afraid of themselves, and to long for a more secure and predictable Ego. No one expressed fascination with their own mysteriousness. Neither did they seem to be delighted in the strangeness of other people.

Self-mystification and faulty self-knowledge are old themes in Western Civilization, but the common apprehensions of our time have heightened insecurity, and demand extraordinary personal qualities. People often behave as if they are on show, and they express a strong need to catch the attention of others, to be assured of their own personal worth. At the same time they claim not to know that self on the scene. An escape from that dilemma is to stop the inner communication and turn to others for reassurance. Surely I am as ordinary as you?

In cultural theory the idea that we create ourselves, at least our so called identities, is popular. But far from all people think that they are manufacturing their individuality by choosing among alternatives. To understand what is going on in the "identity-market" we should also pay regard to less rational aspects. Self-mystification goes public as a culturally formed micro-process when people tell each other about their relation to themselves. As a secret mystification is only potentially part of the cultural flow. If you are prepared to be more open-minded and do not try to hide behind ready-made clichés, you have to work out a reasonable explanation of your feelings and behaviour, in a language that de-privatizes your experience and gives it a form that other people can relate to and work with.

I am odd, the students complain, I am strange, eccentric, and queer, I do not understand myself, so how can I possibly understand other people? Why do I act like this, and who is determining my will and thoughts? I am scared by my feelings and reactions. Why do I want to change other people so that they become more like me, even though I do not know myself?

In front of the mirror, which is one of the most influential tools for seeing oneself as both a strange Ego and a somewhat recognizable person, they confront a familiar stranger. I have seen that person before, many times, but who is she and what is she thinking right now? Some of the students told me that they had broken more than one mirror with their hands, when they could not stand the wondering eyes in front of them. Nobody else looks at me like that, they complained. Some young women compared this experience with destroying the bathroom scale when it shows a weight they cannot accept.

These observations are, as I said, not only about the psyche of other people, but also about communication of shared meanings: how people speak of and symbolize the dilemma of being mysterious in social life, and alone with their thoughts. My somewhat impolite question enacted an emotional drama where people conveyed a painful message about their inner private life, only to find that it evidently is very common to be full of contradictions.

The message is clear. Now you have an opportunity to see your own confusion in the face of others. It is like reading a novel about the inner life of a person and wondering how the author can know so much about my own thoughts and feelings.

In situations like this, self-mystification becomes a moment to detect that other people are as eccentric as I am, which is not always a comforting discovery. By telling others about our own oddities, we are connecting to each other, and drawing a line between the strangeness of oneself and that of other people. Maybe the expression of self-mystification in some way contributes to lower the walls between individuals, people who would otherwise be scared of each other.

But I am not sure. In the human search for meaning, value, identity and love, self-mystification may also rip off any feeling of security in social interaction and make people isolated, unable to accept themselves as just one more contradictory individual. If I cannot trust myself, how can I trust anyone else?

I do think that it could be fruitful to analyse this odd micro-process as a way to see how psychological reasoning in everyday work is transformed into culturally formed ideas of self. As a mostly hidden and numb activity, self-mystification is otherwise easy to overlook in the discussion of what is happening in culturally complex and "multiethnic" societies with their official demands for mutual understanding between strangers.

My idea is that the more we know and tell about the weird things that we think and do, the less reason we have to condemn other people for their strange behaviour. This is a slightly different way of expressing the often misused concept of cultural relativism. The faint hope of respect between people with different values and perspectives does not have to build only upon faith in mutual understanding, something which we may never be sure of reaching. This may be hard for researchers of cultures and social relations to accept.

CAMOUFLAGE*

Kristofer Hansson
Photographs by the author

To camouflage is to adapt in a situation. The word is used in different ways with many connotations and synonyms, as in disguise, mask, hide, conceal, obscure, cover-up and create a façade or smoke-screen. What the words have in common is that they point out how something can give protection from recognition. Camouflage is therefore a good word to use in studying how the individual being can mask and hide differences, stigmas, or abnormalities. Before translating the concept into specific cultural practices, it may be worth noting that it has been developed in two very separate fields: biology and warfare.

Biology and Mimicry
In biology the concept of camouflage has been used to understand how certain species develop similarities with their surroundings to protect themselves from predators. A species can imitate an animal that is dangerous or poisonous to a particular predator. This protective similarity is called *mimicry*. The concept has been translated into a cultural strategy by Homi Bhaba in *The Location of Culture* (1994). He uses the term mimicry to understand style among the Indian middle class in colonial India. The imitation of British habits – clothes, body language and behaviour – created a likeness, but with a certain slippage. It was *almost* right, and this 'almost' created an unsettling difference. It allows the imitated to sneer at the lack of perfection of those trying to live up to the ideal; but they can also feel that they are the victims of parody. Cultural mimicry may become a strategy that plays on the tensions between trying to

pass and mockery. Is this a real gentleman or someone just posing as one? As I look at him (or her) I see a copy of myself, distorted or exaggerated.

Warfare and Camouflage Dress
The military concept of camouflage can help us understand how individuals engage in masking and

concealment. When firearms increased in firing rate and range during the latter half of the nineteenth century, it became more important to protect troops with some form of disguise. The idea was to deceive the human eye. The British developed a camouflage uniform they named khaki, an Indian word for dust. During the First World War camouflage techniques became more and more sophisticated. With the help of modernist artists – like German artist Franz Marc (1880–1916) and the French artist Lucien Victor Guirand de Scevolas (1871–1950) – patterns were developed that would blend into the surrounding landscape, water or sky. The idea was to use different patterns so that structural lines and sharp edges like the human silhouette were broken up. Boundaries between background and foreground were blurred.

In cultural camouflage one has to identify these sharp edges, the behaviour, traits or ideas that are not accepted as normal, and mask or obscure them. The individual must learn to know when it is important to blur these edges – which can be either a conscious or unconscious process.

We all have bodily and psychological characteristics that we don't want other people to know about. To protect ourselves we use different strategies to blur and hide those unwanted qualities under a surface of acceptable characteristics and qualities. This transformation is sometimes an everyday mundane action allowing us to blend into different social settings. Most of the time we imitate a typical group member and merge into a larger group. Examples include dressing like others, trying to talk about the same topics, and so forth. This is something we often do without any reflection. But sometimes we use a more active form of camouflage.

In military terms there are two ways of talking about camouflage which we can use for understanding general social processes of active and passive concealment. First is permanent masking built into the object, and second is masking that is put on for specific settings. Permanent masking only works in a given setting, so your khaki uniform suddenly stands out when you move out of the desert, and the green painted tank can no longer hide when snow

starts falling. Flexible camouflage uses the chameleonic technique of changing properties as the setting is transformed. In this kind of active applied masking, soldiers have to learn what props to add to their outfit: items including branches, leaves, and face paint. He or she must constantly be aware of the background and how to adapt to it. In this kind of *passing* a person can conceal a stigmatised identity beneath another more accepted identity (Goffman 1963). It is a kind of reflexive camouflage. At the same time this reflexive passing is not always done through individual choice. A person can be forced to act in accordance with a dominated discourse of what is accepted and what is not (Foucault 1987).

In an ethnography of police surveillance of criminals in an urban setting, Ann Kristin Carlström (1999) found that the detectives had developed very different kinds of camouflage styles. Putting on a bright red sports jacket was called 'wearing a stop jacket'. Here the attention was drawn to the bright colours of the jacket which at the same time made the individual's face inconspicuous and less notice-able. People who perfect the techniques of blending in become experts in the cultural analysis of others. They know if you need a wig, a special dress, or just a certain body language or a big smile.

Passing as Normal

Camouflage strategies are constantly at work in everyday life when you have an illness or a handicap that you don't want others to know about. With the use of the military metaphor we can understand that an illness creates, in different ways, sharp edges, features that stand out. To use a camouflage strategy is to break up these sharp edges so that the boundaries between oneself and the surrounding background of normal and healthy bodies are blurred. Georg Drakos (1997) shows how Greek people with leprosy mask their situations in the hospitals so that they can obscure the boundaries between healthy and sick. In this way they can control their own situation and do not need to be categorised.

Doing fieldwork among youth with asthma, I was struck by the ways through which males tried

Ola found asthma a handicap that threatened his understanding of how a masculine body must behave. Asthma could communicate weakness but above all turn the body into an unpredictable machine, because an attack might come all of a sudden in a situation where it caused embarrassment. The boy would then be locked in a handicapped category; to avoid this he needed to conceal his medication (cf. Nilsson 1999).

Another boy talked about a situation in a gym when he realised that he had forgotten to take his medicine. He got stressed and started wondering if he needed his medicine. At the same time he didn't want to stop training in front of everybody. He said:

> If I needed to disrupt the training I needed to disrupt it in front of all the other people in the gym. It would really make me feel stressed, as if everybody would think: 'He can't manage the training.' They wouldn't understand my real reason for stopping.

to camouflage their handicap in public places. The situations when they thought concealment was important, and the camouflage techniques they used, told me a lot about the ideals of a 'normal' masculinity they wanted to live up to.

Ulf Mellström (1999) has discussed the ways in which men in Sweden often think of their bodies as machines that should be controlled, predictable, and efficient. Some of the boys with asthma I talked to said that their bodies were 'constantly letting them down,' not allowing them blend into cultural visions of ideal male bodies. Asthma is an illness that can usually be kept invisible in public. It is only when you are hit by an attack and urgently need medicine that you become vulnerable. One of these boys named Ola, put it like this, when I asked if he openly used his asthma inhalator in public: 'No, I go away. If people around me don't know I have asthma it feels too dramatic for me to take the medicine openly. People might think you are going to collapse any minute...'

Many of these young men almost obsessively focus on male ideals and worries about behaving abnormally. This can make them 'more normal than the normals'. They have to use many techniques to blend in. They even repress thoughts about their illness, and take up smoking as a way of distancing themselves from their asthma problems, even though they know this will just create more health issues. In some ways this is mimicry overdone as camouflage, which creates a situation in which boys constantly have to monitor their own behaviour and think through all of the possible reactions by others. Can they detect my handicap?

There are also gender differences at work here. Young men seem to be more afraid of showing physical weakness. A girl with allergy spoke about a different strategy she used. When I asked if it was hard for her to talk about her illness she answered:

No. It's better that they know, so they don't need to do anything. That is one of the first things that I tell if I visit somebody: 'I am allergic to that and that' and then they know. And I don't need to worry...

Concealment, disguise, and camouflage are all cultural techniques that require careful observation and analysis of the group or setting you want to blend into or hide something from. They all require reflexive monitoring of your own behaviour.

The concept of cultural camouflage has proven to be productive in my ongoing study of young people with asthma and allergies. Many of these boys and girls are eager to pass as 'normal' teenagers and they develop all kinds of strategies to hide their handicaps. In this process they become very observant and reflexive about cultural concepts of normality, and the problems of blending in or standing out. They have revealed many aspects of cultural standards and ideals in teenage life which would otherwise remain hidden or taken for granted.

Note

* This article is a part of a Ph.D. study at European Institution of Ethnology and Vårdal Institute, at Lund University. The people on the photos, taken by the author, have nothing to do with the text.

References

Bhaba, Homi 1994: *The Location of Culture*. London: Routledge.

Carlström, Ann Kristin 1999: *På spaning i Stockholm. En etnologisk studie av polisarbete*. Institutet för folklivsforskning, Stockholm.

Drakos, Georg 1997: *Makt över kropp och hälsa. Om leprasjukas självförståelse i dagens Grekland*. Stockholm/Stehag: Brutus Östlings Bokförlag/Symposion.

Foucault, Michel 1987: *The History of Sexuality,* vol. 2: *The Use of Pleasure*. London: Penguin.

Goffman, Erving 1963: *Stigma: Notes on the Management of Spoiled Identity*. New Jersey: Prentice-Hall.

Mellström, Ulf 1999: *Män och deras maskiner*. Nora: Bokförlaget Nya Doxa.

Nilsson, Bo 1999: *Maskulinitet. Representation, ideologi och retorik*. Umeå: Boréa Bokförlag.

SILENCE

Sarah Holst Kjær

In the midst of a busy Copenhagen neighbourhood the exclamation 'SILENCIO' is written on a wall. Taking up much space, the writing can be seen from afar. For years the city council's graffiti squad has for some reason decided to leave this particular piece alone. One can only speculate if the word is meant as an imperative.

Passing the wall every day, it makes me smile. The silencing effect of the exclamation is at best a reminder that things can be different. In the street, cars, people, trucks and shopkeepers go about their business. Every hour the bell from a nearby school rings through the hustle and bustle. Children are playing in the schoolyard. Whenever they get the chance, they cross the street in large and noisy groups to buy candy bars for lunch. A competing bell from the church on the other corner makes people hurry in the morning and again in the evening. An extended melody from the church tower is underlining the eight o'clock hour in the morning as particularly important – it's time to go to work!

Every Friday evening the classic, blue coloured ice cream van rings its bell, and children and their families gather around. 'Old and nostalgic noises' already have permission to communicate in public space, while 'new noises', such as calls to prayers from the mosque, have to be approved. It is not easy being a newcomer to the city's soundscape, and rumour has it that the application from the mosque has not (yet) gone through.

Particular forms of activities, working procedures, forms of public communication, indoor and outdoor cultures of leisure, and the norms of different groups occupy and negotiate the 'right' balance between comfortable silence and entertaining noise. But what happens when everything falls silent? What accompanies the phenomenon of silence, how is it interpreted, and with what meanings is it impregnated?

Moving from a public soundscape to a private one, I am going to discuss how silence is narrated and defined in connection with intimate relationships. Silence engages in a storyline of coupling and in this context it can be understood as a phenomenon that tells you something about a current condition in a relationship, and creates a space for the cultural imagination and fantasies of that relationship.

Relationship Research, Reflexivity and Silence as Pause

In my field of study – contemporary, heterosexual, white, Western, middle class, adult couple's relationship narratives – silence seems like something either to be avoided or to become involved with in particular ways.

The interpretation and meaning installed in silence is understood differently when they intersect with larger identity categories such as age, class and sexuality. Furthermore, silence as a phenomenon involves polarized relational concepts, for instance silence–talk, known–unknown, hidden–visible, dream–reality. In relationship research a strong presupposition is that 'fundamental things are hidden and must remain hidden for those concerned' (Kaufmann 1998: 8).

Still, the ability and desire to narrate and listen to relationship stories occupies the centre of my field of study. Silence in this sense becomes both a pause and a space in the relationship narratives, and is defined through an underlying and secretive narrative that contains certain (undefined) 'truths'.

The sociologist Anthony Giddens has interpreted late modern heterosexual relationships through the storyline of the romance, a story with a beginning, a middle and an ending (Giddens [1992]1995: 31, 44). In the process of building up and 'working on' the relationship story – how we met, what kind of obstacles we had, how we overcame them, where we will go in the future, what we will do in old age – silence expresses ideas about causality. A pause here changes and comments on a preceding narrative and affects what will come after. The beginning and/or end of the present storyline changes because an underlying storyline is added on to it, either maintaining, disengaging, or making space for another one.

What is being included in, and what is being excluded from the storyline of a relationship, can be difficult to examine. In what follows, I will examine how silence – when approached in the field of intimate relationships – is sometimes created as a space of the fulfilled, fearful, and marginalized. A silent space is sometimes supposed to be hidden, or approached and accepted as hidden, and thus suggests meaning and non-meaning. It becomes an interpretation in which the conditions of an intimate relationship can be defined differently by persons and couples. This kind of silence contains embedded cultural meanings and fantasies.

Still, silence – being silent – has a practical dimension when studying relationships through ethnographic interviews. Remaining silent becomes difficult – perhaps annoying to the interviewer. In order to get silence across to the reader, researchers need to describe and define silence with specific words and/or codes. In this sense, the definition of the pause of 'nothing' evokes the definition rather than the content. An ethnologist wrote:

At our meeting Jonny and Jeanette talk about themselves and their reality in a quiet way. There are many things, they say, they have never thought of. My questions are answered briefly or not at all. But what they say, and what they keep silent about, shed a certain light on my other interviews with informants who are more than eager to talk about their lives up front with me (Martinsson 1997: 71, *my translation*).

Silence – to be silent or quiet – is thus judged against the researcher's expectations that coupling is a talkative and highly reflexive field so when couples are silent it is difficult to deal with. Jonny and Jeanette have working-class backgrounds. I cannot know how this colours the researcher's expectations of this couple's self narrative. I can only point out that *something* happens in this example with Jonny and Jeanette that places them as a couple at the margins of coupling. They do not seem to fit expectations about how 'coupling' is supposed to be done, namely performing a particular style and praxis of talking about relating. When placed at the margins, this couple is also marginalized. It seems that a couple, in order to be placed at the centre with all the other 'similar' (and here referred to) couples, has to practise talk, communication and reflexivity. This practise is supposed to reflect a cultural and social ability to relate, handle and develop an intimate relationship. Communicative style thus becomes crucial in understanding relationship building.

As researchers we may be trapped in studying relationships through words, and thereby participate in creating a strong verbal storyline in coupling narratives. All that remains is a little room for pauses and silences, narrative by-products that contest reflexivity, leaving an undefined, marginalized space, outside the 'proper' form of coupling and therefore often remaining outside coupling research. When it is mentioned by researchers, silence often is interpreted and impregnated with fantasies about the conditions of the relationship, defining silence either as relationship ease or unease.

In the following examples from movies and my own fieldwork observations I will examine how the phenomenon of silence, closely connected with general and cultural understandings, can be understood as the relational and imaginable 'content' of a close relationship.

Silence in the Bedroom. Cultural Imaginations of the Adult Couple

The archetypical bedroom scene of couple trouble in an American Hollywood film relies on the formalities of the chamber-play: In the closed environment two people depend on each other to move the story along, and silence between them points towards something wrong and imperfect in the storyline of the relationship. Silence is narrated as a tension, a break in the order of things, a lack of communication and intimacy and thereby a lack of togetherness.

In a classic scene like this, the light is turned off at one side of the bed, the back of a person is turned towards the room and eyes are gazing emptily towards the dark skies outside the window. The other side of the bed is empty, the lights are on, and water is running in the bathroom. These ten seconds of the film feels like a lifetime. The silence is evaluating the couple's relationship. What is the matter? What is going on?

This between-ness of tension is orchestrated as a silence that points towards an obstacle, a shift in the storyline of intimacy and relating. Something needs to be said, everything has been said, but nothing has come of it, and the man and the woman's storylines have gone different ways. As the One returns from the bathroom, the spectator (me) finds herself hoping for a big fight that can either clear the air or make a clean break. Either way, get the story straight!

This form of silence is playing on the cultural imagination of what is *missing* in the scene: The bedroom is a strong marker of the (noisy) intimacy between the two. The bedroom is the place where the voyeur of this kind of mainstream film expects to see the various elements of belonging. There are just the two people at night, leaving all others – children for instance – out of the scene till the morning, so the bedroom is a cultural place founded in the imagination and order of adult heterosexuality. This order connotes the couple's claim to the future legitimated by association with the 'correct' meaning of being together, namely reproduction. In contrast with this interpretation of the bedroom, need I say that same-sex couples are silenced in the mainstream bedroom scene? Homosexual couples are not even supposed to be there.

The manner in which adult age and silence are combined can be infused with a certain (wishful or unwishful) imagination of togetherness, which locates the adult couple within the centre or matrix of ideas about how an intimate relationship should be lived, and even by whom. The 'long' pause and the expectations of the bedroom scene indicate that intimacy has a whole range of micro-elements attached to it. Right and wrong tempos and rhythms in the events describe and expose the idea of a 'natural' and 'normal' adult intimate relationship, which flows forward with ease.

The Undisturbing Silence. Becoming an Old Couple – to Others

At the opposite end of a couple's life path is a narrative of the old couple. Silence in old age defines other kinds of expectations to an intimate relationship. This is exemplified in my field notes by an incident in which Carlo and Gerda, a couple in their eighties, moved away from their home and into a home for the elderly. This is the story of a couple who lived a full life, raised children, helped with their grandchildren, and grew old together, they stood by each other's side though ups and downs and have thus followed the lines of classic values, not because they had to, but because they wanted to. In old age this 'version' of a lifelong relationship is explained though their primary recognition and remembrance of each other:

> Together with two grandchildren I am packing up Carlo and Gerda's house. They have lived in the outskirts of Copenhagen for almost fifty years. At that time, they moved to a group of very modern one-floor houses, in green areas, with common leisure facilities. The houses belonged to a Danish beer factory where Carlo used to work. Gerda has worked most of her life in a factory making carton boxes. Carlo and Gerda are socialists and realists; the everyday care they gave to their

grandchildren, when they were little, getting them to sports, picking them up, helping them with homework 'without it never getting dull', a particular dessert Gerda made out of ice-cream and a mild spirit they brought back from a vacation in Spain, is part of the stories the grandchildren tell me, as we are clearing out their home. Pictures in the family album show different holidays, birthdays and festivities. We divide the china – 24 settings into six sets.

Two other grandchildren return from the home where Carlo and Gerda now live, telling us that the moving has confused their grandparents. The grandchildren say that because the couple are old and cannot remember much, they now only recognize each other. The grandchildren had them sit together in a sofa. Holding hands, Carlo kissed Gerda on the cheek. The grandchildren had counted 23 kisses. This is the only thing spoken of as we pack up. Otherwise everyone is quiet. Carlo and Gerda do not return (Field-note observation. November, 2003).

The way I imagine this old couple through the stories of their grandchildren is viewed from the perspective of a younger generation. The phenomenon of age defines silence as a retreat, an undisturbed and quiet condition of being together. They are not expected to do anything – it has all been done. Here the category of class is also active, even romanticized, placing the couple in the centre rather than at the periphery of proper behaviour. Evolving around the metaphors and realities of working class life and of old age, the doing, the deed and the leading of life is the authentic, good, and true relationship.

In this image of the old couple, silence is a bodily sensation of both amnesia and the remembrance of what is understood as important in a relationship – togetherness, kissing, and holding hands. The silence while packing up the house works as an end to the storyline, not as a disturbing break and pause in the story as discussed earlier. The silent end is ordering the past, having an impact on rather than defining the events of the story. The younger generation thus places their grandparents at the end of a lived storyline where their relationship is mutually agreed upon, fulfilled, and settled, a life lived with ease despite the possible hard work, with a sense of knowing each other without the need for words.

It is our preoccupation with the situation at Carlo and Gerda's house that leads us to create an atmosphere of quietness that correlates with our imagination of the old couple. Navigating, understanding and negotiating the fragments of life, the rightful end of coupling is defined. Everything has been said and done and something has come of it; a common past of difficulty and joy that the true couple balanced out.

Organizing all of the events of living to reach this condition, where our silence defines their silence, can only in retrospect turn out as an ideal coupling story. The togetherness of the old couple falls into place at the end: the pair becomes a couple by fitting together. They have grown together, and now they share a synchronic form of silence where the one is the other and the other is the one. The old couple points to one of the strongest motivational themes in relationship stories: staying together.

The Silent Phone and the Undoing of the Couple
In the 'straight' and 'natural' story of the couple, elements of silence, except those at the end of the life path, connote a lack of engagement, activity and development. Cultural imagination of a constant process toward greater intimacy are contested when an intimate couple in the middle of the life path is seen as separated, while doing other things, apart and elsewhere. The lack of togetherness points toward the disintegration of, not only the storyline, but also the entire relationship. When the telephone suddenly stops ringing in a relationship, the expected process of communication, interrelatedness, sharing of words and the continuing of the relationship is suddenly cut off, and the discontinuity and inactivity can lead to fearful stagnation.

In the relationship storyline, this fall of silence indicates a liberating or frustrating pause of a possible 'until', including what has happened before the silence, and a happy or unhappy ending, moving towards the beginning of a new storyline. In this sense the silence reflects on the disengagement and disidentification of two people (Ebaugh 1988: 10): The lack of doing, causes the undoing of the intimate couple. When everything else has been tried; waiting, calling friends and family, the hospital, the police, the two-ness of the couple is undone and cut off by the unspeaking of the one. As a shared cultural code, 'the unspoken' generates an interpretation of a change in the condition of the relationship and thereby gives meaning to silence. Silence in the middle of the life path and storyline is like an 'unnatural death'. The words, thoughts, and presence that remain silent have never happened, and will never happen between the two. The French philosopher Lisa Block de Behar describes this deliberate and intended cutting off:

> Voluntary silence, which is doubly suspicious – because it is suspicious of the word, and is at the same time itself an object of suspicion – has its counterpart in the silence of the others, a conspiratorial silence, which the Germans, before the second decade of this century [20. Cr.], called with proleptic precision *Totschweigentaktik*, or, much more recently, what in Spanish has come to be known as *ningueneo* (de Behar 1996: 9).

The techniques of silencing something – the relationship, or someone – the other, to death (*Totschweigentaktik*) or the refusal of expressing oneself (*ningueneo*) is presented as the praxis of isolation and isolating. They organize social and cultural space, creating an interrelated condition between the two that evokes and/or maintains disappearance (Virilio 1996: 36).

The condition of isolation or meaningful noneness is perhaps a sanctuary of silence, depending on the other not to access or define the undefined. Standing outside this undefined space, the Danish poet, Inger Christensen writes:

> Så alt hvad der er til i sin forsvinden forbliver sig selv og aldrig farer vild.
> [So everything there is in its disappearance remains itself and never gets lost] (Christensen 1991: 484).

When the phone has stopped ringing, silence is a phenomenological condition and bodily sensation of being captured or liberated outside the two-ness and within the undone-ness of the couple. This creates an over-activity of couple nostalgia; sentimentality, melancholy or forgetting is entangled with moods and feelings of freedom and absence. The one leaving or left waiting by the phone engages with a void of over-hectic silence. This is a state of disintegration and disappearance, no matter if it is willing or unwilling; creating a vulnerability where the one left behind has a tendency to run into Freud, God or Death – all wanting to talk. Engaging with abstract figures of speech and thoughts sharpens the sense of solitude and intensifies a practical 'what now,' desperately trying to leave the twilight zone.

Club Silencio and the Silence of Definite Loss

The phenomenon of silence can be an unintended and unmarked zero-sign, possibly described as 'nonsense' or 'nothing' (Kurzon 1998: 5–7), while at the same time silence can be understood as meaningful and embedded into everything. Still, silence in and of the relationship, when it has not followed the lines of a 'natural' ordered life path and storyline, is left to fantasies and feelings of unease. These uneasy meanings of silence are impregnated with imaginable contours of every possible state of being and relating in and outside the relationship; how it was, how it is, how it could be. At the same time it includes nothing, desertion and disengagement – how it is not, what it was not, and never will be. The relatedness between these two poles of silence hovers dreaming and awake, known and unknown, and everything and nothing.

In David Lynch's film *Mulholland Drive* (2001), Club Silencio is a place in Hollywood where all the sleepless people go. At two o'clock in the morning the whispering of the word 'SILENCIO' calls them to the club. This club has no band, the music is recorded, not live, and the musicians are only pretending to play. When a beautiful singer falls dead on the stage, her voice is still heard. Here at Club Silencio the show and performance are presenting a twisted world between the real and the unreal, life and death. Far from the causal order of time, Club Silencio is a place where existence contains several modes of times and spheres overlapping each other.

The main character of the film, a woman, is watching the show together with her girlfriend, but at the same time this reality is contested by another reality, namely the woman's sudden realization that earlier on she has killed the girlfriend she is sitting next to. In the twisted course of events, jealousy has stirred up time and reality. The girlfriend fell in love with a man and left her.

Her feelings of loss and love at the same time have mixed the real with the unreal, so times and spheres are intertwined. The illusion of her dream world falls apart when the song is sung without the beautiful singer. She has been living a perfect love relationship but with a dead girlfriend.[1] After this sudden realization of murder and death the film continues, but now the presence becomes an affair of recollection. Searching with her imaginative (living *and* dead) girlfriend, together they find her missing, dead, lost, disintegrated and gone. A mystical and metaphysical level of existence discloses an unreal relation between the woman and her dead girlfriend taking place between waking and dreaming.

The storyline of the film and the relationship is messy and chaotic, without linearity, changing times and is altering the 'natural' order of the life path. This disordered form points to the hidden, unreal, unnatural and undiscovered crime of passion. Not only does the disordered storyline underline the wrongness of Club Silencio with its false pretend music, and twisted causality of time. The club also symbolizes the organization of dramatized silence in a foul death, founded in the emotion that has put this whole distorted storyline in motion, namely the jealousy of the woman losing a girlfriend to a man; the most important figure of the 'right' and 'natural' relationship with a woman.

Meanings and Non-meanings of Silence

Putting the phenomenon of silence to the test in few examples as I have done, perhaps even over-dramatizing or over-interpreting its meanings in intimate relationship, reminds us that silence is de-fined (and protected) as both a zero-sign and a sign of underlying meaning. Silence can imply ease or unease, it can be stressful or relaxing, it can symbolize order or disorder, and it can be used to imagine and fantasize about an intimate relationship. As I have shown, this depends on the context in which silence occurs and who is performing the silence or pointing to it.

The end of coupling as in the case of Carlo and Gerda is a narrative of old age and mutually agreed upon restful silence. The narration of the mainstream 'bedroom-scene couple' has on the contrary little space for silence as a relational condition, nor has Jonny and Jeanette in the given example when perceived through the expectations of styles and communication practices of coupling.

Different forms of silences presented in the middle of the storyline and life path thus point to a break in relationships, to the undoing of a couple, and breaking up the twosome. They point to the 'wrong' order of causality and even the 'wrong' kind of sexual and intimate relationship. Furthermore they point toward what is missing in the relationship and could even be associated with what socially and culturally, coupling is *not* supposed to be: namely 'un-reflexive, quiet, marginalized or unnatural'. The silent couple becomes the not 'quite right couple'.

Furthermore the tight storyline of causality that occupies couple narratives in the field of popular culture, and is typically at the centre of heterosexual relationship research, sometimes suggests an underlying narrative of the hidden. Implicating ideas of secrecy, this fearful silence, when understood as a concealing practice, has connotations of inexplicable wrongness, darkness and distortion. Silence may be a camouflage for nothingness while, at the same time, it is charged with strong meanings. It is this uncertainty that makes silence such a provocative phenomenon for both couples and researchers.

Note
1 An extended interpretation of *Mulholland Drive* by Allen B. Rush is offered on the website: http://www.themodernworld.com/mulholland_drive.html.

References

de Behar, Lisa Block 1995: *A Rhetoric of Silence and Other Selected Writings*. Berlin: Mouton de Gruyter.

Christensen, Inger 1991: *Samlede digte*. Copenhagen: Gyldendal.

Ebaugh, Helen Rose Fuchs 1988: *Becoming an EX: The Process of Role Exit*. Chicago & London: The University of Chicago Press.

Giddens, Anthony 1995 [1992]: *The Transformation of Intimacy: Sexuality, Love & Eroticism in Modern Societies*. Polity Press. [*Intimitetens omvandling*. Nora: Bokförlaget Nya Doxa.]

Kaufmann, Jean-Claude 1998: *Dirty Linen: Couples and their Laundry*. London: Middlesex University Press.

Kurzon, Dennis 1998: *Discourse of Silence*. Amsterdam/Philadelphia: John Benjamin's Publishing Company.

Martinsson, Lena 1997: *Gemensamma liv. Om kön, kärlek och längtan*. Stockholm: Carlssons Bokförlag.

Virilio, Paul 1996: *Försvinnandets estetik*. Uddevalla: Bokförlaget Korpen.

SANCHISMO

K. Anne Pyburn

The Possibility of the Unrational

Substantivism and formalism have been tossed around by anthropologists for many decades. Are people basically rational and guided by the logic of their cultural context, or irrational and guided by belief at the expense of observation? So far the answer appears to be "yes." These two perspectives have never died out of anthropology, and one of these two beliefs about human nature can be teased out of most treatises (Wilk 1996). Hobbes vs. Locke, Weber vs. Durkheim, Lévi-Strauss vs. Evans-Pritchard; for Bruno Latour (1993), we have never been rational; for Marshall Sahlins natives think differently (1995); for Eric Wolf it is the anthropologists who are irrational (1982).

In this paper I argue for a third possibility, the possibility of the non rational. I contend that a significant portion of human behavior cannot be understood as the result of any sort of logic whatsoever, including culture, error, stupidity, fanaticism, or addiction; but instead results from decisions outside the explanatory realm of traditional anthropological approaches. Although these actions are not explicable either through anthropological analysis of the internal working of a particular culture or as an intelligible consequence of some irrational belief, they do have a strangely predictable nature. These are the actions that invoke the familiar reaction, "I knew you were going to do that!" and the angry, unbelieving, unanswerable rejoinder, "How did you know?"

For example, in my own experience, being significantly behind in my work invariably produces in me a very strong desire to watch television and play computer games. This choice to do so is not based on a misunderstanding of the consequences of procrastination or from an irrational hope that the work will disappear. Nor is it explained by the logical need for a break from work that drives me to take some time for entertainment, since I frequently watch shows and play games I dislike, while avoiding "work" that requires a type of effort that I do like. Even a modest amount of pleasure is spoiled by my constant worrying about the consequences of not working. For years I thought this was a personal peculiarity, but having confessed my sin to friends, I have found to my astonishment that most of them experience the same thing. Certainly there are psychological explanations for procrastination, but what does the existence of non rational behavior mean for cultural analysis? What I have given is a minor example, but there are other behaviors that are best understood as non rational, some of which are much less trivial in their consequences.

Cervantes' Creations

Non rational behavior is difficult to identify at first, since the traditional categories of rationality and irrationality can be applied *ex post facto* to anything humans do and make any action appear to have a cultural function; sometimes both categories apply at once (Jarvie 1965). By far the easiest way to exemplify non rational behavior is to create a fictional actor, since in doing so the artist can resist the earmarks of explicability that are so easy to interpolate.

Cervantes did a particularly fine job of this in the character of Sancho Panza.

Don Quixote can be understood as irrational, possibly insane, or rational, possibly allegorical, but most likely both. His insanity made sense, his actions were predictable, and his irrational decisions were rational within his own system of logic. On the other hand, Señor Panza knew that Rosinante was a nag, that the giant was a windmill, that Dulcinea was a hag, and that his master was not going to succeed in his quest. We are not convinced by Cervantes that Panza saw the allegorical value of his master's actions, or that his assistance was given to his master due to the compulsion of fealty. It appears instead that with full knowledge of imminent failure, with a rational understanding of Quixote's irrationality, Panza repeatedly helped him fail. We are not told that Panza thought success was possible with each new quest, nor do we suspect him to be *a saboteur*. We also imagine that he might have escaped his delusional master had he been determined to do so. None of these rationalizations quite fits Panza's behavior; nor does he seem to be the victim of irrational hatred or love of his master. Sancho Panza is the epitome of the non rational, which I refer to from here on as "sanchismo," a word that captures not only the essence of the non-process I want to describe by using Cervantes' character as a metaphor, but also hints at latent aggressiveness.

The question here is whether such behavior actually exists outside fiction. Do people in various cultures, including western ones, act in ways they cannot explain? Do people do things without bothering to justify them or consider the consequences? Of course. But do we also consider and understand the consequences and still do things that make no rational sense without any helpful intervention from the irrational?

The Inexplicable

Since it cannot be predicted by ordinary reasoning or anthropological analysis, the only way to describe sanchismo is through examples. At the most inconsequential level are the acts of whimsical self destruction common in pop culture. Any trip through the

internet will turn up abundant pictures of famous, infamous, and unknown people dressed in idiotic and compromising outfits who are also wearing looks of defiance that make it clear they are aware of their error, even embarrassed about it, but are not going to back down. Celebrities singing songs with idiotic lyrics or espousing beliefs in public better left in private regularly show that not all publicity is always good publicity.

Sanchismo rhymes with machismo, and the two categories are linked, as Sanchismo is often aggressive, or at least passive aggressive. The hypocritical choices of people who openly flout the ideals they espouse have this passive-aggressive quality, as when they wear sweatshop clothing to charity balls, bring a mistress to church, or put a "Greenpeace" bumper sticker on a gigantic SUV. This aggressiveness is neither rational (nobody believes the argument that huge vehicles are safer, since statistically they are not), nor irrational (these vehicles show up in university parking lots, where rationalism is supposed to be king); it is clearly non rational.

Aggressive sanchismo may create unhappiness and damage. Unfortunately the most common examples of aggressive sanchismo are heinous and dreadful; there must have been someone among the light brigade who was not consumed by nationalistic zeal, someone riding into the canyon behind Custer whose hatred of Native Americans did not blind him to his own immanent death. Patriotism is often pasted over sanchismo to make sense of the senseless, or create value from valueless loss. No doubt some canon fodder is made up of patriots, irrational idiots, and rational self sacrificers, but not all.

Within this class of actions is the category of "mob behavior", once a popular target of analysis. While variously explained as de-individuation, conditioned response, or copycatting, none of these explanations seem adequate and the residual consensus seems to be either that there is some superorganic influence with an almost mystical influence on rowdy groups, or that the manner of categorizing behavior has created a false data set.

Of course I would argue that this is a category of sanchismo. Intelligent people aware of the consequences of their actions and aware of the inevitable failure of their apparent goals will, nevertheless, contribute *en masse* to something evil such as lynching, rioting, and vandalism, or participate in self immolation on a grand scale. The question that scholars have not been able to answer is why is the group behavior different to individual behavior? Why do people do things in mobs that they would never do alone? My answer is that people DO do these things individually, but they have been misidentified as acts of stupidity or bravado or irrationality, rather than simple sanchismo.

Implications for Anthropology

Michael Jackson (1998) says that Western culture's emphasis on the explanation of events as due to human action and causal forces that can be predicted and generalized is a means of controlling the world. He proposes that some non western people do not explain their actions or the characteristics of others in general terms as a deliberate avoidance of authoritarianism. The power to name, to interpret, to generalize is a type of social power so fundamental to western thought that westerners have difficulty recognizing any other type of intellectual existence. Refusal to generalize or explain things was once dubbed prelogical (Lévy-Bruhl 1925) and continues to be considered a stage of mental development that educators identify as a prelude to adulthood (King & Strohm 1994; Piaget 1970).

Recognizing sanchismo precludes insistence that all human behavior is explicable; even predictable behavior may be inexplicable. Jackson and others have described and even filmed the blank look on the face of a non western person asked why he did something or why something happened. The concept of sanchismo democratizes this response by pointing out that despite our overt dedication to cause and effect, westerners sometimes use a logical explanation to cover Sancho's tracks. Freed of a western cultural imperative, the honest answer to why is probably more often "I don't know," than anthropologists are willing to accept.

What this means for the "Interpretation of Culture" is that there is a wild card in the deck. Some of the patterns we see in culture are probably false ones, while others are less visible and muddied by the inclusion of behavior that is not really patterned at all, that cannot be adequately dealt with as either rational or irrational. Although sanchismo appears to be cross cultural, it is possible that it mainly appears in contexts where rational or rationalized behavior is considered normal. Sanchismo may be a reaction against the boundaries of explanation or against the boundaries of ordinary irrational behavior. But if we can explain it, then by definition, the behavior in question is not sanchismo.

References

Jackson, Michael 1998: *Minima Ethnographica: Intersubjectivity and the Anthropological Project.* Chicago: University Of Chicago Press.

Jarvie, I. C. 1965. Limits to Functionalism and Alternatives to it in Anthropology. In: Don Martindale (ed.), *Functionalism in the Social Sciences: The Strength and Limits of Functionalism in Anthropology, Economics, Political Science, and Sociology.* Monograph 5 in a series sponsored by the American Academy of Political and Social Science. Philadelphia: The American Academy of Political and Social Science.

King, Patricia M. & Karen Strohm 1994: *Developing Reflective Judgment: Understanding and Promoting Intellectual Growth and Critical Thinking in Adolescents and Adults.* San Francisco: Jossey-Bass.

Latour, Bruno 1993: *We Have Never Been Modern.* Cambridge: Harvard University Press.

Lévy-Bruhl, L. 1925: *How Natives Think* (Les fonctions mentales dans les sociétés inférieures). New York: A.A Knopf. Original text published in 1910.

Piaget, Jean 1970: *Genetic Epistemology* (translated by Eleanor Duckworth). New York: Columbia University Press.

Sahlins, Marshall 1995: *How "Natives" Think: About Captain Cook, For Example.* Chicago: University of Chicago Press.

Wilk, Richard R. 1996: *Economies and Cultures: Foundations of Economic Anthropology.* Boulder, Colorado: Westview Press.

Wolf, Eric 1982: *Europe and the People without History.* Berkeley: University of California Press.

SLEEPING

Mikkel Venborg Pedersen

Did our forefathers ever sleep? They must have done, sleep being an elementary body function. But sleep displays cultural variations and has cultural meaning as well. Sleep is staged with different artifacts, rooms and by different performances, culturally informed and individually decided. Like eating, dressing and housing, sleeping is a common human feature. Modern science tells us that we sleep at least 1/3 of our lives. A life of 70 years includes about 23 years sleeping and dreaming. Modern science also informs us that there are four periods of sleep interrupted by REM (Rapid Eye Movement) sleep, when we dream. Of the 23 years of sleep we might dream during as many as five or six of them. We remember very little of this (Alvarez 1995: 84).

Those who sleep are always a mystery. They are absent and present alike, apparently in peace but in reality (during REM-periods) engaging in wild adventure of the most private nature. Sleep is private; many modern people are shy about looking at a sleeping person. This may be in part because they sense that there is something going on which they can never be part of. People may also show many of the unflattering physical movements taking place. A sleeping person turns, groans, snores, talks in his/her sleep, usually quite unawares. Sleep thus constitutes a phenomenological paradox. It is a phase in which none of the waking life's rules are kept – including the rules that tell us what it is to be awake (Alvarez 1995: 101). Yet, if not forgotten, sleep is poorly accounted for in the discipline of European Ethnology.

Sleep is both a cultural process itself, and it is subject to other cultural processes; including time-space processes, conceptualisations of sleep itself, of order and chaos, public and private. For example, the private feeling of sleep is affiliated to a cultural process of making things intimate. This process is probably a child of Middle Age courtly culture wandering through times to be celebrated in the bourgeois classes of the eighteenth and nineteenth centuries (Frykman & Löfgren 1979; Elias 1980). "Intimatisation" often leads to feelings of shame when looking at a sleeping person. At the same level of thought, some feel tender, caring love when looking at a treasured one sleeping. Also, a sleeping female, nymphet, or goddess has for long been a common motif in European art. Beautiful and peaceful, but also promising for the wondering (male) mind, she is usually portrayed surrounded by wild nature. Sleep is also paradoxical because we make it so. Heraclitus said: "For the awake there exists only one world, but when we sleep each of us turns to our own private world."[1]

The Night

Sleep usually takes place at night. Sleep can appear as a flimsy topic for European Ethnologists who are used to cultural studies and ethnographic detail tied to specific places, historical periods, and social strata. We are more at home with the subject of "the night". There are two ways to make the night inhabitable. We can either close it off and go to sleep, dreaming sweet dreams. Or we can enlighten it. Several studies on this subject have considered the meaning of the

electric light, which changes the centuries-old relationship to the night to a point where we find it difficult to understand the nightly fears and anxieties of our forefathers (Schivelbusch 1983). The curious thing is that we tend to see this process as rather new, at the oldest after World War II. However, in 1914 the Danish cultural historian Hugo Matthiessen wrote a fascinating book on the night in medieval and renaissance towns, in which he says that we can hardly imagine the darkness of the dark in old times. Nor can we imagine the fears. The towns were fortified and locked up. Fire, thieves and night prowlers threatened decent citizens of the towns. Their worst fears were embodied by the people of the night; "dishonest" people, culturally and legally speaking, like the town-executioner, gypsies and vagrants (or other people in the broad early-modern category of "dishonest people"). Witches' foul rituals happened at midnight (Matthiessen 1914; Henningsen 1984). In these early modern towns garbage collection was taken care of by night men who carried their stigma in their name. Just like witches they did "dishonest" work at un-Godly hours.

The night *is* dark. In our European tradition we celebrate sun and light. One of the finest treasures in the Danish National Museum prehistoric collection is a bronze sun-chart pulled by horses, interpreted as a Bronze Age celebration of the sun and light. In classical Greece, Apollo drove the sun-chariot as well. Dawn meant the resurrection of order. In our Christian tradition, Christ is the *Lux Mundi*, the light of the world, and morality is built through dichotomies (so beloved in cultural studies) which oppose: light, goodness, order, sense, and God to darkness, evil, chaos, impulses and Satan (in some traditions the fallen angel of light). In the Greek tradition, the last dichotomy perhaps Apollo versus Dionysus.

The night is also a time of fear. Hunting animals come out and attack, and ill-minded people are up and about. The senses of "honest" people are slowed down and people must cope with nightmares. The night contains almost anything one puts into it. Lacking clear vision, fantasy wins free and finds the strangest places to wander. Just ask Romantic era writers who were famous for their intimate re-

lationships to dreadful dreams. Ghosts and malign spectres come out at night too. When electric light arrived, to a certain degree it gave fear a name and a face, and it became, as Hannah Arendt would say, banal. Chaos turns to order. But we still fear the night, especially our uncontrolled minds when we sleep and dream. Fortunes are made in the medical industry because of this fear. More sleeping disorders are being treated (or lulled away) today than ever before.

The Bed

In Western culture we sleep in a bed, where we also take refuge in case of illness, where we make love and where we often choose to die. Sleeping rooms and beds are distinct artefacts telling us about this basic process in human life. Perhaps these material things are the most promising ethnological avenue to follow in understanding the cultural process of sleep, which otherwise seems to slip through our fingers. Material culture has the advantage of tying together many free-floating cultural processes into something more concrete. In scholarly research the study of artefacts is a promising way to understand sleep as a cultural, rather than biological process. Artefacts usually have an obvious central function; a bed is to sleep in. Its style can signify a time-period and socio-economic context. At the same time, a bed can be a complex cultural symbol for the meaning of sleep, and all its embedded and referred-to larger processes of privatisation, creating order, making the world possible for people to live in. All three meanings go together in a cultural analysis of an artefact (Gerndt 1986: 117ff.; Venborg Pedersen 2003: 92).

In my daily work at the Open Air Museum I come across beds all the time. Each season we make up about 120–130 beds, alcoves, benches, and cradles to illustrate sleeping habits from about 1650 to 1930, the period represented by the museum buildings. Some of the beds (as an all embracing term for the different pieces of furniture that were used for sleep) are very well equipped, others are modest. The beds also served as displays of wealth. A featherbed demanded the material from perhaps 10 to 15 geese, and in the eighteenth century bed linen was worth as much as silver by weight (Venborg Pedersen 2004: 125ff.). It was a form of conspicuous consumption, just as today, we might buy a big car and make sure it is parked right by our house. However, in some places the bed is still a forceful sign of wealth. During a trip to the northeastern parts of the Balkans in the mid-1990s, I often saw beds made up for display in the best room of farm houses. Even there, modern times have come to farmers, though. Above the display of sheets and pillows, there was usually a shelf full of pots and pans in bright-coloured enamel. I believe the bed and the shelf of pots and pans had the same purpose as the displays of wealth.

Research on houses and historic dwellings has seldom given as much attention to beds and sleeping rooms as to kitchens and drawing rooms (Dröge 1999: 9–11). But in studies of elite culture, beds seem more important; after all Louis XIV of France governed from his bed and made his *lever* and *coucher* into important state ceremonies. Most ladies of higher social strata in the elegant eighteenth century would receive people in the morning while still in (or on) their bed. But when it comes to early modern peasant culture, beds are usually considered in terms of art history and folk-crafts (Dröge 1999; Steensberg 1949; Erixon 1938).[2] A bed is basically simple in construction, so it allows for many different modes of decoration. In European private homes and in museums one fantastic piece after another can be seen. As important as this approach is, it seldom tells us much about how people slept or otherwise used beds. The German ethnologist Gottfried Korff has done some work in this field (Korff 1981, 1986), but we have to turn to the museum researchers to find more elaborate work (Eder Matt 1994; Heidrich 1988).

There are good reasons to focus on the materiality of sleep – in the bed, in the house, in the heart of everyday life. In the house, cultural values meet technology, economy, and ecology. Here we also see personal choices and compromises that organise the reality of life (Roche 2000: 81–82). The house is a protected and protecting place providing shelter against the elements, against wild animals and ill-minded people. It is the place were work is done,

where artefacts and possessions are kept. Here time is fixed in frames of remembrance and daily routines broken by times of celebration. Here one can connect the present and the past, and become a person in a cultural context (Venborg Pedersen 2003: 96ff.).

In the home work, rest, food and social life meet, and the wheel of life is symbolised by the bride's chest, the bed, the table and the chairs, the clock, and the deathbed. Public and private meet; from the pump in the courtyard to the street door; from the warmth of the fire and to bed. Production, reproduction and consumption intermingle. In short, here life is lived! More than any other furniture, the bed is a symbol of life. Many everyday artefacts may be symbols; the table can be a ceremonial item for celebration – the altar. A chair may be the seat of a judge or the throne of a king. The bed can be conceived as a token of fulfilment. In early modern culture as well as in the traditional anthropological perception of Mediterranean societies, the bed is the very place where conception is proven. There were eye-witnesses at the bedside, or bed linen was displayed to tell its own silent story. Childbirth, engagements, consummation of marriage, and wills before death are just the most prominent events that had the bed as a focal point (Mørch 1972: 6).

The Metaphor

So, did our forefathers ever sleep? Biologically yes, they must have done. Culturally – again yes. They slept and they put meaning into it, changing from time to time, between social strata, and from place to place. The study of sleep (in this view) will not follow a certain place or a specific condition, but will follow the metaphor, the meaning of sleep, its extension, use, and history, in social, economic and ecological contexts (Marcus 1995). Sleep has always been important because it is biologically necessary. Hence humans have always needed a way to perceive it, make it speakable, including sleep in cultural discourse. However, culture at any given time is often like the debris or "fall-out" of past ideological systems, rather than a system or a coherent whole, as the British-American anthropologist Victor Turner has pointed out (Turner 1974:

14). Hence we must follow the idea of sleep down twisted roads.

Let us turn towards Europe's classical heritage once more. According to the Roman poet Ovid, Morpheus was the chosen son of the god of sleep, Hypnos – we recognise the name in the concept of hypnosis. Is it good or bad to be under the influence of hypnosis? If one sleep walks through life, today we would see this as a negative quality. Though we could also connect it to the idea of a free man who has not surrendered to modernity's busy life. Hypnosis is a tool for laughter at cabarets and side-shows. But it is also a tool in psychoanalysis, drawing on the classical wisdom that Hypnos is a gift. For Homer in the *Illiad*, Hypnos and Thanatos (Death) were twin sons of the Night (Nyx); and Hypnos donates the gift of sleep to man. With wings he hovers above the ground, touching the tired with a small twig dripping with dew, or pouring sedative juices from a horn. This is overwhelmingly positive. The needy are given the chance to rest.

In the Greek tradition most phenomena are made objects, carried by the gods. This is a way to make them speakable! But we do not necessarily see objects most clearly though. In an enquiry from the newspaper *Le Figaro* around World War I, the novelist Marcel Proust was asked about the power of habits and our way of perceiving the world. Proust's most thought-provoking answer may have been an aside about Noah and his Ark. Proust should have answered (according to Alain de Botton) by telling a small story about his childhood's understanding of Noah. When he was a small child, no one in the Bible seemed more pitiable than Noah forced to be in the Ark for forty days. Later, when Proust became ill and often had to stay in an ark (that is, his bed) he understood that Noah would never have been able to see the world as well as he did from the Ark, even though he was shuttered up and it was night (Botton 1998: 173–175). To make one see what one usually cannot see is Proust's strength. But how could Noah have seen anything of the planet sitting in his Ark with his Zoo? For the first time, because he could not see bushes and trees, Noah really *saw* trees and bushes, and for the first time in six hundreds years

of life he really understood the *meaning* of trees and bushes – that is the point of Proust's short story.

In other words, Noah was able to create cultural images of all the things he could not see. Giving them status as images, symbols, and metaphors, he was able to understand them. In the Western realm of thinking, sleep provides the same advantage. As Proust could walk to the Dukes of Guermantes or Swann, and found the two roads eternally intertwining, metaphors may help all thought. A metaphor is a meta-symbol collecting the manifestations of cultural values expressed by symbols. They are, as the famous anthropological phrase goes, "good to think". The word metaphor is often used to mean "figure of speech," but it may just as well be a "figure of thought", the "web of significance" as Clifford Geertz' famous phrase goes. Symbols and metaphorical relations are, in this line of thought, both models for and of reality, they take part in creating reality and they are used to express the cultural understanding of reality. Perhaps most important, and where we return to Proust, they are "tangible formulations of notions, abstractions from experience fixed in perceptible forms, concrete embodiments of ideas, attitudes, judgements, longings or beliefs ... they are as public as marriage and as observable as agriculture" (Geertz 1993 [1973]: 91ff.).

The analysis of metaphor is a useful and proven approach when dealing with the, for us as European Ethnologists, familiar fields of peasant culture, material culture, and cultural systems. It is also not difficult to see how this approach can be applied to the study of sleep as a condition. But we are familiar with the idea in another way as well.

During the last fifteen to twenty years the ethnological and historical study of nations, nation-states and nationalism has drawn much attention. European ethnology's own history has also drawn interest as it relates to nationhood. The metaphor of sleep and sleeping does not just deal with beds and sleepy peasants. It is a cultural metaphor for what could be called a kind of "culture hiding yet not being away", a culture of hibernation playing the tune of the "nationalisation of culture" performed during the nineteenth and twentieth centuries (Löfgren 1989) and which gave birth to nationality studies (Stoklund 1999). The basic idea of romantic nation building was that the people of the nation were asleep, and needed to be awakened to see and fulfil their role as Frenchmen, Germans, Danes, and Swedes. The idea of latency is close to the idea of sleeping, taken the metaphor to its broadest extent. It seems to me that the metaphor of sleep not only can provide an entry into the study of sleep but is indeed a thought-figure appearing at the most unforeseeable places both in the world we claim to study and in our own studies themselves. Scholars and scientists are, after all, in and not outside the world they study.

The Sleep

In this article I have already discussed sleep as a field for science and medicine. We have also seen sleep as an expression of the private, as a condition more than a process. In sleep we turn ourselves over to the merciful peace of Hypnos. We say we "sleep like a child". Doing so, we are approaching the unspoiled condition of nature, turning towards a state dreamt of by Rousseau. But this happens according to our own rules, or to sleep's own rules (we remember Heraclitus), to a kind of returning Charivari, which through creating an intimate culture turned upside-down, makes us safe in public culture during day, and brings us through the daily menace of life.

Cultural change is often slow, but is usually felt as being very quick by those who experience it. As today also in early modernity people felt that during their lifetime the world had changed far too much, far too quickly, and far too thoroughly. Studies of modernity have celebrated change, often rapid change, as a token of the speedy process of modernisation and, hence portray slowness and sleepiness as belonging to pre- or early modern conditions, or as defense strategies by individuals. However, this is only the case to a certain degree. "Festina lente" (hurry slowly) may have been the wise words of Augustus, Caesar of Rome, and perhaps because of this affiliation caution is still considered a virtue today. But the sluggish, slow, inert, slack peasant of the eighteenth century is hardly an ideal in the modern world. The Enlightenment killed this cultural ethos' positive connotations (Christiansen 2002).

Small phenomena speak to large issues. A project following the lines above is being conducted at the Danish National Museum, the Open Air Museum. Our study of the cultural history of sleep includes such artefacts of sleep as beds. We are not trying to solve the eternal riddle of sleep, but to understand a bit of what our ancestors thought about sleep, how they solved the problem of sleep and, hopefully, thus make our selves a bit wiser. This means using phenomenological sensibilities, and seeking interpretations, in the broadest possible ways. In what way does sleep fit into the cultural creation of order, making the world possible for people to live in?

Notes

1　Heraclitus' statement is translated by me. The same is the case later in the essay.
2　Steensberg's and Erixon's studies are mentioned just as examples of this way of studying peasant furniture – and hence beds. Others could have been mentioned but it appears fair to say that the lines of study laid out by Steensberg and Erixon are still broadly followed when dealing with peasant furniture.

References

Alvarez, A. 1995: *Natten. Om nattens liv, nattens sprog, søvn og drømme*. Copenhagen.
Botton, Alain de 1998: *Sådan kan Proust forandre dit liv*. Copenhagen.
Christiansen, Palle Ove 2002: *Lykkemagerne. Gods, greve, forvalter og fæster i 1700-tallets verden*. Copenhagen.
Dröge, Kurt 1999: *Das ländliche Bett. Zur Geschichte des Schlafmöbels in Westfalen*. Schriften des Detmold.
Eder Matt, Katharina 1994: *Wie sie sich betten. Eine Ausstellung zur Kulturgeschichte des Schlafens*. Basel.
Elias, Norbert 1980 [1939]: *Über den Prozess der Zivilisation. Soziogenetische und psychogenetische Untersuchungen*. Frankfurt am Main.
Erixon, Sigurd 1938: *Folklig möbelkultur i svenska bygder*. Stockholm.
Frykman, Jonas & Orvar Löfgren 1979: *Den kultiverade människan*. Lund.
Geertz, Clifford 1993 [1973]: *The Interpretation of Cultures: Selected Essays*. London.
Gerndt, Helge 1986: *Kultur als Forschungsfeld. Über volkskundliches Denken und Arbeiten*. Munich.
Heidrich, Hermann 1988: *Das Bett. Notizen zur Geschichte des Schlafens*. Bad Windsheim.

Henningsen, Gustav 1984: *Fra heksejagt til heksekult, 1484– 1984*. Copenhagen.

Korff, Gottfried 1981: Einige Bemerkungen zur Wandel des Bettes. *Zeitschrift für Volkskunde* 77(I), 1–16.

Korff, Gottfried 1986: Wie man sich bettet, so liegt man. Überlegungen zur Schlafkultur auf der Grundlage des Betten-bestandes des Rheinischen Freilichtmuseums Kommern. In: Konrad Berdahl & Hermann Heidrich (eds.), *Freilichtmuseum und Sozialgeschichte*. Bad Windsheim, pp. 57–75.

Löfgren, Orvar 1989: The Nationalization of Culture. *Ethnologia Europaea* 19, 5–23.

Marcus, George E. 1995: Ethnography In/Of the World System: The Emergence of Multi-Sided Ethnography. *Annual Review of Anthropology* 24, 95–117.

Matthiessen, Hugo 1914: *Natten. Studier i gammelt byliv*. Copenhagen.

Mørch, Ibi Trier 1972: *Senge*. Copenhagen.

Roche, Daniel 2000: *A History of Everyday Things: The Birth of Consumption in France 1600–1800*. Cambridge.

Schivelbusch, Wolfgang 1983: *Lichtblicke. Zur Geschichte der künstlichen Helligkeit im 19. Jahrhundert*. Munich.

Steensberg, Axel 1949: *Danske Bondemøbler*. Copenhagen.

Stoklund, Bjarne (ed.) 1999: *Kulturens nationalisering. Et etnologisk perspektiv på det nationale*. Copenhagen.

Turner, Victor 1974: *Dramas, Fields, and Metaphors: Symbolic Action in Human Society*. London.

Venborg Pedersen, Mikkel 2003: Material Culture: A Source Material to Everyday Life in Early Modern Eiderstedt, Schleswig. *Kieler Blätter zur Volkskunde* 35, 89–104.

Venborg Pedersen, Mikkel 2004: *Ejdersted. Skitser fra et landskab 1650–1850*. Copenhagen.

ABOUT THE AUTHORS

Lynn Åkesson is associate professor of European Ethnology at the University of Lund. She has recently edited a book on waste and abundance and one on burial
rituals in Sweden today, both in Swedish. Her current
research is mainly on waste and waste-handling.
(Lynn.Akesson@etn.lu.se)

Gösta Arvastson joined Uppsala University in 1988,
and is currently a professor at the Department of
Cultural Anthropology and Ethnology. He has studied globalization and urban change as well as the
"New Economy". A major study on European car industries was published in 2004. Together with Tim
Butler he edited the special issue of Ethnologia Europaea 2004:2 Multicultures and Cities.
(Gosta.Arvastson@etnologi.uu.se)

Russell Belk is the N. Eldon Tanner Professor of
Business Administration at the University of Utah.
He is the editor of the forthcoming books The Hand-
book of Qualitative Marketing Research and Research
in Consumer Behavior, and author of prior books
and other work including Collecting in a Consumer
Society (2001). He is currently working on projects
on the concepts of cool consumption, clutter, and
beauty and skin color in Asia.
(mktrwb@business.utah.edu,
www.business.utah.edu/~mktrwb/)

Regina Bendix is professor of Cultural Anthropology and European Ethnology at the University of
Göttingen, Germany. Among her recent publications are The Senses (edited as a special issue of Etnofoor, 2005, with Don Brenneis) and Sleepers, Moles
and Martyrs (edited as a special issue of Ethnologia
Europaea, 2003, with John Bendix). She is currently
working on a number of different projects in disciplinary history.
(rbendix@gwdg.de,
www.kaee.uni-goettingen.de/)

Billy Ehn is professor of Ethnology at the University
of Umeå. Among his recent publications are books in
Swedish about methodological curiosity and wonder
(2005), emotions in Academia (together with Orvar
Löfgren 2004), and how to handle crises in working
life (2003). He is currently working on a book about
monuments in a cultural perspective (together with
Jonas Frykman).
(billy.ehn@kultmed.umu.se)

Jonas Frykman is professor of European Ethnology
at Lund University. Among his recent publications
are Being There: New Trends in Phenomenology and
the Analysis of Culture (2003 with Nils Gilje), Ar-
ticulating Europe: Local Perspectives (2003 with Peter
Niedermüller), and a book on European monuments
(in press, with Billy Ehn). Research fields are post-
socialism in Europe and the role of contributions
from the well-fare state for local culture.
(Jonas.Frykman@etn.lu.se)

Güliz Ger is a professor of Marketing at Bilkent University, Ankara, Turkey. Her articles appeared in Jour-

nal of Consumer Research, Journal of Material Culture, Journal of Economic Psychology, International Journal of Research in Marketing, and elsewhere. She co-edited *Consumption in Marketizing Economies*. Ger's recent work investigates consumption in transitional societies and among immigrants, cultural products and globalization, tradition and modernity. (ger@bilkent.edu.tr, www.bilkent.edu.tr/~ger)

Kristofer Hansson is a Ph.D. student of European Ethnology and The Vårdal Institute at the University of Lund. Recent publications discuss pharmaceuticals as fetishes and the popularisation of biomedicine (2004, 2005). He is currently working with a project on young people living with asthma. (Kristofer.Hansson@etn.lu.se, www.etn.lu.se/Etnologi/hemsidor/KristoferHansson/_www/default.html)

Ella Johansson has recently left a guest professorship at Humboldt University in Berlin and started working as head of the research unit at the Multicultural Centre in Botkyrka near Stockholm. Her latest publication is an article on workers in a book about modernity and masculinity in Scandinavia 1840–1940 and her latest book is an anthology about playfulness and material culture (*Kulturen* 2005). Other publications are mainly in the fields of social history, modernity, gender, masculinity, landscape and cultural heritage. (ella.johansson@mkc.botkyrka.se, www2.hu-berlin.de/skan/personal/ej.html, www.mkc.botkyrka.se, www.angersjo.lu.se)

Lars-Eric Jönsson is associate professor of European Ethnology at the University of Lund. Among his recent publications are a book on problematic cultural heritages (edited with Birgitta Svensson) and "Home Women and Children: Social Services in Postwar Sweden" (In: *Home Cultures* 2/2005). He is now working with two projects: one on ideal and problematic homes in post-war Sweden and another one on literary accounts of psychiatric institutions. (lars-eric.jonsson@etn.lu.se, www.etn.lu.se/Etnologi/hemsidor/LarsEricJonsson/om.htm)

Sarah Holst Kjær is a Ph.D. candidate in European Ethnology at the University of Lund. She is working on her dissertation about man–woman relationships. Her specific interests are on how cultural imaginations, practices and habits create a couple. (Sarah.Holst_Kjaer@etn.lu.se, www.etn.lu.se/Etnologi/hemsidor/SarahHolstKjaer)

Sven-Erik Klinkmann is associate professor of Folkloristics, especially popular culture, at the University of Åbo Akademi. His research interests deal with representations of popular culture, especially in relation to popular imagination, cultural clichés, nostalgia and anachronisms. At the moment he is working on a project called tradition and innovation in Swedish Finland and bilingual rock and pop in Vaasa during the time period 1960–2005. A book in Swedish with his essays on dream figures and icons of popular culture is due this autumn. (sven-erik.klinkmann@netikka.fi, www.netikka.net/sek/index.html)

Orvar Löfgren is professor of European Ethnology at the University of Lund. Among his recent publications are *Magic, Culture and the New Economy* (edited together with Robert Willim 2005) and a book in Swedish on emotions in Academia (together with Billy Ehn 2004). He is currently working with a project on the cultural production of the inconspicuous. (Orvar.Lofgren@etn.lu.se, www.etn.lu.se/Etnologi/hemsidor/OrvarLofgren)

Kirsti Mathiesen Hjemdahl is assistant professor of Cultural Studies at the University of Bergen in Norway, and a senior researcher at Agder Research. Among her recent publications are a book on Nordic theme parks (2003), studies of "The Experience Economy" in Norway (from 2004 and 2006), and an anthology about Tito (edited together with Nevena Škrbić Alempijević 2006). Currently she is working on the project "Political places in change. A comparative study of Croatia and South Africa".

(kirsti@kulturviter.no,
www.kulturviter.no)

Tom O'Dell is an associate professor at the Department of Service Management, Lund University, Helsingborg Campus. Previously he has published *Culture Unbound: Americanization and Everyday Life in Sweden* (1997). He has also edited several volumes on tourism and the experience economy, including *Experiencescapes: Tourism, Culture, and Economy* (2004, together with Peter Billing). He is currently working on a project investigating routines, mobility, and the home.
(Thomas.odell@msm.lu.se)

Mika Pantzar is an economist (Ph.D.). Currently he is research professor at National Consumer Research Centre (Helsinki). He has published within consumer research, design and technology studies, rhetoric of economic policy, food studies, systems research, future studies etc. Among his books are *Domestication of Technology. From Science of Consumption to Art of Consumption* (in Finnish 1996) and "Manufacturing Fun: Innovations in Happiness, Well-being and Fun", *NCRC publications* 1/2005 (Mika Pantzar and Elizabeth Shove eds.).
(Mika.Pantzar@ncrc.fi,
www.kuluttajatutkimuskeskus.fi/files/4717/publications_2005_1_manufacturingleisure)

K. Anne Pyburn is professor of Anthroplogy and Gender Studies at Indiana University and director of the Center for Archaeology in the Public Interest. She co-edits *Archaeologies: Journal of the World Archaeological Congress* with Nick Shepherd. Her field work is in Belize (Chau Hiix) and Kyrgyzstan (Koch Kor). Recently she has been writing about gender (*Ungendering Civilization*, 2004), ethics, community archaeology, and early cities.
(apyburn@indiana.edu,
www.research.indiana.edu/centers/capi.html)

Per-Markku Ristilammi's research has focused on processes of cultural inclusion and exclusion in urban settings. He is associate professor in Ethnology at the department of IMER (International Migration and Ethnic Relations), Malmö University. His recent publications are Spectral Events: Attempts at Pattern Recognition (in Löfgren & Willim eds. *Magic, Culture and The New Economy*, 2005), and a book on urban life from 2003.
(per-markku.ristilammi@imer.mah.se)

Katarina Saltzman is researcher at the Department of Ethnology, Göteborg University. Her research interests are within the sphere of landscapes, everyday uses and understandings of nature, rural-urban relations and heritage. Her thesis on coexisting and conflicting uses of contemporary rural landscapes was presented at Lund University and published in 2001. In her current work she is studying ephemeral landscapes at the rural-urban fringe.
(katarina.saltzman@ethnology.gu.se)

Elizabeth Shove is professor of Sociology at Lancaster University. Recent publications include *Comfort, Cleanliness and Convenience: the Social Organization of Normality* (2003). She is currently working on issues of design, consumption, practice and everyday technology.
(E.Shove@lancaster.ac.uk,
www.lancs.ac.uk/fss/sociology/staff/shove/shove.htm)

Nevena Škrbić Alempijević is a senior assistant at the Department of Ethnology and Cultural Anthropology, University of Zagreb, Croatia. She is currently doing research within the project on the reinvention of the "traditional" in the frame of Croatian cultural politics. She has recently published articles in Croatian, on the construction of Istrian identities (2002/2003) and on carnivalesque practices on the island of Rab (2006). Together with Kirsti Mathiesen Hjemdahl, she is editing an anthology in Croatian and English on the birthplace of Josip Broz Tito.
(nskrbic@ffzg.hr,
 www.ffzg.hr/etno/Skrbic)

Kathleen Stewart is associate professor of Anthropology and director of the Center for Cultural Studies at the University of Texas, Austin. She has just finished a book of experimental writing called Surface Tensions (forthcoming) which traces the ordinary affects, experimental subjects and dream worlds that animate everyday life. Her current work, Las Vegas Chronicles, describes how the twisted strands of influence from nuclear testing and nuclear waste to gambling and new beginnings have defined this city as a working class nightmare and dream world. (kstewart@mail.utexas.edu)

Birgitta Svensson is professor of European Ethnology at the University of Stockholm. Among her recent publications are *Landscape Values of Rural Inhabitants in the Öresound Region* (together with Jette Hansen-Møller and Katarina Saltzman) and *Inmates in Motion – Metamorphosis as Governmentality. A Case of Social Logistics* (together with Kerstin Svensson). She is currently working with projects on cultural deregulation, city culture and on the cultural economy of passion. (birgitta.svensson@etnologi.su.se, www.etnologi.su.se)

Mikkel Venborg Pedersen, Ph.D., is curator and senior researcher at the National Museum of Denmark, Open Air Museum. Together with John Erichsen he is editor of a four-volume work on Danish estates and manorial culture. Recent publications are a book on aristocratic identity from 2005 and a study of a particular group of international cattle-breeders and cash-crop farmers in early modernity. He has published numerous articles on the subjects of elite culture, landscape perception, material culture and theory in cultural history. He is currently working on a project on the process and phenomena of sleep(ing) in Early Modernity and its artefacts. (Venborg@natmus.dk, www.natmus.dk)

Jojada Verrips is professor of European Anthropology at the University of Amsterdam. He has written and edited a number of books in Dutch and is currently working on a book titled The Wild (in the) West. (j.verrips@uva.nl)

Richard Wilk is professor of Anthropology and Gender Studies at Indiana University. His most recent book is *Home Cooking in the Global Village* (2006), and his edited *Fast Food/Slow Food* (2006). He is currently working on rhythms and routines of consumption. (wilkr@indiana.edu, www.indiana.edu/~wanthro)

Robert Willim, Ph.D., is researcher in European Ethnology at Lund University. Among his recent publications are *Magic, Culture and the New Economy* (edited together with Orvar Löfgren 2005) and a number of articles dealing with a concept called industrial cool. He is currently working with a project on the cultural production of the inconspicuous. (Robert.Willim@etn.lu.se, www.robertwillim.com/)